A NEW RHETORIC

A NEW RHETORIC

Francis Christensen
LATE, THE UNIVERSITY OF SOUTHERN CALIFORNIA

Bonniejean Christensen
THE UNIVERSITY OF NORTH DAKOTA

Harper & Row, Publishers
New York, Hagerstown, San Francisco, London

Sponsoring Editor: George A. Middendorf
Project Editor: Eleanor Castellano
Designer: Emily Harste
Production Supervisor: Francis X. Giordano
Compositor: American Book–Stratford Press, Inc.
Printer and Binder: The Murray Printing Company
Art Studio: J & R Technical Services Inc.

A NEW RHETORIC

Library of Congress Cataloging in Publication Data

Christensen, Francis.
    A new rhetoric.

    Includes index.
    1. English language—Rhetoric.   2. English language—
Grammar, Generative.   I. Christensen, Bonniejean, joint
author.   II. Title.
PE1408.C475   808'.04275   75-35948
ISBN 0-06-041282-8

For Ellen and Maggie
Lyn, Bonnie, and Jonathan Francis

Acknowledgments

Acknowledgment is made to the following:

Bobbs-Merrill, for passages from *Company Manners*, by Louis Kronenberger, copyright 1954.

Columbia University Press, for articles from the *Columbia Encyclopedia*, copyright © 1956 and 1963.

Doubleday, for the selections from *The Identity of Man*, by Jacob Bronowski, copyright © 1965; and for the selection from *The Octopus*, by Frank Norris, copyright 1901; and the selections from *Linguistics and Your Language*, by Robert A. Hall, Jr., copyright © 1950, 1960 by permission of author.

Harcourt Brace Jovanovich, Inc., for a paragraph from "The Knot Hole," by Dorothy Canfield, in *A Harvest of Stories*, copyright © 1956; for an excerpt from *The Origins and Development of the English Language*, 2nd Edition, by Thomas Pyles, copyright © 1964, 1971, by Harcourt Brace Jovanovich, Inc. and reprinted with their permission; for an excerpt from *Main Street*, by Sinclair Lewis, copyright 1920 by Harcourt Brace Jovanovich, Inc., copyright 1948, by Sinclair Lewis, reprinted by permission of Harcourt Brace Jovanovich, Inc.; for excerpts from "The Leaning Tower," in *The Leaning Tower and Other Stories* by Katherine Anne Porter, copyright © 1941, 1969, by Katherine Anne Porter, by permission of Harcourt Brace Jovanovich; for excerpt from "The Patented Gate and the Mean Hamburger," by Robert Penn Warren, copyright © 1947, 1975 by Robert Penn Warren, in *The Circus in the Attic and Other Stories*, by permission of Harcourt Brace Jovanovich, Inc.; for four lines from "The Waste Land" by T. S. Eliot in *Collected Poems*, copyright © 1962, Harcourt Brace Jovanovich, Inc.

Harper & Row, for the selection from Erich Fromm, "The Creative Attitude" and the selection from Abraham H. Maslow, "Creativity in Self-Actualizing People," from *Creativity and Its Cultivation*, edited by Harold H. Anderson, copyright © 1959.

Harper's, for the passage from an article by David Boroff in the April 1960 issue and for the passage from "The Easy Chair" by McGeorge Bundy in the January 1962 issue.

Houghton Mifflin, for passages from "The Blue-Winged Teal" in *The City of the Living*, by Wallage Stegner, copyright © 1957.

Knopf, for excerpts from *Pigeon Feathers and Other Stories*, by John Updike, copyright © 1962.

Macmillan, for selections from *Windswept*, by Mary Ellen Chase. Copyright 1941 by Mary Ellen Chase, renewed 1969 by Mary Ellen Chase.

Pacific Spectator, for an excerpt from " 'The Fault, Dear Brutus': Poetic Example and Poetic Practice Today," by Theodore Morrison, in the Summer 1957 issue. Reprinted by permission by the author.

Penguin, for the paragraph from *Our Language*, by Simeon Potter, pp. 107–108. Copyright © Stephen Potter, 1959 and 1960.

Philosophical Library, for an excerpt from "The Craft of Writing," by John Erskine, in *Twentieth Century English*, ed. William S. Knickerbocker, copyright 1946. Reprinted by permission of the publisher.

Prentice-Hall, for a paragraph from *The Ways of the Poem* by Josephine Miles, copyright © 1961.

Random House, for selections from *The Ox-Bow Incident*, by Walter Van Tilburg Clark, copyright 1940.

Saturday Review, for the passage from "Quick, Frankie, the Needle," by Arthur Knight in the December 17, 1955 issue, and for four lines from "Ensnare the Clouds," by Elizabeth Coatsworth, in *Saturday Review*, February 19, 1949, p. 38.

Scribner, for excerpts from *For Whom the Bell Tolls*, copyright 1940, "The Snows of Kilimanjaro" in *The Short Stories of Ernest Hemingway*, copyright © 1955, and "Big Two-Hearted River (Part II)" in *In Our Time*, copyright 1950 by Ernest Hemingway; and sentences from *Look Homeward, Angel*, by Thomas Wolfe, copyright 1952.

May Swenson, for quotation on page 66 from "One Morning in New Hampshire," by May Swenson. Reprinted by permission of the author from *To Mix With Time*, copyright © 1963 by May Swenson and Charles Scribner's Sons. The poem originally appeared in *The New Yorker*, 1961.

Contents

Preface xiii

PART I THE PROCESS OF WRITING 1

1. *Introduction* 3

2. *Basic Principles* 6
   Addition 6
   Direction of Movement 7
   Levels of Generality 8
   Texture 9
   EXERCISE 15

3. *Two-Level Narrative Sentences* 19
   Representational Writing 20
   Grammatical Elements 22
   Rhetorical Elements 24
   Bringing the Grammatical and Rhetorical Together 25
   Advice for Writing 28
   EXERCISES 29

4. *Multilevel Narrative Sentences* 32
   Relationship of the Additions 33
   Graphic Representation 36
   Discrimination of Levels 38
   EXERCISES 39

5. *Description—The Appositive Noun Phrase* 42
   Base Clauses 42
   Free Modifiers 43

The Noun Phrase   45
EXERCISES   51

6. *The Language of the Senses*   55
Visual and Nonvisual   56
Sound   58
EXERCISES   64
Smell   66
EXERCISES   70
Touch   71
EXERCISES   75
Taste   77

PART II THE LARGER UNITS OF COMPOSITION   83

7. *A Short Narrative*   85
The Assignment: A Paragraph   85
Student Examples   88
EXERCISES   93

8. *Dominant Tone*   97
Techniques   98
Subjects   100
EXERCISES   103

9. *The Longer Narrative*   110
Techniques   110
EXERCISES   114

10. *Paragraphing—An Introduction to Discursive
Writing*   126
Structural and Supporting Sentences   126
The Cumulative Nature of Extended Sequences   126
The Problem of Paragraphing   127
Graphic Devices   128
Organization   128
Punctuation by Paragraph   132
Ordering a Series   133
Like Things in Like Ways   133
EXERCISES   134

11. *The Structure of Paragraphs*   142
Simple Coordinate Sequences   143
Simple Subordinate Sequences   147
Mixed Sequences   149
Mixed Coordinate Sequences   150
Mixed Subordinate Sequences   153

The Topic Sentence 154
Paragraphs with Extrasequential Sentences 159
EXERCISES 164

12. *Methods of Support 166*
Identification 170
Details, Particulars 172
Examples, Instances, Illustrations 173
Definition 175
Elimination, Negation 176
Restatement, Repetition 178
Comparison-Contrast, Analogy 179
Explication 181
Causes or Reasons; Effects or Consequences 183
Evidence and Authority 185
Other Methods 187
The Writer's Obligation 187
EXERCISES 188

Index 195

Preface

This book has been written to permit teachers of composition to share in what has been called the "most exciting educational development" of our times—"the widespread efforts to improve the quality of instruction in several basic academic subjects, mainly in identifying and concentrating more directly upon their central principles and by bringing their content more nearly into line with current knowledge of the particular disciplines." This quotation shows the influence of Jerome S. Bruner's *The Process of Education*, and it comes from Albert H. Kitzhaber's *Themes, Theories, and Therapy: The Teaching of Writing in College*. Any book about writing that is copyrighted after 1963 must reckon with these two books. One is an inquiry into the learning processes, based on the revolutionary developments in teaching some of the sciences but equally applicable to the humanities; the other is an inquiry into the teaching of college composition that finds most English teachers still "doing business in the same old way at the same old stand."

Our effort to identify and concentrate on central principles and to bring the content of the course in composition into line with current knowledge of the relevant disciplines makes this book different from its predecessors in several important ways. It is only fair to be explicit about where the differences lie.

The major practical problem of the basic academic subjects is how to make them count outside the classroom and after the course is over. The solution Bruner reports as favored by those who have been working on the new curriculums lies in giving the students an understanding of "the most fundamental structure" of the subject. This means that the course does not concentrate on skills and techniques but on the most basic and general ideas underlying the subject, not on repetition and drill to fix in the memory but on principles and attitudes. In this way the student is most likely to understand the subject, remember it, and apply it; and with a curriculum so structured he is less likely to have to un- learn at later stages what he learned at the elementary ones. "Subject matter presented so as to emphasize its structure will perforce be of that generative kind that permits reconstruction of the details or, at very least, prepares a place into which the details, when encountered, can be put" (J. S. Bruner, *On Knowing*).

What are the most basic and general ideas that constitute the struc- tures of composition in language? Not any of those, we believe, found in our rhetorics and handbooks. Not the four forms of discourse, though the conception is useful. Not unity, coherence, and emphasis. These are evaluative, not constitutive. In the first chapters we have offered a statement of what we take to be the most fundamental constitutive principles of writing. (These principles are explained in Francis Christen- sen's "A Generative Rhetoric of the Sentence," in *College Composition and Communication*, October 1963, reprinted in *Notes Toward a New Rhetoric*.) They sum up the results of an inductive study of prose style that began years ago when we concluded that we could not teach com- position by the principles then available in handbooks and rhetorics. We could go through the motions, we could expect students to write better; but we could not teach them to write better. (Some other results of this study have been published in two articles in *College English*, October 1963, and also reprinted in *Notes Toward a New Rhetoric*.)

Any book on writing must present rhetorical principles—whether or not they prove to be basic and fundamental. These principles, it ap- pears, may be arrived at in two ways—by observing the process, in one's own writing or in the reports of others; or by analysis of the product rather than the process. The latter is the usual procedure; and the usual, but not necessary, consequence is that books on writing present the *results* of the analysis. But, as Sidney Cox has said (*Indirections*), "Analysis gives you components; the thing it cannot give is the com- position. And composition happens to be the one thing needful, the only thing that counts." The teacher who uses the book, or perhaps the student himself, has to translate the blueprint into a sequence of opera- tions.

It may be that we have to get along with ad hoc improvisation ac- cording to the needs of a given class or the bent of a given instructor. It may be that writing is too complex for the course to be given an orderly sequence. "When someone teaches composition, he is trying to cultivate in the student a bafflingly complex intellectual skill. Instruction in it does not proceed in a systematic and sequential way, where one thing must be learned before the next; instead, a student needs all things at once whenever he composes anything as long as a paragraph" (Kitzhaber, *Themes, Theories, and Therapy*).

In spite of such pessimism we have tried to treat writing as a process, an activity; we have tried to present not so much a blueprint as a set of directions for operations. In order to do this, we have started with the sentence. Even a single paragraph does precipitate almost all the problems of writing. But the sentence is a manageable unit; and in descriptive-narrative writing the sentence is an isolable unit—moreover, one that involves all four of the basic principles of what we have called a generative rhetoric. The strategy, thus, is to begin with one-sentence finger exercises reporting sense impressions. Such exercises have proved for us an ideal starting point for a sequential and cumulative treatment of writing as a process. The training they give in sentence structure and diction carries—or can be made to carry—over into the next stage of the process, paragraph structure in expository writing. And all three—diction, sentence structure, and paragraph structure—carry over into the last stage, the strategies of longer expository essays.

Our choice of a starting point represents a sharp break with tradition, and we have not made the choice lightly.

One consideration has been the reluctance of instructors to tangle with the sentence. We are like the ingenious architect of the Grand Academy of Lagado, who had contrived a new method for building houses by beginning at the roof and working down to the foundation—except that we go him one better by starting at the roof and working upward. The cause of our reluctance, apart from the reluctance of graduate departments to provide training relevant to the teaching of composition, is that we have no effective way to teach sentence improvement. The chapters on the sentence in our handbooks and rhetorics all adduce the rhetorical classification of sentences as loose, balanced, and periodic. But the term *loose* is taken as a pejorative, our students have little occasion for balanced sentences, and some of our worst perversions of style come from the attempt to teach them to write periodic sentences. The traditional grammatical classification of sentences is equally barren. Its use in teaching composition rests on a semantic confusion, equating complexity of structure with complexity of thought and vice versa. But very simple thoughts ("I don't know who done it") may call for complex grammatical constructions.

The chapters on the sentence all assume that we think naturally in primer sentences, progress naturally to compound sentences, and must be taught to combine the primer sentences into complex sentences—and that complex sentences are the mark of maturity. We have tried to work out a rhetoric of the sentence that will do more than combine the ideas of primer sentences—one that will *generate* ideas.

Such a generative rhetoric of the sentence shifts the emphasis from the complex and the periodic to what we have called the *cumulative* sentence. This is a new name for the loose sentence, but a name without its pejorative connotations and one justified by modern practice. If we are correct in our historical deductions, modern writers have given us teachers of composition the slip. The complex and periodic sentences we prescribe are largely archaic. While we urge the subordinate clause, they work largely with verbal constructions and an array of appositives that our grammars seem not to have noticed; while we urge variety in sentence beginnings (and get dangling modifiers), they put the sentence modifiers at the end. Of course, they still use subordinate clauses (the restrictive ones are obligatory), but the nonrestrictive ones do not count for much in the practiced writer's repertory of sentence elements.

Another consideration has been sentence length. The cumulative sentence not only uses structures unfamiliar to our impoverished grammar, but it is longer than the sentences dictated by our impoverished rhetoric. Our emphasis on the plain style—short words in short sentences—is the same as the educator's emphasis on limited vocabulary in primer sentences or on simplified versions of the classics. Short words in short sentences is the Flesch doctrine, and a doctrine is the same whether it is packaged by the college of letters and arts or the school of education. The course in composition is a course in reading as well as in writing, and much of what a student has to read is cast in long sentences. Long sentences do not all make equal demands on the reader. More depends on structure than on length. Long cumulative sentences are generally easy to read; long periodic sentences are often hard to read; and long simple sentences, with long noun and verb clusters, are the really hard sentences to read. Moreover, the long sentence is necessary if the writer is to write concretely, with an eye to the needs of the reader, if he is to get into his writing the concrete details that we seldom define and never tell him how to manage. Again, the writer cannot vary the length of his sentences unless he can write long sentences, nor vary them effectively unless his long sentences come where the context demands them. We ought to do our utmost to develop syntactic dexterity, to make our students sentence acrobats. "No bird soars too high if he soars with his own wings."

Another consideration, and a major one, has been that to begin with the sentence as an isolable unit we have found that we had to begin with descriptive-narrative writing—and today in most composition courses we teach only expository writing. We deplore this limitation as we do the limitation to the plain style. Both are confessions of inadequacy, both signs of our willingness to sell our liberal heritage for a pot of utilitarian message. In both we undercut our own discipline.

In part, at least, the sellout is traceable to confusion. One source of confusion is the traditional notion of the four forms of discourse. This notion leads us to think of pure blocks of description, of stories as pure narration (with perhaps interspersed blocks of description), of essays as pure exposition, and of arguments as all argument. Instead, we should think of writing as either *discursive* or *representational* in form. If discursive writing (exposition) is *talking about* a subject and if representational writing (description and narration) is *picturing* a subject, the one the *appearance* of things and the other the *behavior* of things, then all three may appear even in a single sentence. There are stories and novels that are almost purely expository in methods; there are essays, expository in intent, that are almost straight narrative or narrative alternating with description or interwoven with it in the modern manner; and there is little effective exposition (except in some modes of scientific and commercial writing) that does not have a strong infusion of the other two modes. Thus, the attempt to teach exposition without reference to the other two modes is like trying to paint with only one primary color or to get high-fidelity reproduction with a band width of 100–4,000 cycles.

Another source of confusion comes from teaching descriptive-narrative (or imaginative or creative) writing as self-expression. Thus a piece of writing becomes an emanation of an inviolable soul—untouchable and unteachable—or it becomes banal rambling on about "My Summer Vacation," usually *talking about* the subject and thus exposition rather than description or narration, or it may be, really, a flight of fantasy. But the prevalence of such abuse is a measure only of our own slackness. Representational writing can be managed so as to afford a far more rigorous discipline than discursive writing does. Flaubert was not writing, or teaching Maupassant to write, essays on tension, texture, and tone in *Tartuffe*.

Defined, limited, and ordered as we have attempted to present it here, descriptive-narrative writing makes an effective starting point. It solves for the first few weeks the problem of what to write about. Every student has something to communicate—his immediate sense impressions, which need a bit of exercising. Unlike other kinds of materials, sense impressions are not already verbalized; he has to match language to his sense impressions. His acuteness in observation and in choice of word can be judged with a fair degree of objectivity—is the sound of an empty milk bottle being set down on a concrete step suggested better by *clink* or *clank*?

But these are utilitarian considerations. The discipline we are proposing carries over of itself into the study of literature. It is a paradox that certain aspects of literature cannot be studied effectively in a literature class. "A man does not begin to savor the words, the rhythm, the details, the metaphors, the structure, *or* the experience which they were chosen to communicate until he has tried to wrestle his own experience into words. To real-ize as a creative reader, one must real-ize as a creative writer" (Rev. William J. O'Malley, S.J., in *Convention Concerns*,

NCTE Convention, November 1962). The material cause, the linguistic matrix, can hardly be studied without turning the course in literature into a course in language. But it can be studied in a class in writing where the writing itself is representational. It helps the student thread the syntactical mazes of much mature writing and it gives him an insight into that elusive thing we call style. For many students, moreover, such writing makes life more interesting and it gives them a way to share their interest with others. When they learn to put concrete details into a sentence, they begin to look at life with more alertness. If it is a liberal education we are concerned with, it is just possible that this by-product of a few weeks of sensuous seeing, instead of conceptual identification, is more important than anything we can achieve by concentrating on the plain style in expository prose. "The art of seeing," Erich Fromm says, "is about the most important act one can perform in one's life." "The greatest thing a human soul ever does in this world," Ruskin says, "is to see something, and tell what it saw in a plain way."

Besides trying to identify the underlying principles operative in the writing process and to treat writing as a process, we have tried to bring the content of the course into line with current knowledge. This means primarily the new knowledge about language from linguistic science. We have rejected the school tradition and embraced the scholarly tradition. We have not tried to compromise. Insofar as we know what linguists think about language, we have accepted and applied it—consistently and openly. The relevance of grammar to teaching and learning writing is much disputed but without much logic. It is irrelevant that many professional writers know little formal grammar. The professional is not in the same situation as the student in the classroom; he has other motivations, other resources, and a lifetime to learn his craft. It is irrelevant that many students who write well have little knowledge of formal grammar. Most such students have been from an early age voracious readers; they have learned to write by osmosis from reading literature. But, again, their situation is not the same as that of the student in the classroom. Osmosis is a slow process, and what can be absorbed from the amount that can be read in the composition course is negligible. The instructor who argues that writing can be learned only by osmosis is arguing himself out of a job. He is also inviting some questions that could be embarrassing about the writing of those who read literature the most. It is equally irrelevant that many students who have studied grammar and liked it and learned it well do not write well. One does not learn to write by osmosis from grammar any more than from reading. Grammar is not likely to have any bearing on writing unless there is a teacher or a textbook to bring it to bear. It is irrelevant, even, that controlled experiments have shown no correlation between knowledge of grammar and ability to write. We have seen no experiments where the grammar—either the kind used or the way it was used—could be expected to produce results. The problem is how to bring the grammar to bear and what grammar can best be brought to bear. If there is anything truly original in this book, it is in the solution of this problem.

In this context linguistics also means usage. The school tradition has always confused grammar, usage, and rhetoric and multiplied the confusion by insisting on an absolute and unchangeable standard of correctness and stultified language study by making such correctness its be-all and end-all. The ironic consequence has been to make the English class a school for conformity.

The effort to treat writing and learning to write as a sequential and cumulative process has dictated the form of the book. Part I outlines the process; it constitutes in itself a rhetoric. It is an attempt, first, to persuade the student to think of himself as the key man in a three-way collaboration with text and teacher and, second, to explain the four basic, underlying principles that control the process and, third, to aid the student in developing exact observation and syntactic fluency. Part II presents the process, moving from narration and description to exposition and persuasion, and from sentence, to paragraph, to the longer sorts of expository writing. Throughout this book, our approach is positive, our aim consistent—to help make good work better, not to make botched work presentable.

The death of Francis Christensen in 1970 ended the life of a good man, a great teacher and scholar. He did not see the final drafts of these chapters, but the results of his research and insights are here, a memorial to one who brought joy to his family, vast learning and great compassion to his students, and new understanding to his profession.

B. C.

The University of North Dakota
October 1975

PART I
THE PROCESS OF WRITING

1

Introduction

Writing is an art: its medium is language. The very commoness of language—and the commonplaceness of what we use it for—makes it difficult to see what is involved in the art of writing, and thus to see clearly what to try for in a course such as this. We all speak, frequently and freely—some people almost incessantly; and we usually contrive, with a good deal of arm waving and backing and filling and frequent demands for assurance ("You see what I mean"), to communicate with others. Many students, when they have a paper to write, simply dictate to themselves and are hurt and confused when the instructor declares that the meaning is not clear. Both may be honest people—the student when he says it is clear (meaning clear to him) and the instructor when he says it is not clear (meaning not clear to him), but here the instructor is right.

For there is a fundamental and inescapable paradox about language: we would not be human without language, and because of language it is hard to be fully human. The art of writing is to use language, with all its limitations, so as to overcome its limitations. With a clear grasp of this paradox, we can appreciate better the strategies of effective writing and speaking. Let us start with a look at the paradox itself, beginning with this quotation.

Let us assume that a person sees a rose and states: "This is a rose," or, "I see a rose." Does he really see a rose? Some do indeed, but most do not. Then, what is the experience of the latter? I would describe it this way: they see an object (the rose), and state that the object they see falls under the concept "rose," and hence they make a correct statement in saying: "I see a rose." Although it seems that the emphasis in this statement is on the act of *seeing*, it is really on the act of cognition and verbalization. The person who thus states that he sees a rose is actually stating only that he has learned to speak, that is, to recognize a concrete object and to classify it under the proper word for its class. Seeing, here, is not really seeing, but an essentially mental act. What, then, is seeing in the real meaning of the word?

. . . If we are fully aware of a tree at which we look—not of the fact that it is correctly called a tree, but of *this* tree, in its full reality, in its suchness—and if we respond to the suchness of this tree with our whole person, then we have the kind of experience which is the premise for painting [or describing] the tree. Whether we have the technical skill to paint [or describe] what we experience is another question, but no good painting [or writing] is ever done unless there is first a full awareness and responsiveness toward the particular object.

To view it from still another angle, in conceptual knowledge the tree has no individuality; it stands there only an example of the genus "tree"; it is only the representative of an abstraction. In full awareness there is no abstraction; the tree retains its full concreteness, and that means also its uniqueness. There is only this one tree in the world, and to this tree I relate myself, I see it, I respond to it. The tree becomes my own creation. [Erich Fromm, "The Creative Attitude," in Harold H. Anderson, ed., *Creativity and Its Cultivation*]

This sounds odd—"The tree becomes my own creation." It is probably what Blake meant, when he said "A fool sees not the same tree a wise man sees." How can this be and how can one be a wise man and not a fool?

We are assailed by so much data—the world impinges upon us so insistently—that we have to be shielded from overload. Indeed, we have defenses in depth. We have come to see that the receptive nervous system is not a simple one-way communication system carrying messages to the brain to be processed there into our representations of the world. Rather, it is selective. "The eye is blind to what the mind does not see," an Arabian proverb asserts. The mind has a program of its own; it sends out to the sense organs and the relay stations orders that specify priorities for different kinds of messages. As one psychologist has put it, the nervous system is as much an editorial hierarchy as a transmitting system. Thus, intent on writing, we are not open to experience from other quarters. We see, and do not see, the three red roses in a blue mug on each desk in our study. We *know* that they are Will Rogers roses and we *know*, without looking, some of their more obvious qualities. But this is only cognition; they are for the moment only the representatives of the abstraction, Will Rogers roses. Such cognition is passive, not creative. It is not the intense and vivid encounter that sets the mind working in such a way that the internal representation seems less a mirror image of the rose that grew in the garden than a rose that has flowered in the mind. A person may be creative in this way without being able to paint or describe the rose, but one wouldn't be able to paint or describe the rose without this kind of creative seeing.

Another layer of shielding is the selective memory and still another is language. How language shields us from naked experience is expressed neatly in Robert Graves's poem "The Cool Web." There is a cool web of speech, he says, that winds us in, a retreat from too much gladness, too much fear, a retreat that saves us from madness.

We human beings are thus in a dilemma. For it is language that sets us apart from the rest of animal nature. It is language that makes us human, that binds us together in complex social groups, that binds us together over untraveled reaches of space (only the word has to post) and binds us together over untravelable reaches of time (only the word has to survive to give us our history). By means of language each individual internalizes his own experience and carries it about with him. Language "at its highest development becomes the power to catch the world in a net of symbols, to possess it, to manipulate it in new and wondrous ways, to master it, and to recreate it" (Joseph Church, *Language and the Discovery of Reality*).

Yet in the act of mastering it, we may lose it. We may lose contact with things and people and move about in a world of words and symbols, words and symbols that stand for classes, not individuals, and much less for the qualities and details of the individual. This is a kind of divorce from reality that makes us treat the people who move into our schools and neighborhoods not as individuals, who of course may be good or bad, but as outsiders, whether we say "whitey" or "nigger" or some other mindless term. There are people, on the other hand, for whom words do not spell away the overhanging night ("It's only the sky, silly!"); naming it takes away the irrational terror, but not the wonder.

These people can see the fresh, the raw, the concrete, the ideographic, as well as the generic, the abstract, the rubricized, the categorized, and the classified. Consequently, they live far more in the real world of nature than in the verbalized world of concepts, abstractions, expectations, beliefs, and stereotypes that most people confuse with the real world. [Abraham H. Maslow, "Creativity in Self-Actualizing People," in Harold H. Anderson, ed., *Creativity and Its Cultivation*]

A course in English cannot afford to start with a pad of paper, a typewriter or pen, and a list of 182 errors to be avoided in word, sentence, paragraph, and the whole composition. It must help you, while using language, to outwit language, to free yourself from what has been called the tyranny of words: first by using words to intensify rather than to replace sensory perception, and second by treating writing as a strategy for using words in such a way as to give the reader the sense that his transactions are with things more than with words.

2

Basic Principles

We are now ready to consider the underlying principles of a writing program that will use language in such a way as to overcome the disabilities of language. We want to use language as an opening to reality and not as a "cool web" to shield us from reality.

ADDITION

For a starting point let us take a statement from an essay, "The Craft of Writing," by John Erskine, one of whose courses at Columbia led to the Great Books courses, and who was himself a craftsman, a novelist:

> Let me suggest here one principle of the writer's craft, which though known to practitioners we have never seen discussed in print. The principle is this: When you write, you make a point, not by subtracting as though you sharpened a pencil, but by adding. When you put one word after another, your statement should be more precise the more you add. If the result is otherwise, you have added the wrong thing, or you have added more than was needed.
>
> This principle is provocative enough even in a bare statement, but if you think it through, if in practice you reach the conclusion it forces, you see the startling gulf between the grammar which is taught and learned and the grammar which is used. In a loose way grammar concedes that speech is a process of addition; at least grammar distinguishes between the noun substantive and the noun adjective. But the grammarian leaves with the unwary the impression that the substantive, since it can stand alone, is more important than the adjective, that the verb is more important than the adverb, that the main clause is more important than the subordinate.

6

In the use of language, however, the truth is precisely the reverse. What you wish to say is found not in the noun but in what you add to qualify the noun. The noun is only a grappling iron to hitch your mind to the reader's. The noun by itself adds nothing to the reader's information; it is the name of something he knows already, and if he does not know it, you cannot do business with him. The noun, the verb, and the main clause serve merely as a base on which the meaning will rise.

The modifier is the essential part of any sentence. [John Erskine, "The Craft of Writing," in William S. Knickerbocker, ed., *Twentieth Century English*]

This is the foundation for all that is to come in Part 1, The Process of Writing: writing is essentially a process of *addition*.

DIRECTION OF MOVEMENT

But speech is linear, moving in time, and writing moves in linear space, which is analogous to time. When you add a modifier, whether to the noun, the verb, or the main clause, you must add it either before or after what it is added to—that is, before or after what we will call the *head* or *headword*. If you add it before the head, the direction of modification can be indicated by an arrow pointing forward; if you add it after, by an arrow pointing backward.

Noun Head: a slight limber BOY of seventeen with auburn hair

Verb Head: usually WALKED with more activity than result.

Clause Head: At dusk, FISH LEAPED IN THE CHANNEL, making sounds like flat stones thrown in edgewise.

Thus we have the second principle—the principle of *direction of modification* or *direction of movement*.

There are practical limits to the usefulness of this principle. If the head is a noun or a verb, the position of the added modifiers is largely fixed. The writer can choose whether to add and what, but not where to add. An adjective added to a noun head comes before it; a phrase or clause comes after it. Such close or limiting modifiers of words are said to be embedded rather than added. They are not set off by junctures in speaking or punctuation. Although embedded modifiers are frequent and important, we will not spend much time on them or on direction of modification within the phrase or clause.

It is with modifiers added to clauses or sentences and set off from them by punctuation, the so-called sentence modifiers, that the principle comes into full play. The typical sentence of modern English, the kind we can best spend our efforts trying to write, is what we will call the *cumulative sentence*. The main or base clause, which may or may not have sentence modifiers like this before or within it, advances the discussion or the narrative. The other additions, placed after it, move backward (as in this sentence), to modify the statement of the base clause or more often to explain it or add examples or details to it, so that the sentence has a flowing and ebbing movement, advancing to a new position and then pausing to consolidate it. In contrast to embedded or *bound modifiers*, we will call those that are added and set off *free modifiers*.

We will see that the principles of addition and direction of movement apply equally to sentences and to the groups of sentences we call paragraphs. Beyond that, it applies to the group of paragraphs we call an essay, a chapter, or whatever.

LEVELS OF GENERALITY

Addition and direction of movement are structural. To bring in the dimension of meaning, we need a third principle—that of *levels of generality* or *levels of abstraction*. The main or base clause of a sentence (or the topic or base sentence of a paragraph) is likely to be stated in general or abstract or plural terms. With the base clause or the topic stated, the forward movement of the sentence (or paragraph) stops. The writer, instead of going on to something new, shifts down to a lower level of generality or abstraction or to singular terms and goes back over the same ground at a lower level.

Two terms here call for definition—*abstract* and *general*. We call some words concrete and others abstract, defining concrete words as representing things we can see, hear, touch, taste, or smell (*tree, rose, car, book*) and abstract words as representing qualities abstracted from —that is, drawn out from—things and our experience with things (*graceful, fragrant, durable, interesting*). But in another common sense of the term, all words are abstract. They are not themselves things but our internal representations of things and, moreover (except for some proper names), not of individual things, as we have seen, but of classes of things. *Car*, meaning "automobile," stands for all the millions of individual cars the world over, of all makes and of all series, models, and types, with all color and equipment options, in all conditions and in all degrees of obsolescence, planned or unplanned. Thus *car*, although a concrete word, is general. Imagine someone saying, "I just bought a new *car*, a *Ford*, a *Galaxie*, a fastback *hardtop* with a four-on-the-floor shift." You would understand, of course, that he bought just one vehicle—that is, that the four terms are not a parallel series to be added up, but that each one after the first is the name for a smaller class than is the one before it. (You could draw a set of four nested boxes to make this graphic.) Each term is more specific, less general, than the one before it: there are more cars than Fords, more Fords than Galaxies, and more Galaxies than Galaxie hardtops. As a corollary of this, cars in general have less in common than Fords have, and so on; in other words, the specific word is closer to the thing because it represents fewer things.

But note, too, that the last item in the sequence has had something added to the head *hardtop*. You can go only so far in the search for a specific word; then you must resort to addition: the fastback and the four-on-the-floor shift are *parts* or *details* of the hardtop.

Let us reduce this topic to a simple example, a sentence from *The Grapes of Wrath:*

1 Joad's lips stretched tight over his long teeth for a moment,
         and
1 he licked his lips,
    2 like a dog,
      3 two licks,
        4 one in each direction from the middle.

This is a compound sentence; it presents two actions, the lips stretching and the lips being licked. Steinbeck is not much interested in the first, but he is in the second, as the additions show. Note that what follows "he licked his lips" does not go on to a new action; the sentence pauses to examine more closely the lip licking. The indention and the numbering indicate the number of levels—or layers of structure, to use grammatical terms. Why add these extra levels? Is Steinbeck interested in dogs or Joad or the reader or in piece work, so much a word? We might imagine a dialog like this: Q. How did he lick his lips? A. Like a dog. Q. But how does a dog lick his lips? A. He makes two licks. Q. How, two licks? A. Well, one in each direction from the middle. In dialog an inquisitive person might have to wring such information out of an uncommunicative informant. But a speaker or writer who knows his business (and his dogs) anticipates the reader's state of mind and adds level after level, as his purposes require and his sensibility permits, with each added level making the image more precise. There is no theoretical limit to the number of levels.

TEXTURE

We come now to the fourth, and last, principle, that of *texture*. Texture provides a descriptive or evaluative term. If a writer adds to few of his nouns or verbs or clauses and adds little, the texture may be said to be thin. The style will be plain or bare. The writing of most students is thin—even threadbare. But if he adds frequently or much or both, then the texture may be said to be dense or rich. In our course, we have to work for greater density and variety in texture and greater concreteness and particularity in what we add.

These four principles—addition, direction of movement, levels of generality, and degree of texture—are basic, fundamental principles of composition. One of the most important things to learn in learning to write is to move easily and freely up and down from level to level. The key to such learning is to recognize *when* to pause, in order to down-shift to a lower level and let the reader know what it is you have been talking about. The *signal* for the shift should be any high-level statement or term, and your response to such signals must become automatic. It must enter into the very movement of your mind.

In examining these principles, we have been examining the strategy for using language to outwit language. We can't escape language; even the extremest experiment at outwitting language, such as Joyce's in *Finnegan's Wake*, must use language. As Humpty Dumpty said, it's just a question of who is master. The obstacle makes the opportunity.

At this point it would be convenient to have a set of such transparencies as you may have seen in hygiene textbooks, with which the several systems of the body, each depicted in a different color, can be laid over one another until all can be seen working together. But since we are working to improve our use of language, we had better see what we can do with our own medium. Here, stripped down to the bare skeleton, is a passage from a well-known book by an eminent American writer.

1. The sky was changing now; it was coming on to storm, or I didn't know signs.   2. Before it had been mostly sunlight.   3. Now it was mostly shadow.   4. And the wind was down to earth and continual. 5. The smoke from houses where supper had been started was lining out to the east and flowing down.   6. It was a wind with a feel to it.   7. Out at the end of the street, the look of the mountains had changed too. 8. Before they had been big and shining.   9. Now they were dark and crouched down, and it was the clouds that did matter.   10. And they weren't spring clouds, or the kind that mean a rain, but thick, shapeless and white.

If, in spite of the buildup, you think this is rather flat, you are a sound critic. There is, though, something to be said for it. The changes that are the signs of coming on to storm are presented in an orderly way—first the sky before (mostly sunlight) then the sky now (mostly shadow), then the changes in the wind, finally the mountains before and the mountains now and the clouds on the mountains. The action that is to ensue will take a posse of townspeople down the street, out of town, and into the mountains, into a snowstorm that has symbolic overtones.

Besides this, two sentences do have a bit of life—the fifth, with two well-chosen verbs, and the last, with three predicate adjectives describing the storm clouds.

But still the passage is flat and lifeless. The texture is about as thin as possible. The only way to pare further would be to cut down the compounds: *and continual, and flowing down, and crouched down, and shapeless and white.* The ten sentences average 11.6 words, but since two of them are compound (the first doubly compound), the thirteen base clauses average 9 words. There are only three subordinate clauses, all restrictive. The style, in short, is what we call primer style, the style of the books you learned to read from as a child and probably grew bored with even as a child.

It may be worth a paragraph to consider what, of all you learned about writing in school, you might offer to improve such a passage. You were surely taught to avoid the repetition of words, and you might want to avoid the repetition of *clouds.* Since there is no synonym for *clouds,* you would have to find the name for the specific kind of clouds in the last sentence (probably cumulonimbus) or you would have to resort to what is called elegant variation (say, *galleons of the sky*). But neither the technical nor the pseudoliterary term would be right for the cowhand who is reading the weather signs. You were probably taught not to begin sentences with *and* or *but* and might want to delete the two *ands* or replace them by *furthermore.* But consider that in this you would be putting the rule of thumb of a textbook before the practice of an eminent writer and replacing a simple and unobtrusive word by an obtrusive one. If you kept one *and* and deleted the other or replaced it to avoid repetition, you would have overlooked that the two *and* sentences have exactly the same position and function in the first and last parts of the paragraph; like things should be put in like ways (note the *but* sentences in this paragraph). If you were taught to avoid sentence patterns based on *be,* you would have to recast eight of the thirteen main predicates and would certainly turn the plain into the contrived. If you have been taught such things, you have been taught crude rules of thumb that may have minor and occasional relevance in polishing a manuscript but have no relevance here and do nothing at all to flesh out the skeleton.

You might want also to replace *like* by *such as. Such as* may be right for you, but would it be right for an unlettered cowhand? This is a matter of social dialect; and a social dialect merits accuracy in its transcription.

Let us now insert the single-word modifiers (all but two of them embedded modifiers) the author actually used.

The sky was *really* changing now, *fast*; it was coming on to storm, or I didn't know signs. Before it had been mostly sunlight. Now it was mostly shadow. And the wind was down to earth and continual. The smoke from houses where supper had been started was lining *straight* out to the east and flowing down, *not up*. It was a *heavy* wind with a *damp, chill* feel to it. Out at the end of the street, the look of the mountains had changed too. Before they had been big and shining. Now they were dark and crouched down, and it was the clouds that did matter. And they weren't firm, spring clouds, or the *deep, blue-black* kind that mean a *quick, hard* rain, but thick, shapeless and *gray*-white.

The fifteen words do not make a great difference. Four of the first (*really, fast, straight,* and *up*) are adverbs that add intensity to the verbs. (Note how a comma has been used to emphasize *fast* and *not up;* these are free modifiers.) The other words (except *not*) are adjectives —descriptive adjectives that indicate a quality of the object designated by the noun. Whatever you may have been taught about adjectives (which somehow are always called "flowery") you must concede that they do give you the feel of the wind and do differentiate the three kinds of clouds and the kind of rain that falls from the deep, blue-black kind.

The next set of modifiers consist each of more than a single word —that is, they are various sorts of phrases and clauses; and they are all free modifiers—they are all set off by punctuation. And it is no accident that they all come at the end of the sentences.

The sky was really changing now, fast; it was coming on to storm, or I didn't know signs. Before it had been mostly sunlight, *with only a few cloud shadows moving across fast in a wind that didn't get to the ground, and looking like burnt patches on the eastern hills where there was little snow.* Now it was mostly shadow, *with just gleams of sunlight breaking through and shining for a moment on all the men and horses in the street, making the guns and metal parts of the harness wink and lighting up the big sign on Davies' store and the sagging white veranda of the inn.* And the wind was down to earth and continual, *flapping the men's garments and blowing out the horses' tails like plumes.* The smoke from houses where supper had been started was lining straight out to the east and flowing down, not up. It was a heavy wind with a damp, chill feel to it, *like comes before snow, and strong enough so it wuthered under the arcade and some-times whistled, the kind of wind that even now makes me think of Nevada quicker than anything else I know.* Out at the end of the street, *where it merged into the road to the pass,* the look of the mountains had changed too. Before they had been big and shining, *so you didn't notice the clouds much.* Now they were dark and crouched down, *looking heavier but not nearly so high,* and it was the clouds that did matter, *coming up so thick and high you had to look at them instead of the mountains.* And they weren't firm, spring clouds, *with shapes,* or the deep, blue-black kind that mean a quick, hard rain, but thick, shapeless and gray-white, *like dense steam, shifting so rapidly and with so little outline that you more felt than saw them changing.* [Walter Van Tilburg Clark, *The Ox-Bow Incident*]

It must be evident by now that the meaning is (or may be) in the modifiers. Of the 318 words here, 193 are in the added free modifiers, and it is these additions that make the difference between a bare primer style and a rich-textured mature style. They give the scene what can be called "solidity of specification." One would read the skeletonized version (except for the fifth and last sentences) with a vacant mind, merely recognizing the features alluded to. "Mostly sunlight" and "mostly shadow" are highly generalized; one would read them either forming no image at all or perhaps drawing from his own experience of sunshine and shadow inappropriate images. What is added is concrete and specific; it gives the particulars; it gets down to details. These particulars and details *real*-ize the scene, so that instead of skimming over it with a distant nod of recognition, the reader experiences it. He *sees* the cloud shadows "like burnt patches on the eastern hills" and the gleams of sunshine that make the guns and metal parts of harness wink and the sign and the white veranda gleam. He *sees* and *feels* the wind flapping the men's garments and blowing the horses' tails. And he *feels* rather than sees the shifting of the thick but shapeless blue-black clouds. All these details are so exact and precise, so accurately observed, that they also *authenticate* the scene. They compel the reader not only to participate but to accept. They create the illusion of reality.

This example shows why our strategy for getting the upper hand of words, which stand for categories and types (in life "there are no types, no plurals"—F. Scott Fitzgerald), is to concentrate on the modifiers, especially phrases and clauses. Anyone—well, almost anyone— can turn out narrative as effective, if not as orderly, as the stripped-down version, and do it with his eyes shut, spinning it out of his own fantasy. The additions, if they are to give life—and if our imaginary gardens, as the poet Marianne Moore urged, are to have real toads in them—must come from that intense encounter with the world that we have called creative. For most young people this means that the additions must come less from memory than from immediate observation. The problem is less how to say than how to see. Indeed, Robert Frost once asserted that "all there is to learning to write or talk is learning how to have something to say." The faith of this book is that learning how to say it is a stimulus and guide to learning how to have something to say. One can see what he knows how to say.

Learning how to have something to say is learning to be what Henry James called the kind of person on whom nothing is lost. "Nothing seemed to escape him," the painter Joseph Severn said, describing Keats's astonishing powers of observation,

> the song of a bird and the undernote of response from covert or hedge, . . . the motions of the wind—just how it took certain tall flowers and plants—and the wayfaring of the clouds: even the features and gestures of passing tramps, the colour of one woman's hair, the smile on one child's face, the furtive animalism below the deceptive humanity in many of the vagrants, even the hats, clothes, shoes, whenever these conveyed the remotest hint as to the real self of the wearer. [William Sharp, *The Life and Letters of Joseph Severn*]

For those who were not as surely born to be poets as Keats was, the best help a book like this can offer is the two lessons on observation that Flaubert enforced on de Maupassant:

1. *The unrealized in the familiar.* Since we are accustomed to using our eyes only with the memory of what we have already thought about the thing we are looking at, every least thing contains something as yet undiscovered. The writer must contemplate what he intends to express intensely enough to discover an aspect never seen or described by anyone else. "This is how one becomes original."

2. *No two things are alike.* Since in the whole world no two grains of sand, two flies, two hands, two noses are absolutely alike, the discipline of the writer is, with the utmost economy, to distinguish individuals perfectly.

> "When you pass," he told me, "a grocer seated in his door, or a porter smoking his pipe, a cab station, show me that grocer and that porter—their pose, all their physical appearance, containing, as shown by the skill of the description, all their moral nature—and in such a way that they will not be confused with any other grocer and any other porter; and make me see, in a single word, just how one cab horse does not resemble fifty others that follow and precede him." [Guy de Maupassant, Preface to *Pierre et Jean*]

At this stage you should not hanker after a big subject. The subject is unimportant; the treatment, the rendering, is all. A hand lying quietly in a lap is a better subject than a sunset. The lighting of a match is a better subject than the blast-off of an ICBM. At this stage, too, the details, accurately observed and vividly presented, may be regarded as an end in themselves, just as beauty may be its own excuse for being. In a story or in the kind of personal writing you are likely to undertake, such details are necessary to authenticate and to share the experience, but in a great story every detail is also a means to an end, and in the greatest stories selected details may rise to the level of symbolism. In this course it will be enough if we can create and sustain the illusion of reality.

EXERCISE

This is a brief exercise in identifying free modifiers. These are so important in all that follows that the first step is to learn to spot them automatically whenever they appear.

There will be two problems for you to solve. First, initial free modifiers—those that stand before the base clause or whatever it is they modify—are free simply because of their position, whether or not they are set off by punctuation.

Second, the comma is a mark of internal punctuation that serves two quite different functions. It is essential to see which of these functions each comma serves. Some are used to separate *coordinate* elements, these ranging from a pair of adjectives, for instance, to a pair of base clauses in a compound sentence. Others are used to *set off subordinate elements*—that is, the free modifiers. Our concern is with the second sort, but we have to be able to distinguish between marks of coordination and marks of subordination in order to examine the second sort, the free modifiers. Let's examine a passage that is marked for analysis. From Carson McCullers' "The Jockey":

The jockey had left the wall and was approaching the table in the corner. He walked with a prim strut, swinging out his legs in a half-circle with each step, his heels biting smartly into the red velvet carpet on the floor. On the way over he brushed against the elbow of a fat woman in white satin at the banquet table; he stepped back and bowed with dandified courtesy, his eyes quite closed. When he had crossed the room he drew up a chair and sat at a corner of the table, between Sylvester and the rich man, without a nod of greeting or a change in his set, gray face.

We see that initial free modifiers are underlined once. These are not set off by punctuation (though another author might choose to do so), but are free nonetheless because of their position—they stand before what they modify.

The medial free modifier is underlined twice. It has a pair of marks, here commas, to set it off. Medials are marked at both ends, with a pair of commas, or a pair of dashes, or a pair of parentheses, depending upon emphasis.

The final free modifiers are underlined three times. It is common to have more than one final free modifier attached to a base clause. They are set off from the base clause, and from each other, by a mark of punctuation, the comma being the most common mark—but not the only one possible.

The analysis suggests also the function of the marks of internal punctuation. The semicolon separates two base clauses. The first three commas set off free modifiers from the constructions they modify. The pair of commas in the last sentence sets off a medial free modifier. The final comma separates a pair of adjectives.

Here is a passage from Isaac Bashevis Singer's *The Estate* describing the events of a Yom Kippur in the eastern Europe of a distant past:

There had been a time when Nowolipki Street had been a Gentile street, but now only Jews lived there. Yom Kippur candles shone from the windows. Jews were on their way to prayer. The men were dressed in white robes and slippers, and wore their prayer shawls under their coats. The women wore beaded capes, silk or satin dresses with trains, and their most precious jewels. In a top hat and a frock coat, his beard combed into two silver-white points so sparse that every hair could be counted, an enlightened Jew was on his way to the German synagogue, escorting a woman in a hat trimmed with ostrich plumes. In Wola, the large red sun set among purple clouds, like plowed furrows. All the shops were shuttered and bolted. Even the Gentiles walked by with muted steps. The horse-drawn trolley rode past, half empty. Not far away, on Krochmalna Street, the "Pure Prayer" was being read to Ezriel's father, who had become blind. His mother wept at the lighting of the candles.

The analysis shows a coordinate conjunction designated by a box drawn around it. A coordinate conjunction will stand between sentences or between the base clauses of a compound sentence. It is not counted as a free initial modifier; it stands between coordinate structures, but is not part of either.

Notice initial free modifiers here are set off unless they are single-word adverbs or adjectives; punctuation of initial modifiers is often a matter of individual choice. When there are initial free modifiers in narrative-descriptive writing, they tend to be adverbial in function.

There is no medial free modifier. In narrative-descriptive writing this is usually the smallest category; in expository writing it is a larger, and much more significant, category.

Let us examine one more example, a paragraph from Lawrence Durrell's *The Dark Labyrinth:*

As for Fearmax, he was concerned with problems of a different order. He lay for hours in his cabin with his eyes fixed on the ceiling. His door was always open, so that whenever he passed Baird could look in and see him there, hands crossed on his breast, collar open, staring at the paintwork. He did not appear to any meals for the first twenty-four hours and Baird wondered idly if he were having a severe bout of sea-sickness; yet his door stood open, and whenever Baird passed it he saw him lying there. Led by the promptings no less of curiosity than of courtesy, he at last tapped at the door and put his head in, asking Fearmax in his pleasant way if he could be of any use to him. For a time he did not seem to hear— but at last, with an effort, he turned in the bunk and raised himself on one elbow.

No new problems are presented here, except perhaps the subordinate clause beginning *so that.* The subordinate clause is a construction necessary to exposition, not so frequent in narration-description. The *so that* is part of the modifier.

Notice the number of coordinate conjunctions—three in one compound sentence, standing between the base clauses.

And notice the dash in the last sentence—it is used to separate two base clauses.

The following exercise is a passage from John Steinbeck's *The Grapes of Wrath.* When you have identified the initial free modifiers, and when you have distinguished the two functions a comma may serve, you can mark the free modifiers in any convenient way. One way is to underline, the number of lines depending on position. Another way is to use transparent marking pens, a different color each for initial, medial, and final. Such marking gives a rough notion of the proportion of free modifiers in each position and of the proportion of free modifiers to base clauses.

You could go on to counting to make these proportions more exact. There are 156 words in the base clauses and 122 in the free modifiers, not counting the five instances of *and* standing between base clauses. You yourself can count the number of words in the modifiers in each position. When, as here, there are fewer words in the free modifiers than in the base clauses, the texture is on the thin side. In all word counts in this book, each part of a hyphenated compound word has been counted as a separate word; thus *high-domed* was counted as two words.

1. The sun lay on the grass and warmed it, and in the shade under the grass the insects moved, ants and ant lions to set traps for them, grasshoppers to jump into the air and flick their yellow wings for a second, sow bugs like little armadillos, plodding restlessly on many tender feet.   2. And over the grass at the roadside a land turtle crawled, turning aside for nothing, dragging his high-domed shell over the grass.   3. His hard legs and yellow-nailed feet threshed slowly through the grass, not really walking, but boosting his shell along.
4. The barley beards slid off his shell, and the clover burrs fell on him and rolled to the ground.   5. His horny beak was partly open, and his fierce, humorous eyes, under brows like fingernails, stared straight ahead.   6. He came over the grass, leaving a beaten trail behind him, and the hill, which was the highway embankment, reared up ahead of him.   7. For a moment he stopped, his head held high.   8. He blinked and looked up and down.   9. At last he started to climb the embankment.   10. Front clawed feet reached forward but did not touch.   11. The hind feet kicked his shell along, and it scraped on the grass and on the gravel.   12. As the embankment grew steeper and steeper, the more frantic were the efforts of the land turtle.   13. Pushing hind legs strained and slipped, boosting the shell along, and the horny head protruded as far as the neck could stretch.   14. Little by little the shell slid up the embankment until at last a parapet cut straight across its line of march, the shoulder of the road, a concrete wall four inches high.

3

Two-Level Narrative Sentences

The discussion of writing is hampered at every turn by the lack of suitable terms for the various kinds of writing. It is customary to speak of the "four forms of discourse"—description, narration, exposition, argumentation. These four terms, or modes as they are now called, group naturally into two more inclusive kinds, for which we lack commonly accepted and familiar terms. Even without familiar terms, we will find it necessary to distinguish these two main kinds. In speaking or writing, you can either *picture* the object or *talk about* it.

When you picture, or represent, an object, you can picture either its *appearance* (description) or its *behavior* (narration). Description and narration can be called *representational* writing—as we use that term in speaking of representational sculpture or painting. It is a clumsy term, but *creative* and *imaginative* do not either limit or characterize the mode. The contrasting term for the other pair of modes is *discursive*. When you talk about an object or an idea, you can try in a neutral way to *explain* it (exposition) or, taking up an issue, try to *convince* your hearer or reader (argumentation or persuasion).

A minor example will help you to see the difference. If you say "She was wearing a *pretty* dress," you are talking about the dress, not picturing it. *Pretty* is an abstract adjective. Its choice may derive from a close scrutiny of the dress, but it does not offer the evidence, only a conclusion or a judgment. The word does not assist the reader much in forming an image of it; it gives him full leeway to clothe the girl in whatever answers to his notion of what is pretty in a dress. In this, it is like "mostly sunlight." But if you say "She was wearing a *red* dress," you are making a start toward picturing it, because *red* is a concrete adjective. It is only a start, of course, because *red,* though concrete, is general—there are reds and reds. Besides, a single adjective doesn't carry you far in picturing.

REPRESENTATIONAL WRITING

Description and narration both picture, and we have distinguished the two by saying that description pictures the *appearance* of things and narration pictures the *behavior* of things. In the world as science now describes it, this distinction is probably not valid; everything is in constant flux. But in the world as our senses apprehend it, the distinction is useful. In the course of a class hour, the configuration of our bodies, the form of our features, our coloring, even our hairdos and our clothing remain much the same; this is our appearance. But we are pretty constantly in motion—twisting, turning, writing, gazing out the window, occasionally raising our hands and talking; this is our behavior. Even the posture of the student sleeping in the back row, propped up behind dark glasses, must be counted as behavior. Thus description tends to be static, centering on nouns, and narration, despite the student in the back row, to be dynamic, centering on verbs. The modern writer tries to overcome the static character of description by interweaving it with narration or by attributing action to static things or presenting them as interacting.

The most convenient starting point for us will be narrative sentences, which by definition *picture actions.* Here are eight narrative sentences, by student writers, stripped down like the sentences in the paragraph examined in the last chapter. The verbs have been set in small capitals.

1. The loaded oil tanker THRUST heavily FORWARD, . . .
2. The Corvair SLOWED TO A STOP, . . .
3. When the light changed, the "Caddy" BEGAN TO MOVE AWAY soundlessly, . . .
4. The Model A hot rod STOOD WAITING, . . . and then, . . . LET GO and BURST into the traffic.
5. The next car CAME TO A STOP, . . .
6. The car MOVED steadily FORWARD, . . .
7. The MG STOPPED, . . .
8. The gray Thunderbird GLIDED TO A STOP, . . .

Let us look first at the subjects of the sentences. Two writers have been satisfied with the most general term, *car.* Others have used a more specific one, the trade name (Corvair, MG, Thunderbird) or a function designation (oil tanker). Some writers have added a word describing appearance—the concrete adjectives *loaded, gray.*

The verbs range from the general (*moved, stood waiting, stopped*) to the more specific and more lively (*thrust forward, let go, burst*). Note that *slowed to a stop, came to a stop, glided to a stop,* and *began to move away, thrust forward,* and *move forward* have all been taken, loosely perhaps, as constituting the verb.

Some of the writers have added an adverb to sharpen the picture of the action indicated by the verb—the adverbs can be ranged in a continuum from abstract to concrete—*steadily, soundlessly, heavily.* These are adverbs of manner. In descriptive and narrative writing, adverbs and adverbial phrases and clauses of place and time generally take care of themselves; we are concerned primarily with those that describe the manner. Thus, when we talk about what is added, we will not be talking about such commonplace adverbials as *fast, into the traffic,* and *when the light changed.*

Here now are the sentences students wrote as two-level narrative sentences for the assignment "Watch the Fords Go By." Note the numbers and the indention used to indicate graphically what we will call the two levels. The main or base clause is the first level; what has been added, in each case a phrase, is the second level.

1. 1 The loaded oil tanker THRUST heavily FORWARD,
       2 with a short, sharp jet of released air brakes and a heaving lift of the engine.
2. 1 The Corvair SLOWED TO A STOP,
       2 impressing the muddy road with the scalloped ridges of its tires.
3.   2 When the light changed,
     1 the "Caddy" BEGAN TO MOVE AWAY soundlessly,
       2 mirroring a galaxie of little catch lights on its glazed panels.
4. 1 A Model A hot rod STOOD WAITING,
       2 rolling ever so slightly, and then,
       2 with a blast from its twin pipes,
     1 [it] LET GO and BURST into the traffic.
5. 1 The next car CAME TO A STOP,
       2 the doll in the rear window dancing to the sudden change in momentum.
6. 1 The car MOVED steadily forward,
       2 the spot of light above the windshield moving around the rim and then slipping off the back fender as it passed me.
7. 1 The MG STOPPED,
       2 the glimmering pattern of the wheels in motion unraveling into a loosely interwoven warp and woof of silver spokes.
8. 1 The gray Thunderbird GLIDED TO A STOP,
       2 its taillights glowing like a pair of double-burner hotplates.

It is hardly necessary to insist again that the meaning, or perhaps here the interest, is in the modifiers. We need now a language for discussing them. The next few paragraphs are the foundation of our treatment of the sentence. You should master them so well that you can apply the principles creatively, in writing, and analytically, in the discussion of writing. The language we need is of two sorts—*grammatical* and what we will call *rhetorical*.

GRAMMATICAL ELEMENTS

The grammatical language is not difficult. The simplest of the grammatical elements added to the verb is the single-word modifier, the adverb. Adverbs usually appear within the clause as bound modifiers of the verb, though sometimes they are set off by punctuation as free modifiers. We have already observed that they vary in the degree of concreteness. Adverbs tend to be abstract and thus to talk about, rather than picture, the action. Such abstract adverbs are an indulgent shortcut to be looked on with suspicion as intruding the discursive into the representational. Another adverb to be looked on with suspicion, even though it may be concrete, is that used to shore up a general verb—*walk slowly* instead of the more specific *saunter* or *stroll* or many others.

The grammatical element next in complexity is the prepositional phrase. (See sentence 2 above and the second part of 4.) The preposition is a grammatical device for converting nouns, or nominals, into modifiers. The ones we will encounter most often are *in, with, without,* and *like.* The phrases we will attend to are those set off by punctuation and thus classed as free modifiers and placed on a separate level.

Sometimes what has been observed can be expressed by either a noun or a verbal—with a BLAST of its twin pipes/its twin pipes BLASTING. If *blast* had a modifier, the two forms would appear thus—with a *sharp* blast of its twin pipes/its twin pipes blasting *sharply.* The choice of a noun or a verb depends usually on the availability of modifiers.

These examples bring us to the third sort of modifier, that in which verbs are converted to modifiers (in the form of verbals or verbids—*-ing, -ed,* and occasionally *to.*) These are almost always free modifiers and thus almost always set off by punctuation. There are two types—the verb phrase and the so-called absolute construction.

The verb phrase. Look at sentences 2, 3, 4, and ask what is the doer-of-the-action of the verbids *impressing, mirroring, rolling;* the answer will not be found on the second level, within the modifier, but on the first level, in the head clause—the Corvair, the "Caddy," the Model A hot rod. Although the result would be awkward, each of these modifiers could be converted into a sentence—"The Model A hot rod stood waiting. It was rolling ever so slightly."

The absolute. Now look at sentences 5–8 and ask the same question about *dancing, moving, unraveling, glowing.* The doer-of-the-action, the subject, of each of these will be found within the modifier itself—*the doll, the spot of light, the pattern of the wheels in motion, its taillights.* Each of these could be converted into a sentence—"The gray Thunderbird glided to a stop. Its taillights glowed like a pair of double-burner hot plates." This is not awkward, like the sentence in the preceding paragraph. But the two finite verbs suggest two successive units of time, whereas the glowing is simultaneous with the stopping—it is a part of the stopping.

Our grammar, whether new or old, does not afford us convenient terms for these two constructions. If the first is a verb phrase, the second ought to be a verb phrase with a subject. Since this will not do, we will call it a verbid clause for accuracy, and for simplicity an absolute. You may have met it in Latin as the ablative absolute or in English as the nominative absolute. For writers of modern prose it is an indispensable construction.

If you turn back to the paragraph from *The Ox-Bow Incident,* you will find that all the italicized modifiers fit into the grammatical types just listed except for the *relative clause* (RC) "where it merged into the road to the pass" and the *subordinate clause* (SC) "so you didn't notice the clouds much." Both of these are sometimes called subordinate clauses or dependent clauses. They make sentences, they appear in complete sentences, and it may surprise you to find that in descriptive and narrative writing they are almost negligible. These two can hardly be said to have any descriptive value. Only relative and subordinate clauses that are set off are counted as free modifiers; the three bound relative clauses in sentences 5, 9, and 10 are not italicized.

There are three other kinds of phrases, not illustrated by our samples, that should be mentioned here to complete the roster of grammatical constructions. One is the free *adverbial phrase,* which is exceedingly rare: "Then John said nothing. He sat down on his chair again, *as slowly as an old man whose bones are stiff*" (Mark Schorer). Another is the free *adjective phrase,* which is fairly common: "But her voice went on, *relentless in the thickening blue of the summer dusk*" (Mark Schorer). (One could call this one descriptive of the voice, but there is no need for absolute distinctions between description and narration; the modern practice is to interweave them.) The third is the free *noun phrase:* "Our suite was on the top floor of the dorm, *a long narrow room with bedrooms at each corner*" (Wright Morris). The noun phrase is so important in descriptive writing that a separate chapter (Chapter 5) is given to it.

The last kind of free modifier is the *noun* with *an adverbial function;* it is fairly common—"The gypsy was walking out toward the bull again, walking *heel-and-toe*, insultingly, like a ballroom dancer, the red shafts of the banderillos twitching with his walk" (Ernest Hemingway). This construction is familiar in such expressions as "dancing *cheek to cheek*," "walking *two by two*," "running *neck and neck*," "confronting *eyeball to eyeball*."

RHETORICAL ELEMENTS

The rhetorical analysis provides answers to a question of more importance to the writer than the grammatical forms: when you want to sharpen the image of the action designated by a verb, just what can you do? What can you add that will picture the action and not talk about it? It appears that you can do only three things; and, odd though it may seem, when you want to sharpen the image of the object designated by a noun, you can do only the same three things. But this is not really odd. We have defined description as picturing appearance and narration as picturing behavior, one centering on the noun, the other on the verb. At the risk of some initial confusion, we will call these three things you can do the three *methods of description*. Although we want to distinguish description and narration, one can be said to describe objects, the other to describe actions.

The simplest way to sharpen the image of an object or an action— that is, to describe it—is to use an adjective or adverb to indicate some quality or attribute, as in "*quick, hard* rain" or "moved away *soundlessly*."

A second way is to point to some *part* of the object or action— that is, to use what we will call a *detail*. In the light narrative sentences above, all the modifiers marked as second level point to a part or detail of the action designated by the verb in the main clause. Pointing to a quality effects in the reader's mind an overall modification of the image suggested by the headword; it is like turning the focusing knob and seeing the blurred image spring into sharpness on the ground glass. Pointing to a detail, on the other hand, is like zooming in for a close-up of some part.

The third way is to go beyond the object or the action itself and to sharpen the image by suggesting its likeness to something else. This is the method of description by *comparison*—clouds "thick, shapeless and gray-white, *like dense steam*" and taillights "glowing *like a pair of double-burner hotplates*." An adjective such as *exhilarating* suggests a fourth method of description, by *effect*; but this soon shades off into explanation. The three things you can do, then, whether the headword is a noun or a verb or a clause, the three methods of description, are by quality or attribute, by detail, by comparison.

BRINGING THE GRAMMATICAL
AND RHETORICAL TOGETHER

When we bring the grammatical and the rhetorical analyses together, we see that an attribute is expressed by an adjective or adverb. But all adjectives do not designate attributes; *red-eyed* indicates a detail, *flowerlike* or *flower-soft* a comparison; and an abstract adjective such as *pretty*, as we have said, does not picture, but summarizes and should be regarded as expository. The detail usually calls for a phrase—prepositional phrase (commonly *in*, *with*, or *without*) or a verb phrase or absolute. The comparison usually calls for a phrase with the preposition *like*, but it takes many other grammatical forms (as in *hair the color of wheat straw*). Any of the three can be put instead into the predicate— The clouds were thick, shapeless and gray-white/The wind flapped the men's garments/The clouds were like dense steam.

The two-level sentence has a greater range than we have intimated. It may have two or more free modifiers, logically equal, and using the same or different grammatical constructions. Here the levels and the kinds of modifiers are identified. The method in every one is by detail.

9. 1 "Hyess," Hannah said softly,
    2 sharply inhaling the first of the word, **(Verb Phrase)**
    2 trailing the sibilant to a hair. **(Verb Phrase)**

James Agee

10. 1 A switch engine nosed over the points,
     2 swaying gently as it clattered over the frog, **(Verb Phrase)**
     2 its footboards searching the rails, **(Absolute)**
        and
     1 it shuffled slowly down the siding,
     2 its side-rods clanking, **(Absolute)**
     2 a feather of steam wisping from its idling piston, **(Absolute)**
     2 the red cherry glare of its fire staining the trackside snow. **(Absolute)**

11. 1 The horses were coming,
     2 looking as if their hides had been drenched and rubbed with soap, **(Verb Phrase)**
     2 their ribs heaving, **(Absolute)**
     2 their nostrils flaring and closing. **(Absolute)**
     1 The jockeys sat bowed and relaxed,
     2 their faces calm, **(Absolute)**
     2 moving a little at the waist with the movement of their horses. **(Verb Phrase)**

Katherine Anne Porter

12. 1 Grandmother . . . paused before these candles each Friday
       night,
    2 a clean white napkin covering her head, **(Absolute)**
    2 eyes closed to the tallowy heat, **(Absolute)**
    2 quietly chatting with Him as she might with a neighbor to
       whom she had come to borrow a cup of sugar. **(Verb Phrase)**
13. 1 She stood on the edge of the pool,
    2 resting lightly on sunburned heels, **(Verb Phrase)**
    2 toes curled over the porous stone side, **(Absolute)**
    2 arms slightly bent, **(Absolute)**
       and
    2 fingertips pressing into the fine skin of her upper thighs. **(Absolute)**
14.   2 Wearing only his bagging woolen underwear, **(Verb Phrase)**
      2 his spectacles folded away in the worn case beneath the
        pillow . . . , **(Absolute)**
    1 he lay on his back,
      2 his hands crossed on his breast, **(Absolute)**
        and
      2 his eyes closed while the others undressed and went to bed and
        the last of the sporadic talking died away into snoring. **(Absolute)**

> William Faulkner

15. 1 They had behaved like wild creatures all morning;
    2 shouting from the breezy bluffs, **(Verb Phrase)**
    2 dashing down into the silvery marsh through the dewy cob-
      webs that glistened on the tall weeds, **(Verb Phrase)**
    2 swishing among the pale tan cattails, **(Verb Phrase)**
    2 wading in the sandy creek bed, **(Verb Phrase)**
    2 chasing a striped water snake from the old willow stump
      where he was sunning himself, **(Verb Phrase)**
    2 cutting sling-shot crotches, **(Verb Phrase)**
    2 throwing themselves on their stomachs to drink at the cool
      spring that flowed out from under a bank into a thatch of dark
      watercress. **(Verb Phrase)**

> Willa Cather

There is no need to multiply examples. Other grammatical constructions might emerge, but no new principles or problems, except perhaps the problem of avoiding monotony in the rhythm.

In another way, the two-level sentence is more varied than we
have explicitly stated. The materials for the second level are not limited
to impressions of sight, but may come from the other senses—hearing,
taste, touch, smell, etc.

16. 1 The cushion of the barber's chair lowered with his weight,
   2 breathing itself into firmness. **(Verb Phrase)**
  1 He waited until the barber took away the clippers and sat up more straight,
   2 feeling the inhaling cushion rise slightly as he shifted. **(Verb Phrase)**

17. 2 Sitting in the halted buckboard, **(Verb Phrase)**
  1 Ratliff watched the old fat white horse . . . come down the land . . . ,
   2 surrounded and preceded by the rich sonorous organ tones of its entrails. **(Verb Phrase)**

William Faulkner

18. 1 "I never believed . . . ," said Cousin Eva,/*, "that Amy was an impure woman."
   2/ putting her mouth close to Miranda's ear **(Verb Phrase)**
   and
   2/ breathing peppermint hotly into it **(Verb Phrase)**

Katherine Anne Porter

19. 1 And we'd sit in the dry leaves . . . ,
   2 the rank smell of the lantern fouling the brittle air, **(Absolute)**
   2 listening to the dogs and to the echo of Louis' voice dying away. **(Verb Phrase)**

William Faulkner

20. 1 The stove was warming,
   2 with ** orange light showing around the lids **(Absolute)**
   and
   2 the soft thunder of drafty flame leaping past the open damper. **(Absolute)**

John Steinbeck

21. 1 The kitchen was sweet with tarts,
   and
  1 some of the berries had boiled over in the oven and burned,
   2 making the sharp, bitter-sweet smell pleasant and astringent. **(Verb Phrase)**

John Steinbeck

22. 1 His foot felt the sponginess of the wood worn by many feet before him,
   2 the fibers rolling minutely loose under his tread. **(Absolute)**

Robert Penn Warren

---

* The slash or virgule indicates the position of a medial free modifier.

** *With* is not a preposition and the modifier is not a prepositional phrase. It is a mere "grammatical marker" of the absolute; it can be omitted, as a preposition could not. There are two similar-looking examples in the paragraph from *The Ox-Bow Incident*, but it is hard to tell whether these are prepositional phrases or absolutes.

23. 1 She raised the glass to her lips,
    2 her fingers smarting slightly from the coldness, **(Absolute)**
    2 the rim of the glass awkwardly round against the flatness of her lips, **(Absolute)**
    2 the liquid changing its form almost without motion, **(Absolute)**
    2 only the lemon pulp on top floating toward the back. **(Absolute)**
24. 1 She lit a cigarette,
    2 the sulphuric smart of the match smoke lingering in her eyes, **(Absolute)**
    2 her first puff tainted with its smell. **(Absolute)**
25. 1 Vickers hunched forward,
    2 smelling the damp wool of his sheepskin collar, **(Verb Phrase)**
    2 feeling his breath congealing on the chinstrap. **(Verb Phrase)**

Wallace Stegner

ADVICE FOR WRITING

At the threshold of your first writing assignment, a few negative injunctions may keep you from going astray. These are the commonest beginner's mistakes.

Do not write "As Vickers hunched forward, he smelled. . . ." Such sentences do occur and they may be logical, but they violate the whole-part relationship that is so characteristic of modern writing.

Do not *explain*. Descriptive and narrative writing operates with appearances. The cause and effect relationship is especially likely to intrude—"The driver stepped on the brakes hard, *causing* the front end to dip."

Do not *personify* inanimate things such as machines and natural phenomena; in other words, avoid the "pathetic fallacy." This is the fallacy, so called by John Ruskin, of attributing human feelings, thoughts, intents, purposes to nonhuman phenomena. It is to call the foam, when one is in peril in an open boat, "the cruel, crawling foam." We do not have, in general, a separate vocabulary for the *actions* of nonhuman phenomena; so we may say "the *crawling* foam," just as we say the wind whistles, roars, and so on. The pathetic fallacy means attributing human *feelings* to the inanimate foam, endowing it with a malevolent intent, with cruelty. This is personification, and you can make no progress if you put this sort of fantasy before observation.

Similarly, do not make *inferences*, guesses as to what is going on in the minds of your characters—"The Chevrolet started up, its driver grim and determined in his resolution that the fourteen-year-old vehicle would heed his silent urging and the stern compulsion evinced in his unconsciously clenched teeth." The only thing observed is the clenched teeth, and the clenched teeth must suggest the story. (*Would heed,* incidentally, personifies the car.)

Do not indulge in *elegant variation.* Call a spade a spade, not only once but as many times as you have to mention it, except when you can use a pronoun. A car is a car, always, not first a car, then a highway charger, and then a four-wheeled mechanical conveyance.

Do not be *sentimental.* To be sentimental is to exhibit feelings in excess of what the situation calls for. Just what is excessive is hard to say. Some people are always overwhelmed by babies or children or pets or sunsets, so overwhelmed that they do not see them. And that may be the test; the writer conveys that he is overwhelmed, but does not convey the sense that he is really observing.

Finally, whatever you see to say you must say deftly and briefly; both the base clauses and the modifiers must be kept short or you will seem to have only words, words, words.

EXERCISES

A. Copy these sentences, using indention and numbers to mark the two levels. If your instructor so directs, identify the grammatical constructions used in the second level. Observe the punctuation; put only free modifiers on the second level. You must distinguish between punctuation used to separate coordinate elements and punctuation used to set off free modifiers.

1. The flame sidled up the match, driving a film of moisture and a thin strip of darker gray before it.
2. The horses and cattle in the fields moved quietly, a step at a time, cropping with short jerks of their heads. [W. V. T. Clark]
3. The piano player spanned the keys, his right hand flailing like Garner, his left striding like "Fats."
4. He watched [the stage coach] go by, the four horses spanking along as the driver flicked them, the polished metal gleaming in the sun, the body swaying in the thoroughbraces as the wheels rose and fell in the rough trail. [A. B. Guthrie]
5. The men stood on the siding first on one foot and then on the other, their hands thrust deeply into their trousers pockets, their overcoats open, their shoulders screwed up with the cold. [Willa Cather]
6. Every day she found someone there, sitting upon her desk instead of the chair provided, dangling his legs, eyes roving, full of his important affairs, waiting to pounce upon something or other. [Katherine Anne Porter]

7. She was standing three steps above him, one hand on the banister, the fingers of the other splayed out against the opposite wall, leaning forward as though on the brink of flight. [Aldous Huxley]

8. The ball spun fast down the alley, hugging the right edge, then spinning slightly and curving in a long tapering arc, striking the pins with a loud crash, scattering them all on the floor.

B. Recast these groups of sentences, making each group a single two-level sentence. Indent and number to indicate the two levels.

1. At the beach they waited. They watched the white filigree of foam scrape the gray shore. They listened to the sinking groan of the breakers.

2. They stood together waiting. Their faces were solemn. Their eyes were on the bunch of violets she held in both hands.

3. A little girl hopped up the stairs ahead of her parents. Her blue dress bounced with each hop. The taps on her shoes clicked on the concrete stairs and glinted in the sun.

4. The women sat down below in the theater. Their perfectly dressed hair gleams. Their backs are very straight. Their heads are carried tensely.

5. George and Helen arose and walked away into the darkness. They went along a path past a field of corn that had not yet been cut. The wind whispered among the dry corn blades. [Sherwood Anderson]

6. Savora was bending over her. His fingertips were pressed together in concern. His features were shadowed in attention. [Sylvia Thompson]

7. I padded downstairs in my socks. The boards were smooth and cool and silent to my feet. [Shirley Ann Grau]

8. In the English November fog the leaves dripped with a deadly intensity. It was as if each falling drop were a drop of acid. [Elizabeth Taylor]

9. We walked home in the cold. We walked through cold streets. We clutched our packages and our humiliation. No one dared to complain. No one was old enough to laugh. [N. H. Packer]

10. The gulls dipped and darted on the headland. The soft shine of the sun could be seen on their wings. [Willa Cather]

C. Practice writing two-level narrative sentences in class. Since literally *any* action can be described, it is easy to find subjects—someone writing on the board or erasing the board, entering the room, crossing the room, taking a seat, sitting at a desk, writing notes, raising a hand to speak. Concentrate on details, but try comparisons, too, and adverbs.

D. Assignments to be written outside class should be on actions you can observe. The instructor can set the subjects, if he wishes, and the number of sentences. Hand them in in two forms, with normal margins and with the two levels indicated.

4
Multilevel Narrative Sentences

If you got a bit enthusiastic in writing two-level sentences, if you really caught on to the idea of added levels and your observation was sensitive enough, perhaps your enthusiasm and your sense of awakening technical skill carried you beyond the strict call of duty to another level. Your sentences in that case were what we will call *multilevel*. This term will serve for anything from three-level on. A few lines from a poem by Elizabeth Coatsworth, "Ensnare the Clouds," will provide a clear-cut example:

> a green frog watched me
> put on my shoes, I sitting on a boulder,
> he sitting in the pond, his fingers resting
> upon its edge, his golden eyes upon me.

With the levels indented and numbered the passage looks like this:

1 A green frog watched me put on my shoes,
  2 I sitting on a boulder,
  2 he sitting in the pond,
    3 his fingers resting upon its edge,
    3 his golden eyes upon me.

In the base clause two beings are involved. At the second level, the two are separated, and each is allotted an absolute describing the posture. The third level consists again of a pair of absolutes, but here the subjects (*fingers* and *eyes*) are parts of the frog; thus the third level too presents narrative details, the details of the frog's sitting. Another way to demonstrate the relation is to convert the absolute "he sitting in the pond" into a sentence; then the sentence would be a two-level narrative sentence like this:

1 He was sitting in the pond,
  2 his fingers resting upon its edge,
  2 his golden eyes upon me.

If the author had chosen to do so, she could have added details about the fingers or eyes or both. There is no theoretical limit to the number of levels. (Our file holds sentences with up to ten levels.) The principle is that dogs have fleas and "small fleas have smaller still to bite 'em," to which the rime word is "ad infinitum."

RELATIONSHIP OF THE ADDITIONS

The way to determine the level of each added item is to study its relation—whether it is parallel or in some way subordinate—to what has gone before. In short, what does it bite? *I* and *he* are parallel, hence on the same level; *fingers* and *eyes* are parallel, hence on the same level. But *I* and *he* go back to *me* and *frog,* hence their verbid clauses (which we are calling absolutes) are subordinate and on level 2; *fingers* and *eyes* are parts of the frog, hence their clauses are subordinate to *he,* and on level 3.

In the sentences analyzed below, the predominant method of describing action is by details. But there are a few adverbs describing by attributes and a few *like* phrases and *as if* and *as though* subordinate clauses describing by comparison.

1. 1 John Chapman was sitting alone in the bank,
     2 peeling an apple carefully, **(Verb Phrase)**
       3 the unbroken spiral hanging like a shaving as he turned the fruit. **(Absolute)**

Wallace Stegner

2. 1 I held the cockateel gingerly on my finger, **(Absolute)**
     2 his claws clinging quiveringly, **(Absolute)**
       3 their pads telegraphing the pulse and heat of his timorous mien. **(Absolute)**

3. 1 The shell was a speck now,
     2 the oars catching the sun in spaced glints, **(Absolute)**
       3 as if the hull were winking itself along. **(Subordinate Clause)**

William Faulkner

4. 1 A flag hung in folds parallel with the pole,
     2 unfurling first in one direction then the other, **(Verb Phrase)**
       3 the shadows rippling in vertical lines across the horizontal stripes. **(Absolute)**

5. 1 My grandfather sat across the table from my grandmother,
    2 one hand resting laxly on his knee, **(Absolute)**
      3 palm upward, **(Absolute)**
    2 the other grasping his cane, **(Absolute)**
      3 fondling the handle gently from time to time. **(Verb Phrase)**

August Derleth

6. 1 She picked up one of the sheets, and, / , sent it flying,
    2/ with a sharp snap **(Prepositional Phrase)**
    2 a cascading snowy wave of fresh, washed muslin, **(Noun Phrase)**
      3 its odor of soap and fresh air perfuming the room. **(Absolute)**

7.   2 Heads up, **(Absolute)**
    2 swinging with the music, **(Verb Phrase)**
    2 their right arms swinging free, **(Absolute)**
 1 [the matadors] stepped out,
    2 crossing the sanded arena under the arc-lights, **(Verb Phrase)**
      3 the cuadrillas opening out behind, **(Absolute)**
      3 the picadors riding after. **(Absolute)**

Ernest Hemingway

8. 1 She folded the cloth two times,
    2 end to end, **(Noun Adverb)**
      3 like a quarto, **(Prepositional Phrase)**
    2 matching the angles at each corner. **(Verb Phrase)**

9. 1 He dipped his hands in the bichloride solution and shook them,
    2 a quick shake, **(Noun Phrase)**
      3 fingers down, **(Absolute)**
        4 like the fingers of a pianist above the keys. **(Prepositional Phrase)**

Sinclair Lewis

10. 1 Then he puts down the saw and goes and crouches above the lantern,
    2 shielding it with his body, **(Verb Phrase)**
      3 his back shaped lean and scrawny by his wet shirt as though he had been abruptly turned wrong-side out, **(Absolute)**
        4 shirt and all. **(Noun Phrase)**

William Faulkner

11.   2 Slowly, **(Adverb)**
    2 deliberately, **(Adverb)**
 1 she shifted her weight to the balls of her feet,
    2 heels raised an inch or two, **(Absolute)**
    2 leg muscles hardened, **(Absolute)**
    2 slowly raising her slim arms in front of her, **(Verb Phrase)**

     3 resting one hand upon the other, **(Verb Phrase)**
       4 fingers close together, **(Absolute)**
     3 the soft, supple skin of her chest squeezed gently between
       the tight straps of her swim suit. **(Absolute)**
12. 1 So once more he stood on dry land . . .
     2 he and the woman standing on the empty levee, **(Absolute)**
       3 the sleeping child wrapped in the faded tunic **(Absolute)**
         and
       3 the grapevine painter still wrapped about the convict's
         wrist, **(Absolute)**
       3 watching the steamboat . . . crawl onward up the platter-
         like reach of vacant water, **(Verb Phrase)**
         4 burnished more and more to copper, **(Verb Phrase)**
         4 its trailing smoke roiling in slow copper-edged gouts,
           (Absolute)
           5 thinning out along the water, **(Verb Phrase)**
           5 fading, **(Verb Phrase)**
           5 slinking away across the vast serene desolation, **(Verb
             Phrase)**
         4 the boat growing smaller and smaller until it did not
           seem to crawl at all but to stand stationary in the airy
           substanceless sunset, **(Absolute)**
           5 dissolving into nothing like a pellet of floating
             mud. **(Verb Phrase)**
                                              William Faulkner
13. 1 There they sat,
     2 hypnotized, **(Verb Phrase)**
     2 enthralled, **(Verb Phrase)**
     2 concentrating, / , on Zorro, **(Verb Phrase)**
       3/ with all the power of their developing intellects **(Prepo-
         sitional Phrase)**
     2 two boys, **(Noun Phrase)**
       3 cross-legged on the cold, damp concrete floor, **(Adjective
         Phrase)**
       3 oblivious of their cramped muscles, **(Adjective Phrase)**
       3 unaware of the ice cream cones melting, **(Adjective Phrase)**
         4 making rivulets of chocolate and strawberry down each
           right arm to the elbow, **(Verb Phrase)**
           5 where the sweet, sticky liquid dripped unnoticed to
             the floor. **(Subordinate Clause)**

In their natural habitat multilevel sentences are not all as orderly
as these. The astonishing thing is that, long as they are, most of them
with only commas as clues to the structure, they should yield up the

secrets of their structure so readily. But it will be only fair to point out that there are some difficulties.

GRAPHIC REPRESENTATION

The first sort are those that involve the system of graphic representation by indention and numbered levels. The free modifiers we are concerned with may appear, as we have seen, in any of three positions relative to the head they modify: initial, medial, and final, or before, within, and after. This two-sentence paragraph from D. H. Lawrence's "The Rocking-Horse Winner" illustrates all three positions:

His eyes blazed at her for one strange and senseless second, as he ceased urging his wooden horse. Then he fell with a crash to the ground, and she, all her tormented motherhood flooding upon her, rushed to gather him up.

The initial free modifier is underlined once, the medial twice, the final three times. The sentences can be analyzed visually:

14. 1 His eyes blazed at her for one strange and senseless second,
       2 as he ceased urging his wooden horse.
    2 Then
    1 he fell with a crash to the ground,
               and
    1 she, / , rushed to gather him up.
       2/ all her tormented motherhood flooding upon her

Free modifiers that appear after—the commonest position—ordinarily present no problem.

Nor do those that appear before. Initial free modifiers are the easiest to identify since they are free simply by virtue of their position up front. Many of them, of course, are adverbials of time or place and of no great consequence to us. Sometimes an initial free modifier has free modifiers of its own:

15.   2 Lying there like a corpse in the dead leaves, **(Verb Phrase)**
          3 his hair matter, **(Absolute)**
          3 his face grotesquely smudged and bruised, **(Absolute)**
          3 his clothes in rags and muddy, **(Absolute)**
       1 Will Farnaby awoke with a start.

                                                    Aldous Huxley

A sentence like this with the base clause at the end is called a periodic sentence; it is the opposite of the cumulative sentence. Still, there is no problem.

But the graphic presentation of medial elements does raise problems. The slant line (or slash or virgule) between commas or dashes indicates the position and the punctuation of the medial element; and the slant line beside the number for the level indicates that this is the displaced medial element. A sentence may, of course, have free elements added in more than one position: "The weasel, scenting blood, backed up against the far wall of the box, yellow body tense as a spring, teeth showing in a tiny soundless snarl" (Wallace Stegner).

16. 1 The weasel, / , backed up against the far wall of the box,
    2/ scenting blood **(Verb Phrase)**
    2 yellow body tense as a spring, **(Absolute)**
    2 teeth showing in a tiny soundless snarl. **(Absolute)**

Another sort of problem is presented by this narrative sentence of Hemingway's:

17. 1 George was coming down in telemark position,
    2 kneeling, **(Verb Phrase)**
       3 one leg forward and bent, **(Absolute)**
       3 the other trailing, **(Absolute)**
       3 his sticks hanging like some insect's thin legs, **(Absolute)**
          4 kicking up puffs of snow, **(Verb Phrase)**
           and
       3 finally, **(Adverb Phrase)**
    2 the whole kneeling, trailing figure coming around in a beautiful right curve, **(Absolute)**
       3 crouching, **(Verb Phrase)**
          4 the legs shot forward and back, **(Absolute)**
          4 the body leaning out against the swing, **(Absolute)**
          4 the sticks accenting the curve like points of light, **(Absolute)**
    ? all in a wild cloud of snow.

What sort of construction is the last element? And what level is it—2, 3, 4, or 5 or something else? *All* summarizes the second stage of the action, the turn, and the prepositional phrase describes a condition that prevails throughout the turn. The fact is that any element that represents a deduction from or a survey or condition of what has gone before cannot be conveniently represented by our system of levels; the system works downward only. We will mark this C for conclusion or coda. The same is true of interpolated comments, which we can mark P for parenthetic. Fortunately these do not occur often in sentences. We will meet them again in the chapters on the paragraph, where they are common.

DISCRIMINATION OF LEVELS

Another sort of problem is what constitutes a separate level. Should the two *like* phrases in 17 have been put on separate levels? Is it acceptable to treat the *as if* and *as though* clauses of sentences 3 and 10 differently just because Faulkner set off one and not the other? Should one consider this quotation from Hemingway as a two-level or a three-level sentence —"Then the squirrel crossed to another tree, moving on the ground *in long, small-pawed, tail-exaggerated bounds*"? The prepositional phrase in the verb cluster clearly pictures the squirrel's moving. Our rule, as you have already guessed, will be to follow the author's punctuation, even while wishing that some of it were less capricious. The following sentence was punctuated correctly by its student author and is analyzed according to the punctuation. If one made separate levels of the bound clauses beginning with *until* (level 2), *as* and *that* (level 4), and *as* (level 5) and the prepositional phrase with *like as* and *that* (level 4), and *as* (level 5) and the prepositional phrase with *like* (level 5), he would have a sentence of ten levels. Trial and error supports the simplest analysis possible, the one with the fewest levels.

18. 1 The swells moved rhythmically toward us,
　　 2 irregularly faceted,
　　 2 sparkling,
　　 2 rolling gently at first,
　　 2 growing taller and more powerful until the shining crest bursts,
　　　 3 a transparent sheet of pale green water spilling over the top,
　　　　 4 breaking into blue-white foam as it cascades down the front of the curl,
　　　　 4 piling up in a frothy white mound that the diminishing wave pushes up against the pilings and rocks,
　　　　　 5 with a swish-smash,
　　　　　 5 the foam drifting back like a lace fan opened over the shimmering water as the spent wave returns whispering to the sea.

There remains one final point to be made about the cumulative sentences we have been calling two-level and multilevel. The point will require some examples.

19. Then he reached under his robe and pulled out a small leather-bound prayer book. He opened it at a ribbon marker. The gold edging flashed as it caught the sun. [Edward Fenton]
20. Proceeding down the path, they passed a rocky clearing in which a small herd of cows was grazing, their bells musical in the bright morning air. [Robert Nathan]

In 19 the verbs *reached, pulled out,* and *opened* designate three actions succeeding one another in time; the author has seen fit to present the three in two sentences. But the time of *flashed* is not subsequent to that of *opened;* the time is the same, and logically the flashing is a part or detail of the opening, or at least a circumstance accompanying the opening. In a rich-textured style it would normally appear as an absolute attached to the second sentence: "He opened it at a ribbon marker, the gold edging flashing as it caught the sun." Here "edging flashing" is awkward, and one cannot tell whether the author tried and rejected "the gold edge flashing." In 20, on the other hand, the initial verb cluster does not present a detail or circumstance of their passing the clearing. Chronologically and logically, the passing is included in the proceeding. A more natural form for the sentence would be this: "They proceeded down the path, passing a rocky clearing in which a small herd of cows was grazing, their bells musical in the bright morning air." By contrast, in sentence 7, above, the three initial elements are a part of the action of stepping out and they are simultaneous in time. Thus initial verb phrases are of two sorts. The sort represented by *proceeding* is more frequent in discursive than in narrative prose. It is a device for subordinating one action to another. In the work of professional writers neither type is really frequent; both suggest the classroom and the theme.

Analyzing and writing multilevel sentences is a good way to develop the syntactical dexterity that is as valuable to the writer as digital dexterity is to the dentist. But since you can't add levels unless you have materials to fashion them from, each added level forces a closer interrogation of the action. Each added one is a step away from the habitual, the already generalized and categorized, toward what is individual or unique in the occasion. If depth of exploration, if concreteness, is of value, then work with multilevel sentences is a way to have it forced upon you.

EXERCISES

A. Copy these sentences, using indention and numbering to mark the levels. If your instructor so directs, mark the grammatical character of the levels added to the main clause.

1. Crane sat up straight, suddenly, smiling shyly, looking pleased, like a child who has just been given a present. [Irwin Shaw]
2. For once, the students filed out silently, making a point, with youthful good manners, of not looking at Crane, bent over at his chair, pulling his books together. [Irwin Shaw]
3. She was very old and small and she walked slowly in the dark pine shadows, moving a little from side to side in her steps,

with the balanced heaviness and lightness of a pendulum in a grandfather clock. [Eudora Welty]

4. As he walked into the club he noticed them, objectively and coldly, the headwaiter beckoning haughtily, head tilted, lips in a rigid arc reserved for those willing to pay the price of recognition and attention, the stiffly genteel crowd, eating their food in small bites, afraid of committing a breach of etiquette.

5. [The boy] and Anse are on the porch when I come out, the boy sitting on the steps, Anse standing by a post, not even leaning against it, his arms dangling, the hair pushed and matted up on his head like a dipped rooster. [William Faulkner]

6. He swung up into the saddle, carefully making it an easy-looking mount, slow and all in one move, his back very straight and his right leg, bent at the knee, just sliding over the cantle. [W. V. T. Clark]

7. The vaulter sprinted down the runway, his eyes fixed on the box, his hands gripping the awkward pole, carrying it grace-fully, conscious of the silent tension of the crowd investing itself in his actions; and, suddenly driving the pole into the box, he arced upward, feeling the spring of pole, his muscles pushing his weight toward the sky, his body arching at the crucial instant and jackknifing above the striped bar.

8. They regarded me silently, Brother Jack with a smile that went no deeper than his lips, his head cocked to one side, study-ing me with his penetrating eyes; the other blank-faced, looking out of eyes that were meant to reveal nothing and to stir profound uncertainty. [Ralph Ellison]

9. Some mornings Ellen wakes up by herself and comes on tiptoe down the hall to the big bedroom, her yellow sleepers faded and wrinkled, the worn feet flapping around the ankles like puppies, her fists rubbing her eyes, her senses not quite awake but guiding her surely toward the middle region of the big bed.

10. Hundreds of children with their adult overseers lined the rail behind which, in a malodorous straw-sprinkled enclosure, stood the great beasts, lumbering with heavy grace upon gray tree-trunk feet, their skins the color of fossil rock, folded and creased and pitted like oversized garments on their enormous frames. [Sidney Alexander]

B. Practice writing multilevel narrative sentences in class. The same sort of subjects that you found for two-level sentences will be useful for multilevel sentences. Attend to the action, so that you concentrate on details, but try comparisons and adverbs as well. Developing a good eye is necessary preparation.

C. Assignments to be written outside of class should again describe actions that you can observe. The instructor may prescribe the kind of subjects, if he wishes, and the number of sentences. It will help if you work consciously, level by level, outlining the sentences as you write; hand them in, as before, in two forms, with normal margins and with the different levels indicated.

5

Description— the Appositive Noun Phrase

Narration, even when the sentences are multilevel, is relatively simple. Description is a bit more complicated. Some description is based on sentence patterns with predicate adjectives or nouns after *be* and after such verbs as *seem* and *become*. But such sentences are likely to seem static and when they are interspersed in a narrative they interrupt the narrative movement. They make for a simple style. So most description appears as modifiers, and the most interesting and significant of the modifiers are the free ones.

BASE CLAUSES

We will start again, as we did with narration, by separating the modifiers from their context. Here is a stripped down version of a dense-textured passage by another eminent American writer. To save space, the single-word modifiers have been retained, set in italics. In sentence 13, *once* and the *with*-phrase that follows are not italicized, because they are narrative. The fact that there is only one such adverbial in fourteen sentences is a clue to the way this paragraph differs in style from the paragraph from *The Ox-Bow Incident*.

When stripped down in this fashion, this paragraph like that one is close to primer style. Four commas where another writer might have used them (one each in 3, 5, 6, and 9) would reduce it to primer style, with sentences of ten or eleven words. The escape from the primer prison is by way of the free modifiers.

1. You have seen him a thousand times.   2. You have seen him standing on the street corner on Saturday afternoon, in the *little* county-seat towns.   3. He wears *blue* jean pants, or overalls washed to

a pale pastel blue like the color of the sky after a rain in the spring, but because it is Saturday he has on a wool coat.   4. His *long* wrist bones hang out from the sleeves of the coat.   5. The *big* hands hang *loose* off the wrist bone like *clumsy, homemade* tools hung on the wall of a shed after work.   6. If it is summer, he wears a straw hat with a *wide* brim.   7. If it is winter, he wears a felt hat.   8. His face is long and bony.   9. The flesh along the jawbone is nicked in a couple of places where the unaccustomed razor has been drawn over the *leather-coarse* skin.   10. A *tiny* bit of blood crusts *brown* where the nick is.   11. The color of the face is red.   12. The face does not look alive.   13. It seems to be molded from the clay or hewed from the cedar.   14. When the jaw moves, once, with its *deliberate, massive* motion on the quid of tobacco, you are still not convinced.   15. That motion is but the *cunning* triumph of a mechanism concealed within.

The single-word modifiers are not frequent or prominent; in the base clauses, at least, the description is not by attributes. *Little, big, wide,* and *tiny* indicate size; such adjectives come so trippingly from the pen that in first drafts almost everything turns out to be big or little —often to no purpose. *Clumsy, unaccustomed, deliberate, cunning,* and perhaps *massive* are abstract; they talk about, and the paragraph ends with discursive talk about the man's inertness. *Loose* and *brown* probably belong with *alive* (12) as predicate adjectives; this combination of an active verb with a predicate adjective (*hang loose* and *crust brown*) is a feature of English syntax that permits the blending of narration and description. *Leather-coarse* involves a comparison—as coarse as leather. The attributive adjective *blue* (3) and the predicate adjective *red* (11) are general, but what is yet to be added will make *red* to the last degree specific. Note that the other *blue* in 3 is a noun, with embedded modifiers before and after that make it highly specific.

If you wonder why *street, county-seat, wrist,* and *jean, wool, felt,* and *straw* are not set in italics, a technical answer is easy to give—they are nouns and thus do not designate attributes. The first three of those nouns serve to identify the nouns they modify; the other four identify the material they are made of. Such noun adjuncts can be treated as if they were parts of compound nouns.

FREE MODIFIERS

Here now is the paragraph in full as it appeared in the original. The free modifiers are set in italics.

1. You have seen him a thousand times.   2. You have seen him standing on a street corner on Saturday afternoon, in the little county-seat towns.   3. He wears blue jean pants, or overalls washed to a pale

pastel blue like the color of the sky after a shower in spring, but because it is Saturday he has on a wool coat, *an old one, perhaps the coat left from the suit he got married in a long time back.*   4. His long wrist bones hang out from the sleeves of the coat, *the tendons showing along the bone like the dry twist of grapevine still corded on the stove-length of a hickory sapling you find in his wood box beside his cookstove among the split chunks of gum and red oak.*   5. The big hands, *with the knotted, cracked joints and the square, horn-thick nails,* hang loose off the wrist bone like clumsy, home-made tools hung on the wall of a shed after work.   6. If it is summer, he wears a straw hat with a wide brim, *the straw fraying loose around the edge.*
7. If it is winter, he wears a felt hat, *black once, but now weathered by streaks of dark gray and dull purple in the sunlight.*   8. His face is long and bony, *the jawbone long under the drawn-in cheeks.*   9. The flesh along the jawbone is nicked in a couple of places where the unaccustomed razor has been drawn over the leather-coarse skin.
10. A tiny bit of blood crusts brown where the nick is.   11. The color of the face is red, *a dull red like the red clay mud or red dust which clings to the bottom of his pants and to the cast-iron-looking brogans on his feet, or a red like the color of a piece of hewed cedar which has been left in the weather.*   12. The face does not look alive. It seems to be molded from the clay or hewed from the cedar.   13. When the jaw moves, once, with its deliberate, massive motion on the quid of tobacco, you are still not convinced.   14. That motion is but the cunning triumph of a mechanism concealed within. [Robert Penn Warren, "The Patented Gate and the Mean Hamburger"]

The additions, all in phrases, constitute 40 percent of the words of the paragraph, even though they are added to only seven of the fourteen sentences; in these seven sentences they constitute 60 percent of the words. It is evident immediately that they make it more vivid, more authentic, but you would have to read the story through to see that they are not merely pictorial but functional, even symbolic. Here is a man, rooted in the earth, like generations of his people before him, made what he is by his labor to make a few acres of it his own. When he is up-rooted, transplanted to the little county-seat town, he dies. The solid, massed description roots him in the earth. Even the long rhythms of the sentences are functional, perhaps symbolic, suggesting the slow natural rhythms that measure life by seasons and years, counterpointed by the artificial rhythms of the calendar that bring the family to town on Saturdays.

All three methods of description are evident:

By details. The tendons are a detail, a part, of the wrists; the joints and nails are a part of the hands, the frayed edge a part of the straw hat, the jawbone a part of the long and bony face. Each of these in turn is described by attributes or comparisons so that it can serve its purpose.

By attributes. The attributes are mainly those of color. The appositive adjective *black* and the predicate adjective *red* are both general, but each is modified to make the color quite specific. *Black once* is modified by two added phrases that describe what the black color has become now—the verb phrase *weathered by streaks of dark gray* (detail) and the noun phrase *dull purple now in the sunlight*. The predicate adjective *red* is modified by two long noun phrases; the nouns *a dull red* and *a red* are in apposition to the adjective, and both are modified in turn by comparisons, so that we have multiple levels in description too.

By comparison. The comparison *like clumsy, home-made tools* is embedded in a base clause. The four other *like*-phrases are embedded within the free modifiers. The modifiers also include two more comparisons in compound adjectives—*horn-thick nails* (as thick as horn) *and cast-iron-looking brogans* (looking like cast iron). None of these comparisons is, as we say, farfetched. They all grow out of the stuff of this man's life—the earth he walked, the sky overhead, and the wood he sawed and hewed in order to live between the two.

A grammatical inventory of the ten free modifiers shows one prepositional phrase (*with*), one verb phrase (*weathered*), three absolutes (*the tendons clinging, the jawbone long, the straw fraying*), one adjective phrase, a very minor one (*black once*), and four noun phrases (*an old one, perhaps the coat, a dull red, a red*). Again subordinate clauses seem negligible. Actually there are ten—five adjectival and five adverbial. The adverbial ones are part of the structural framework of the sentences, and the adjectival ones are all bound modifiers, serving like the noun adjuncts mainly to identify. These clauses make their sentences "complex," but from our rhetorical point of view, that fact is quite irrelevant.

THE NOUN PHRASE

As you can see, description is a bit complicated, but we can help ourselves by an exercise in definition and classification and then by concentrating on the few essential structures. The most important of these is the noun phrase. A noun phrase, we know, is a noun headword plus its modifiers on either side. And a noun phrase, we know, can fill most of the positions in the sentence that an unmodified noun or a pronoun can fill. Thus it may be subject, complement (direct or indirect object, subjective or objective complement), object of a preposition, or appositive. The appositive noun is something special. It is not tied down like the others to a given position; it is free to tie up with any other noun (and even words of other classes), and the tie may be the tie that binds (that is, restrictive or limiting—"my uncle the tax assessor") or the tie that does not bind (that is, nonrestrictive or nonlimiting—"my uncle, my mother's brother, a dark man with startling white teeth"). So we have two types of noun phrases—the bound (subject, complement, object of preposition) and the free. But the freedom of the free one is deceptive: it is freed from the sentence in order to become the carrier of the modifiers.

If the analysis of prose style this book is based on is correct, the bound noun phrases, especially the subjects, are likely to be short. The main or base clause is likely to be short. One of the most difficult problems in learning to write is learning how to keep the noun phrases short. One of the most effective devices for keeping them short is the free noun phrase.

Here is an extreme example of the heavily laden subject: "*The hammer-shaped, antediluvian, saurian, earth-colored, as out of the earth, crusted* HEADS OF THE MULES *sagged forward, motionless in the late sunlight*" (Robert Penn Warren). This sentence, one might hazard, is intentionally grotesque—a syntactical parody of the subject it describes, with the long noun phrase for the head and the short adjective phrase for the tail.

No stress analysis is possible, but the following sentences represent about the maximum weight for the bound noun phrase.

1. Subject: . . . *a vast bulging* MAN *with a red face and immense tan ragged mustaches fading into gray hailed them.* [Katherine Anne Porter]
2. Object: All blessed themselves and Mr. Daedalus with a sign of pleasure lifted from the dish *the heavy* COVER *pearled around the edge with glistening drops.* [James Joyce]
3. Predicate noun: She was *a pale snuffly little* GIRL *with a wisp of light braided hair.* [Ruth Suckow]
4. Object of preposition: Fate had been personified by HAT'S ALLIE *in wrinkled white ribbed stockings and a gingham dress too short for her.* [Ruth Suckow]

It is not logical, but it will be convenient, before turning to free noun phrases, to examine the other types of free modifiers used for description. When the noun phrase has its own free modifiers, they will take some of these grammatical forms. You will notice that some of the base clauses are themselves descriptive (e.g., 5–10) but that most of them are narrative. Thus the sentences are hybrids, a narrative base clause carrying the description piggyback. Such interleaving or interweaving of narration and description is a characteristic feature of modern prose.

5. 1 And the eyes were calm,
   2 aware but not interested. **(Adjective Plus Adjective)**

John Steinbeck

6. 1 The freak had a country voice,
   2 slow and nasal and neither high nor low, just flat. **(Adjective Plus Adjective)**

Flannery O'Connor

7. 1 Ricketts was a fine cockney,
   2 bright-eyed and sharp-nosed. **(Adjective Plus Adjective)**

Glenway Wescott

8. 1 The roof was the color of weather,
   2 white with the sun, **(Adjective Phrase)**
   2 gray with the rain, **(Adjective Phrase)**
   2 deep gray with the moon, **(Adjective Phrase)**
   2 rose with the sunset. **(Adjective Phrase)**

Elizabeth Madox Roberts

9. 1 Miss Traymor was a red-haired woman of forty or so,
   2 with lipstick that shimmered wetly and eyelids heavy with smoky-blue mascara. **(Prepositional Phrase)**

Mary Cable

10. 1 She was tall,
    2 with a high, sad face shrunken a little where her teeth were missing. **(Prepositional Phrase)**

William Faulkner

11. 2 Downstairs,
     2 in the kitchen,
        3 cold with the shadow and the obtrusion of dawn, **(Adjective Phrase)**
   1 she was belabored by a chill.

Jean Stafford

12. 1 In the wagon box behind was Ina's white pine coffin,
    2 with frost on the heads of the nails. **(Prepositional Phrase)**

Wallace Stegner

13. 1 The air was motionless,
       but
     2 when you opened your mouth
   1 there was just a faint chill,
     2 like the chill from a glass of iced water before you sip. . . . **(Prepositional Phrase)**

Katherine Mansfield

14. 1 The [snowy] road became polished ice,
     2 stained orange and tobacco-yellow from the teams hauling logs. **(Verb Phrase)**

Ernest Hemingway

15. 1 . . . elephant leaves, / , hung above their heads like parasols.
    2/ streaked with silver snail tracks **(Verb Phrase)**
Truman Capote

16. 1 In a closed drug store stood Venus de Milo,
    2 her golden body laced in elastic straps. **(Absolute)**
James Agee

17. 1 A quartet of taxi drivers, / , surrounded him.
    2/ their little eyes bobbing in dark pouches **(Absolute)**
F. Scott Fitzgerald

18. 1 . . . a chopping block beside the door,
    2 its surface matted and softened from years of chopping.
    (Absolute)
John Steinbeck

19. 1 Nan began to speak again,
    2 her voice soft, slightly high, a little bright from age, **(Absolute)**
    3 with just a trace of quiver. **(Prepositional Phrase)**

20. 1 He slit again and pulled the bag [the womb] open,
      and
  1 there lay a bundle of tiny rabbits,
    2 each wrapped in a thin scarlet veil. **(Absolute)**
  1 The brother pulled these off
      and
  1 there they were,
    2 dark gray, **(Adjective Phrase)**
    2 their sleek wet down lying in minute even ripples, **(Absolute)**
    3 like a baby's head just washed, **(Prepositional Phrase)**
    2 their unbelievably small delicate ears folded close, **(Absolute)**
    2 their little blind faces almost featureless. **(Absolute)**
Katherine Anne Porter

21. 1 Mr. Calhoun brought out four cups . . . and a bowl of sugar,
    2 in which, Jerry noticed, drops of coffee had made little, hard, stained nodules. **(Relative Clause)**
Robert Penn Warren

These sentences are all interesting and effective, but the free noun phrase is far and away the most important vehicle for description. It is the most common of the constructions that permit the description to ride piggyback on the narrative sentence. (Notice that the first three sentences below have a descriptive base.) This keeps the narrative line clean and enables the writer to defeat the kind of reader who wants to "skip the description"; the writer knows the importance of description and tricks the reader into reading it. In the examples that follow, the headwords of the noun phrases have been set in small capitals. Many of the phrases have free modifiers of their own, some of them noun phrases, some the other kinds of free modifiers.

22. The elevator was smooth and metallic, a little upright chromium
    BOX with a panel of four pearl buttons on the wall. [Dorothy Dodd
    Baker]
23. He was a widower of about forty—a high-colored MAN, smelling
    always faintly of the barber shop or of whiskey. [William Faulkner]
24. It was dawn, daylight: that gray and lonely SUSPENSION filled with
    the peaceful and tentative waking of birds. [William Faulkner]
25. She met him at the appointed time in the Plaza lobby, a lovely
    faded, gray-eyed BLONDE in a coat of Russian Sable. [F. Scott Fitz-
    gerald]
26. Judy Jones had left a man and crossed the room to him: JUDY JONES,
    a slender enamelled DOLL in cloth of gold: GOLD in a band at her
    head, GOLD in two slipper points at her dress's hem. [F. Scott
    Fitzgerald]
27. When daylight—a gray and ragged DAWN filled with driving scud
    between icy rain-squalls—came and he could see again, he knew
    he was in no cottonfield. [William Faulkner]
28. The little man pulled at the top of his tie, a small blue TIE with
    red polka dots, slightly frayed at the knot. [Katherine Anne Porter]
29. Tom heard his mother's voice, the remembered cool, calm DRAWL,
    friendly and warm. [John Steinbeck]
30. He waited at the door until the sheriff came out—the fat MAN,
    with little wise eyes like bits of mica embedded in his fat, still face.
    [William Faulkner]
31. Like Paul, like almost all the elders in the Garden, he was chaperon-
    ing a child—a handsome little BOY about Helen's age, with egg-
    shell-brown skin and eyes of an Oriental cast, shining as porcelain.
    [Sidney Alexander]
32. She was dressed in yellow organdie, a COSTUME of a hundred cool
    corners with three tiers of rufflles and a big bow in back until
    she shed black and yellow around her in a sort of phosphorescent
    lustre. [F. Scott Fitzgerald]

Sometimes the relation of the free appositive to the noun it is apposed to is not that of whole to whole (in 31, *boy* = *child*) but that of
whole to a part or parts, as in the next group of sentences.

33. Young LAMBS in a green pasture in the Coombe—Thick LEGS, large
    HEADS, black staring EYES. [Dorothy Wordsworth]
34. The L & N YARDS lay along his left, faint SKEINS of steel, blocked
    SHADOWS, little SPUMES of steam [James Agee]
35. At these times of resentment and injury, I would see MY MOTHER
    clearly and positively—her elegant black HEAD and her hard WRISTS
    volatile with bracelets she had bought all over the world. [Nadine
    Gordimer]

Sometimes the free appositive asserts more freedom than is customarily approved in writing classes. A period takes the place of the comma or dash, and the noun cluster stands free as a sentence.

36. And his EYES seemed to look at her through thick glasses, though he never wore any. Keen, sparkling, pale blue EYES, as cold as icicles. [Willa Cather]
37. Jane and Liddy TALKED LONG IN LOW VOICES, before they went to bed and afterward. A running STREAM of talk like a brook flowing deep and steady at full banks. [Gladys H. Carroll]

The free noun cluster is not always apposed to a noun, though we commonly think of apposition as a noun to noun relation. Occasionally we encounter sentences like this: "They sleep the sleep of the just," where the noun object is etymologically related to the verb; the two are said to be cognates—twin births. But sometimes a juncture, a comma or a dash, slips between the two and frees the object. Such free noun clusters seem to be in apposition to the now intransitive verb, or to its clause. They are fairly common, and therefore interesting. Sometimes the free noun cluster is apposed to still other parts of speech.

38. She KISSED him, a dry, whisking, fearful KISS, and hurriedly stood back. [Lawrence Durrell]
39. Michael WAVED at her mockingly, a child's WAVE, stiff wrist moving fingers. [Shirley Ann Grau]
40. Suddenly the phone RANG, a steady JANGLING that began a little explosively and died almost as abruptly as it began, leaving behind a momentary echo.
41. She was QUIET for a moment, a SILENCE on the edge of tears. [William Styron]
42. She was very DRESSED UP: a new DRESS that she had bought that year on vacation—all heavy tropical GREENS and BLUES. [Shirley Ann Grau]
43. "Abner," his mother said. His father paused and LOOKED BACK— the harsh, level STARE beneath the shaggy, graying, irascible eyebrows. [William Faulkner]

Finally, we may encounter a whole array of these descriptive elements, grammatically diverse but rhetorically parallel and usually very effective.

44. He was a BEER QAUFER, droopy, small, a HUMORIST, wry, drawn, weak, his tone nosy and quinchy, his pants in creases under his paunch. [Saul Bellow]
45. Therefore, this was how we were, in his office, the stout DOCTOR explaining his injection for our lay understanding, fat-faced, dry,

arduous, heavy of breath, his arms hairy, the office stinking of cigars and of his sedentary career in old black leather. [Saul Bellow]

46. All along the front of the house the sun was bleaching the statues. Rain-pitted, damp from the dewfall, with mossy drapery and eye sockets, THEY held out their shells and grapes and cornucopias to dry. [F. Scott Fitzgerald]

47. I can remember the CHOPPIN' BLOCK back home, with a feather caught on it, all criss-crossed with cuts, an' black with chicken blood. [John Steinbeck]

48. Warm, musky-scented, softly rustling with the sound of her bracelets, the touch of her fur, SHE leaned and kissed him. [Elizabeth Taylor]

EXERCISES

A. Be prepared to discuss in class the methods of description (by attributes, by details, by comparison) and the grammatical structures and diction of these descriptions of hands. The principal noun headwords are in small capitals. The great variety in the description of something so small in compass as the human hand suggests a variation on Blake's "Hold Infinity in the palm of your hand."

1. His HANDS were hard, with broad fingers and nails as thick and ridged as little clam shells. [John Steinbeck]
2. Only her HANDS had aged, the palms and fingerpads shining and tight, the backs wrinkled and splotched with brown. [John Steinbeck]
3. She groped with her hand for his. He put IT, plump, pink, silvered with hairs, over her knotted FINGERS with their split and blackened nails. [Ruth Suckow]
4. She put out a HAND to seize him, dry and white with constant soda, the nails cut to the quick. [Graham Greene]
5. She took what I gave her with a big-jointed HAND, seamed and dirty, the skin puckered like the back of salt codfish.
6. He looked at her HAND lying limp on the chair arm, her bent, large-knuckled FINGERS, with the wiry sinews stretching across sunken freckled flesh. [Richard Sullivan]
7. "That'll be fifty cents," said the woman, holding out her HAND, a very old HAND, the skin dry and wrinkled, the blue veins standing out sharply.
8. Tobias had wonderful HANDS, sinewy from his life of action, but smooth-skinned, the smoothness sprigged with crisp brown masculine hair, the fingers steel-hard but tapering long to the deep-set square-cut nails. [Robert Penn Warren]

9. "So you have some amusing memories," said La Condesa, laying her silky HAND over his, the blue veins standing up branched-like like a little tree. [Katherine Anne Porter]

10. She found herself looking intently at his HAND. It was long and pallid and not too clean. The nails were very short as though they had been bitten and there was a discolored callus on his second finger where he probably held his pencil. Mrs. Bishop, who prided herself on her powers of observation, put him in the white-collar class. [Sally Benson]

B. Be prepared to discuss in class the methods of description and the grammatical structures and diction of the following. The principal noun headwords are in small capitals. There may be some narration mingled with the description.

1. He had been a musician in the [Civil] war. There were a PAIR OF DRUMSTICKS, blackened where sweating hands had held them, and a TRUMPET without a mouthpiece. There were the FIFE and the FLUTES; the FIFE like an ebony wand, the FLUTES wrapped in red flannel, their German-silver keys interlaced around the one of cocoawood and the other of a wood called grenadilla. [Glenway Wescott]

2. In some public presentation of Miss Conklin's class Sue had worn a yellow BODICE with a lacing of black velvet ribbon, a bouffant SKIRT OF CHINTZ, covered all over with daffodils, and a COTTON BATTING WIG that smelled of stale talcum powder. [Jean Stafford]

3. For her, just outside the concert hall, lay the black POND with the cattle-tracked bluffs; the tall, unpainted HOUSE, with weather-curled boards, naked as a tower; the crook-backed ASH SEEDLING where the dish-cloths hung to dry; the gaunt moulting TURKEYS picking up refuse about the kitchen door. [Willa Cather]

Notice that in the following sentences (4–9) the noun clusters are free, in apposition to the word in the base clause that is set in capitals.

4. And in the meadows and the lower grounds
Was all the SWEETNESS of a common dawn—
DEWS, VAPOURS, and the MELODY OF BIRDS,
And LABOURERS going forth to till the fields.
William Wordsworth, "The Prelude"

5. She was right; they were in Switzerland then. She kept her eyes fixed to the ground now. There was SO MUCH TO SEE: LAKES like jewels; neat TOWNS spread out, with square

towers and peaked roofs; RIVERS, white with cataracts; RAILROAD
LINES, threading the valleys. [Anne Morrow Lindbergh]

6. He looked through the slightly steamed glass of the FISH
COUNTER: orange SALMON STEAKS with silver-black borders
in rows like French can-can dancers; whipped-puppy TAILS OF
SHRIMP, convict-striped, gray and black; BABY LOBSTERS, evil-
tempered old men despite their bed of glistening cracked ice.

7. I stood in front of the fish counter, an aquarium death-still on
crushed ice, and studied the FISHMONGER'S WARES: SQUID,
ten-armed cephalopods, opalescent and mucous; speckled
TROUT, bright as raindrops on dust, polka-dotted with rainbow
light; CRABS, dull gray, with reaching pliers and brittle shells;
ROCK COD, outsized goldfish, red, bladder-like, and all mouth.

8. The icy fish counter, garnished with curly parsley and trans-
lucent lemon sections, attracted my attention to its DISPLAY:
the headless, split-bellied BARRACUDA, the belly cavity defined
by gothic arching ribs, the spinal fin folded back on the
black skin drawn taut on the frozen flesh beneath; the frozen
FILLETS OF RED SNAPPER, segmented and icy pink, like crushed ice
diluting cherry juice, with irregular patches of silvery-pink
skin binding the segments to bony ribs; and, sprawling
disorderly in a heaped pan, broken CIRCLES OF SHRIMP TAILS, with
red-tinged fanlike tips and a needle-sharp thorn tucked inward among celluloid-like sheaths protruding from the joints.

9. He pulled at the chrome handle of the squat thick refrigerator,
glossy and humming softly, and the plump door clicked open
with a dull, rubber sound, revealing a porcelain interior
lighted from the rear by a frosted electric bulb and the FOOD-
STUFF his vacationing wife had left him to forage on: pale-
yellow BOTTLES OF MILK, beaded with cold and filled to the paper
stopper; a covered PLASTIC DISH OF LEFTOVERS—deflated green
peas, wax-like carrots in a thick, gray juice; FLUTED ALUMINUM
MOLDS OF JELLO, red and shiny, like dime-store costume jewelry;
and PACKAGES OF MEAT—round, folded and tight-wrapped
in bloody brown paper and fastened with strips of sticky tape.

Study the spatial arrangement of the items in this description
of Salt Lake Valley. Note that the noun clusters are free appositives
in the second sentence and subjects of *was* in the last sentence.

10. High up, his arms full of branches of sumac and maple and
yellow aspen, he sat down and smoked a cigarette. West of
him the view opened, framed in the V of the canyon—the broad
valley still green with truck gardens and alfalfa, the *petit
point* of orchards, the broad yellow-and-white band of the salt

marshes, and beyond that band the cobalt line of the lake, the tawny Oquirrhs [mountains] on the south end feathered with smoke from the smelters. At the right, just visible, was the end of Antelope Island, yellow-gold in the blue and white distance, and far beyond that, almost lost in the haze, the tracery of the barren ranges on the far side, almost seventy miles away. [Wallace Stegner, *The Big Rock Candy Mountain*]

C. For the pilot runs in class it will be useful to concentrate on descriptive details and how to get them into words. The contents of a billfold or a purse will provide good materials. What details, for example, can be used to describe a driver's license—identification photo, thumb-print, signature? Consider also the kinds and positions of adjectives. And don't overlook comparisons that make themselves felt.

D. The purpose of the writing assignment is to get practice in using the three methods of description in free noun clusters. Two forms are proposed here, varying in the tightness of their overall structure. Whatever the form chosen, the noun clusters (there will be three to ten) must vary in structure; the same pattern repeated three to nine or ten times would become obtrusive. When you are through, test your writing by ear.

1. Here the series of noun clusters, like those in sentences 4–7, are in apposition to the collective or plural term set in capitals before the colon. The part before the colon, the introduction that motivates the close looking, must be a grammatically complete sentence; the series of noun phrases (three to six items) should be separated by semicolons. They should be varied in structure.

2. Here the series of noun clusters, like those in sentence 10, describe the particulars of a place. The clusters should be ordered in such a way as to show the spatial relations of the several particulars. In this example the progression is from near to far merging into left and right (or south and north). Do not be too explicit in indicating place; it is the bricks that count, not the mortar.

6

The Language of the Senses

Katherine Anne Porter has praised Laurence Stern's *Tristram Shandy* in a way that you might aspire to be praised for the last papers you write for this part of your course.

That book contains more living breathing people you can see and hear, whose garments have texture between your finger and thumb, whose flesh is knit firmly to their bones, who walk about their affairs with audible footsteps, than any other novel in the world, I do believe. Uncle Toby, Corporal Trim, Yorick and Mrs. Yorick, the Widow Wadman, Bridget, Dr. Slop, Susannah, Obadiah, the infant Tristram hovering between breeches and tunic, all live in one house with floorboards under their bootsoles, a roof over their heads, the fires burning and giving off real smoke, cooking smells coming from the kitchens, real weather outside and air blowing through the windows. When Dr. Slop cuts his thumb, real blood issues from it, and everybody has his navel and the proper distribution of vital organs. One hangs around the place like an enchanted ghost, all eyes and ears for fear of missing something. [*The Nation*, July 17, 1943]

The point, of course, is not the number of people in the book, but their living, breathing quality, and this seems to flow from the variety and vividness of the appeals the book makes to the reader's senses— appeals not only to the eyes and ears, but to all the five senses Aristotle allowed us, and perhaps to some of the others a more modern assessment of our sensory equipment has credited us with, such as the senses by which we judge the weight of an object and whether it is warm or cold or wet or dry and whether we are coming or going and whether we are headed up or down.

VISUAL AND NONVISUAL

Although we have not ignored the nonvisual senses (we have seen how narrative and descriptive details may be drawn from impressions of any of the senses), we have up to this point concentrated on the sense of sight. The critical vocabulary we have developed is based on the sense of sight. We have made much of *observation*, which seems to imply visual exploration; and we have defined description and narration as *picturing*, the one appearance and the other behavior. It is natural to think of picturing as representing visual objects. Such terms as *image*, *imagery*, and *imagination*, which we have avoided as far as possible, because of their ambiguity, also suggest visual impressions.

The sense of sight does seem to deliver to us the object itself—its size and shape, its parts or details, its texture, its color, and, besides these, its location and movements. But the object of sight is often remote in space, so that it often seems unsubstantial, not quite real, possibly an illusion. Sometimes we feel the need to touch or handle the object, or we sniff it or listen to whether it is ticking. We are like the boy in Walter Van Tilburg Clark's story "The Watchful Gods," who could not believe that a rifle was his as a birthday present until he held it in his hands and to his nose: "Through his hands, by the weight of the rifle, always so surprising compared to its size, and by the smooth, slippery feel, and also by its smell of cold metal and oil in his nostrils, possession was consummated."

Touch and taste bring us into immediate contact with the object. Sounds and smells are airborne. But sight is lightborne, and in the absence of light we are all dependent, like the blind, on the other senses.

For these and other reasons the practiced writer works with the whole spectrum of sense impressions. If he doesn't picture them, we may say that he *describes* them. But often he only *suggests* them or, more simply, merely *implies* them.

A short passage will show how much in the way of sense impressions can be worked into a narrative that without them would be rather faintly visual.

Nick climbed out onto the meadow and stood, water running down his trousers and out of his shoes, his shoes squelchy. He went over and sat on the logs. . . .

He sat on the logs, smoking, drying in the sun, the sun warm on his back, the river shallow ahead entering the woods, curving into the woods, shallows, light glittering, big water-smooth rocks, cedars along the bank and white birches, the logs warm in the sun, smooth to sit on, without bark, gray to the touch; slowly the feeling of disappointment left him. It went away slowly, the feeling of disappointment that came sharply after the thrill that made his shoulders ache. It was all right now. His rod lying out on the logs, Nick tied a new hook on the leader, pulling the gut tight until it grimped into itself in a hard knot. [Ernest Hemingway, "Big Two-Hearted River: Part II"]

Here the sense impressions are not so much described, really, as suggested or implied. For example, "water-smooth rocks" suggests touch (texture and wetness); "smoking" implies smell, taste, and touch; and "drying in the sun" implies touch (temperature and wetness). All the five senses are alerted here and, besides the Aristotelian five, the senses that register pressure, temperature, wet and dry, and muscular pain. At another level, moreover, two of the sentences and a clause from another sentence describe Nick's mental or emotional state, the waning of the "feeling of disappointment."

When we turn now to the methods of presenting the reports of the nonvisual senses, we can make some interesting observations. The first is that we can treat such reports, like the things we see, as either actions or objects; that is, we can say either "he *sounded* the bell" or "the *sound* of the bell"; "I *smelled* the rose" or "the *smell* of the rose"; "they *tasted* the drink" or "the *taste* of the drink": "she *touched* the fur" or "the *touch* of the fur." What is added to describe the sense impression will thus be added to either a verb or a noun headword. In English we have far more nouns than verbs and the modifiers of nouns are far more expressive than the modifiers of verbs. So in this section we will be dealing more with noun clusters than with verb clusters.*

Another is that there are differences from sense to sense. Our language has an incredibly large stock of both verbs and nouns to designate sounds, and new ones are readily coined. It has a much smaller, but still a considerable, stock of nouns, but very few verbs, to designate smells. And it has few of either nouns or verbs to communicate sensations of touch and taste.

Another is that only two of the three methods of description are applicable to these senses. Then sensations of sound and smell, taste and touch apparently do not have parts; thus the commonest method of describing visual impressions, by details, is not applicable to non-

* A sentence may use both verb and noun to describe the same sense impression: "Outside the window the holly leaves RUSTLED, made thin, dry SCRAPINGS against the screen. . . ." (William Styron).

visual ones.* We must rely on attributes and comparisons. This limitation puts more emphasis on the choice of the headword—the verb or noun naming the sensation.

Finally, the noun headwords are different in character. If, as was suggested before, the sense of sight presents us with the object itself (the rose), then the other senses present us with the qualities or attributes of the object (the SMELL or TOUCH of the rose, the FRAGRANCE or the SOFTNESS of the rose—note the *of* phrase). It is true that sometimes the quality is put first with a visual image: King Lear cries "Strike flat the thick ROTUNDITY of the earth" and Twain, in a different mood, gloats over a watermelon "sunning its fat ROTUNDITY" and Faulkner notes the sunlight dreaming among the "placid ROTUNDITIES" of the silver on the sideboard. Whitman speaks of the "vitreous POUR of the moon," Emerson of "a tumultuous PRIVACY of storm." Hemingway has the late afternoon showing the bridge, in *For Whom the Bell Tolls*, "dark against the steep EMPTINESS of the gorge" and Jessamyn West has a boy fishing "watching the silvery DART and SLIP of minnows and the slower TURNINGS of a big black bass." Faulkner, who seems to command all the syntactic resources of our language, uses this one freely; these examples are all from the early Sartoris: "Beside him on the pillow the bronze SWIRLING of her hair was hushed"; "The fine and huge SIMPLICITY of the house rose among the trees"; "His Roman senator's head was thatched with a vigorous CURLING of silvery hair"; "It was filled with the faintly scented FRAGILITY of garments." This practice is comparatively rare with visual images, but it is the rule with images of sound and smell.

SOUND

And his ears kept the whirlpool's silvery suck
Lyle Glazier, "The Fisher"

Speech itself is sound, and thus language is a natural medium for communicating the sounds that make up a nearly incessant part of our experience in this world—"all this mighty sum of things forever speaking." Language has to provide names for sounds, just as it has to provide names for all the commerce of the senses with the world. But with the names for sounds there is this difference: the names may imitate or echo the sounds. The word *hiss* hisses, the word *murmur* murmurs, but we cannot say that the word *dog* dogs or that the word *smell* smells.

* The only example of the use of detail we have recorded is this by John Steinbeck: "Her voice was the bellow of a bull, a deep and powerful shout *with flat edges* like a circus barker's voice." Note the use of all three methods to describe the shout. Note too the use of both metaphor and simile.

Most of the words of any language are entirely arbitrary designations—a rose by any other name would smell as sweet. But those words that do not merely name sounds but imitate them seem to have a natural relation to the sounds they designate.*

Such words imitative of sounds are called echoic, which needs no explanation, or onomatopoeic (also onomatopoetic), which calls for a close look if you are to understand the word and spell and pronounce it correctly. Notice the two parts—*onomato*, meaning "name," and *poeic* or *poetic*, meaning "making." There was a time when in English poets were called makers.

English is so rich in echoic words that the choice of a precise word for a sound is largely a matter of choosing a word with appropriate sound values. We have many sets of words alike in meaning and in every phoneme but one—*plink, plunk; clink, clank, clonk, clunk; flitter, flutter*. When the choice has been narrowed to such a set, the final choice turns on the appropriateness of a single phoneme. An instructive example is this from Walter Van Tilburg Clark's *The Ox-Bow Incident:* "Now and then in the freshening wind we could hear a meadow lark 'chink-chink-a-link,' and then another, way off and higher, 'tink-tink-a-link.' " The difference in the initial consonants is a function of the difference in distance. This sentence appears near the beginning of the book, when two riders coming in off the range are just getting the feel of the little town of Bridger's Wells. At the end of the book, when they are about to leave, they hear the larks again: "Way off we could hear the meadow larks. . . . Tink-tink-a-link went the meadow lark, and then another one, even farther off, teenk-teenk-a-leenk."

A more instructive example appears in Steinbeck's *The Grapes of Wrath*. It involves not only the phonemes but, as often with onomatopoeic words, the number of syllables. At the beginning of the second chapter "A huge red transport truck stood in front of the little roadside restaurant. The vertical exhaust pipe MUTTERED softly, and an almost invisible haze of steel-blue smoke hovered over its end." At the end of the same chapter, the truck stopped to let Tom Joad off, and while he stood a moment talking with the driver, "The vertical exhaust pipe PUTTERED up its barely visible blue smoke." Many chapters later, the morning Grampa died, huge red transport trucks were moving on the highway, "They rumbled along, putting a little earthquake in the ground, and the standing exhaust pipes SPUTTERED blue smoke from the diesel oil." The three verbs rime and thus are both alike and different. The exhaust of the diesel engine is rhythmic; the two syllables reflect

* One has to say "seems" because the phonemes of such words undergo the same sound changes as the phonemes of any other words in any given language. The cock's crow remains stable; the speech sounds that imitate it follow the drift of the sound system.

its pulsations. The initial phonemes differ in the energy they suggest. *Sputter* suggests well the energy of the laboring engine. Whether there would be a difference in the idling speed to account for the slight difference in energy between *mutter* and *putter* one can't really say; but if there would be, the verbs are in the right places. Did Steinbeck compare the three instances and consciously work out the contrasts, or did he only keep his ear on the ground (as Wordsworth said he kept his eye on the object), detect differences, and, without comparing, choose unerringly the words to reflect them? No matter how he worked, or how we do, we could try to equal the fidelity of his recording.

In spite of the vast array of words for sounds that our language affords, we often resort to word coinage—we become word makers ourselves. In our headlong society we coin words at a dizzy rate—new nouns and verbs and occasionally adjectives and adverbs; but the new words are coined mostly from Latin and Greek materials to name new objects and new actions. Yet even the humblest student may feel free to coin one new word for a sound he has heard as no one else has ever before heard it. The language will suffer no harm; such coinages usually turn out to be what we call nonce words.

Another sort of words for sounds is the translation into human words of the sounds of birds and beasts. Here is how Donald Culross Peattie hears the whitethroat: "Some say he sings of 'Sweet Canada, Can-a-da, Can-a-da!' where he goes to mate, but to me he seems to cry 'Oh, long ago, long ago, long ago!' "

These observations can be confirmed by study of the following examples.

Verb Headword

The verbs range from the literal to the metaphorical. Only two or three sentences have anything added to the verbs.

1. The insects began to CHIRR again. [Jessamyn West]
2. . . . the sheep-bells CLONK dully around her. [Lawrence Durrell]
3. They heard a rifle bolt SNICK as it was drawn back. [Ernest Hemingway]
4. . . . the warm needle stream of milk HISSED into the gleaming pails. At first it SANG against the hollow tin drum of the base, but as the pail filled it MURMURED with a frothy surr-surr. [Herbert Read]
5. I heard the water TITTLE-TATTLING away in deep shadow below. [D. H. Lawrence]
6. Beneath [the bridge] the water was clear and still in the shadow,

WHISPERING and CLUCKING about the stone in fading swirls of spinning sky. [William Faulkner]

7. Outside a dry-fly RASPED the brooding silence up and down with its fret-saw refrain. [I. J. Cobb]

8. A cicada . . . TEARS THE SEAM OF SILENCE furiously at every third minute. [Odell Shepard]

9. Outside, in the pine trees the cicadas HARPED on the theme of their existence. [Aldous Huxley]

10. The deep-toned bell of Independence Hall BRONZING the hours is part of our harmony here. [Christopher Morley]

Noun Headword

The noun headwords are of several sorts. They are much more likely than verbs to have description added to them.

LITERAL NOUN HEADS

11. . . . the soft watery BURBLE of a night hawk came from across the fields. [John Steinbeck]

12. . . . sometimes we came up with horsemen and left behind the SLAP of iron shoes and the loose CHANGE and SLASH of harness. [Saul Bellow]

13. . . . every few hundred yards there was a heavy plank bridge where the waters flowed under from one part of the marsh to the other, and the CHOCK of the horses in the mud, or the PLOP-PLOP on the sod, deepened into a hard, hollow THUNDER for a moment. [W. V. T. Clark]

14. The man who said that spurs jangled was insane. Spurs have a mellow CLASH-CLASH-CLASH. [Stephen Crane]

15. He fired [on the tank] and he could hear the SPANG against the steel. [Ernest Hemingway]

NOUNS ENDING IN -*ing* DERIVED FROM VERBS

16. . . . a chipmunk making its pebbly CHITTERING somewhere out of sight. [W. V. T. Clark]

17. . . . the far-off TWANGING of the red-wing blackbirds in the tule marshes was clear though faint. [W. V. T. Clark]

18. [The sea] filling the beaches with the passionate SCRABBLING of pebbles sucked back in the dark undertow. [Lawrence Durrell]

19. . . . danced quietly together to the monotonous SQUIBBLING of a clarinet played by an old man. [Lawrence Durrell]

METAPHORICAL NOUNS

20. The child's light, faint breath was a mere shadowy MOTH of sound in the silver air. [Katherine Anne Porter]
21. . . . the new baby wailing in a thin THREAD of sound that hurt the ears with its persistence. [Bernice Thorpe]
22. They heard the loud steady STROKE of crickets in the grass outside. [Mary Deasy]
23. [The crickets and cicadas] made little WATCH-FIRES of sound in counter-point, changing tone with distance. [W. V. T. Clark]
24. The unshod hoofs of the two ponies . . . made a soft, muffled COUNTER-POINT. [W. V. T. Clark]
25. He heard the cock's bright MINSTRELSY again. [Thomas Wolfe]

ABSTRACT NOUNS, MORE OR LESS METAPHORICAL

26. . . . the dry, unwearying INSISTENCE of the insects in the trees of the lane. [Robert Penn Warren]
27. In the pear tree the mockingbird's idiot REITERATION pulsed and purled. [William Faulkner]
28. . . . the shadow of the great refectory with its high roofs where the swallows were building, their soft AGITATIONS echoing in the silence like breathing. [Lawrence Durrell]
29. In the spaces of the wind the ear picks up the dry morse-like COMMUNICATION of the cicadas high above on the cliffs. [Lawrence Durrell]

COINED NOUNS

Such coinages are usually italicized. Here small capitals are omitted and italics are used or not according to the practice of the author.

30. I hear now and then the *flup* of a pike leaping out, and rippling the water. [Walt Whitman]
31. The *rucketty-coo* of the pigeons.
32. A little later the thud and scrabble of hooves and the *pad-scrit! pad-scrit!* of dogs' feet on gravel. [R. P. Harriss]
33. He heard the *ca-ra-wong!* of Wilson's big rifle and again in a second crashing *carawong!* [Ernest Hemingway]
34. Then he heard a noise come *sweeeish-crack-boom!* The boom was a sharp crack that widened in the cracking. . . . *Sweeeish-crack-boom!* It came again, the swishing like the noise of a rocket. [Ernest Hemingway]
35. As the twilight fell . . . , an owl somewhere the other side of the creek sounded *too-oo-oo-oo-oo*, soft and pensive (and I fancied a little sarcastic) four or five times. [Walt Whitman]

This is enough, perhaps to show what can be done with the choice of headwords. Notice what has been added to sharpen the image—actually very little—a few adjectives and comparisons, more to the nouns than to the verbs. The sentences that follow rely more heavily on adjectives and comparisons. Some of the sentences have more than one level. One or two examples show a noun modifying another noun (in the position of the attributive adjective) or an adjective from some sense other than sound. The last sentence shows sound treated as impact; this is description by effect.

36. He heard the sound of an ax stroke on wood, a sound thin but satisfying and clean in the emptiness of the afternoon. [Robert Penn Warren]
37. He could hear her level tones, sharp and dry, bitter as old tea. [Robert Nathan]
38. His voice rang over the lisping papery rustle of the grass. [Wallace Stegner]
39. . . . the rockers gave out a cobbling noise on the boards of the porch, and the chair squeaked gently. [James Agee]
40. . . . the blind fiddler's son has begun his acrid tunes on the violin. [Lawrence Durrell]
41. He listened, and heard the nighthawk strike its copper notes, two high and two low . . . listened to the nighthawk sound its copper gong in the valley. [Christine Weston]
42. He picked up the Baby Ben, with its face of pale yellow ringed about by a strip of muddy brown, and listened to its muted heartbeat, a gentle, pulsing *pik pik, pik pik,* like some tiny animal's throbbing breast.
43. We waited in the shade [of the hangar], listening to the wind outside, gentle, persistent, continuous, like a distant line of breakers. [Anne Morrow Lindbergh]
44. Behind her hung the deathly silence . . . with now and again the whisper of her sister's breathing like the flight of a mouse across the room. [Kay Boyle]
45. No wind, yet the musical low murmur through the pines, quite pronounced, curious, like waterfalls, now still'd, now pouring again. [Walt Whitman]
46. I love our rain crows . . . and their stuttering *cuck-cuck, cuck, cook . . . cook . . . . . cook . . . . cook,* like a clock running down, when the skies are black with coming rains. [D. C. Peattie]
47. He held his breath, and heard his own heart like a drum slowly beaten with one finger. [Glenway Wescott]
48. . . . the pine siskins unite in little flocks, conferring together in voices fine as the whisper of a small watch. [D. C. Peattie]

49. . . . the clock in the tower of the courthouse struck. It struck four times, the resonance of each impact dying away, thinning into a drowsy hum like the sound of distant bees. [Robert Penn Warren]
50. The battery fired twice and the air came each time like a blow and shook the windows and made the front of my pajamas flap. [Ernest Hemingway]

Sentences 48 and 49 exemplify one of the most effective uses of impressions of sound, as narrative details. Here are a few more examples.

51. The snow was falling fast, the last sodden leaves lying in mounds, the pigeons uttering their guttural clotted noises. [Lawrence Durrell]
52. An owl went by, extinguishing sound, absorbing the trill of cricket and locust in its soft feathers. [Jessamyn West]
53. As they spoke, the owl flew between the trees with the softness of all silence, dropping past them, then rising, the wings beating quickly, but with no noise of feathers moving as the bird hunted. [Ernest Hemingway]
54. By night the snow might be moving up the broad valley, the flakes hissing at the surface of the river, swarming dryly among the leafless black branches on the ridge. [Robert Penn Warren]

EXERCISES

A. Be prepared to discuss in class the choice of verb and noun heads and the methods of description used in these passages.

1. He stood stock-still a minute; it took a while to separate the cooing of the pigeons from the rustling in his ears. When he had focused on the cooing, it flooded the vast interior [of the barn] with its throaty, bubbling outpour: there seemed no other sound. They were up behind the beams. . . .
   A pigeon appeared in one of these holes, on the side toward the house. It flew in, with a battering of wings, from the outside, and waited there, silhouetted against its pinched bit of sky, preening and cooing in a throbbing, thrilled tentative way.
   Now others shook loose from the rafters, and whirled in the dim air with a great blurred hurtle of feathers and noise.
   The cooing was shriller now; its apprehensive tremolo made the whole volume of air seem liquid. [John Updike, "Pigeon Feathers"]
2. Dunamara under its hill was a sleepy place. The noise of the waves was hypnotic in its slow repetition of soft long notes: the

falling cadence of the break, the tinkle of the thrown spray, the sigh of the flow upwards across the shingle, and the hollow murmur of the ebb sinking back into the roots of the next wave. We [children] nodded to it over our Ballantine or Henty, draughts or chess; and fell upstairs to bed in its echo, muffled like an orchestra heard through two walls. But when we were in our room and Aunt Hersey had heard our prayers, tucked us up, said good-night, and opened the windows, it burst upon us again with an immense noise, not overwhelming, but soft and enveloping, like an orchestra heard from a stage box. Its music carried us away with it into a sea dream; a sleep which had no clear division between a dream-like delight in the sea sounds, the wave-marked walls of Dunamara to which we fell asleep, and the sound of falling waves, the sight of waves of light, all about us on the walls and ceiling, to which we gradually awoke. [Joyce Cary, *A House of Children*]

B. Subjects for practice in class do not have to be imported. It is only necessary to listen to sounds within the room, in the adjoining halls and rooms, and from outside.

C. Since most descriptions of sounds are based on noun headwords, we can use the same sort of written exercises as the first two in the last chapter.

1. In place of "Street Scene," you could try "Street Sounds" or "Beach Sounds."

2. Write an "inventory" on the pattern of the following. Note that all four "sentences" are simply noun clusters.

> Dry friction of cicada from the palm-tree across the road. Eucalyptus leaves breaking their wrists with a small click as they begin to plane down over the tombstones. The maceration of pebbles by sea-water, mingling with the noise of coffee being ground and the shearing noise of a pot being scoured. An inventory of sounds from a late morning walk. [Lawrence Durrell, *Reflections on a Marine Venus*]

3. This sentence has the same pattern as that of sentences 4–7 in Exercise B in Chapter 5. Write a sentence or two, as your instructor directs, using this pattern.

> Sitting on the hill, I could hear the FLOCK OF SHEEP in the valley below me: the strange, flat RINGING, between a clanking and a tinkling, OF THE BELL ON THE "LEADER"; the quick little TINKLE OF THE DOG'S BELL; the soft CRUNCH OF DRY STUBBLE; the high clear VOICE OF THE SHEPHERD calling out

in Spanish, only so many meaningless syllables to me; and, mingled through it all, the intermittent BLEATING OF THE SHEEP, one invariable syllable voiced with an amazing variety of pitch and tone.

SMELL

Here's a crop for the nose:
fume of cobwebbed stumps, musky roots,
resin tincture, bark palm, dayspring moss
in stars new pricked (vivid as soft).
May Swenson, "One Morning in New Hampshire"

Of the canonical five senses, the sense of smell is the most primitive, older than hearing or sight, the first of the telereceptors to put the primitive animal in contact with the world—with food or mate or enemy—at a distance. Whether he knew this or not, Thoreau held that the sense of smell was "a more primitive inquisition" than the other senses. It was "more oracular and trustworthy"; it showed what was concealed from the other senses. The physiology of this "chemical" sense is a fascinating subject to explore,* but that is not our concern here. And there is no need to say anything about the effectiveness of appeals to the sense of smell in writing. Anyone who reads Shakespeare and Keats can bring examples from these two who more than others of the English poets speak the language of the senses. The reader of Hemingway and of Faulkner is aware on nearly every page of the primitiveness of their inquisition of the world, a primitiveness that is one of the sources of their strength. What we are concerned with is still the language problem—how sense impressions can be expressed in words.

The first thing we learn is the poverty of our vocabulary for talking about smells. It is said that the Polynesians are capable of expressing "several thousand shades of meaning" through their words for smells. Whatever "shades of meaning" may mean, the size of the vocabulary is probably a measure of the concern with smell of the people who have developed it; the vocabulary of a people (as of a person) is a pretty good index of what it preoccupies itself with. Perhaps we should import from Japan, in place of so many cameras and binoculars, the materials for a parlor game the Japanese are said to play: "objects are passed around carrying some one of two hundred standardized odors and the participants are asked to name the substance."

Recognizing the source of a smell and naming the source bring us to the language problem; they don't solve it. We have almost no verbs—

---

* See, for example, Ralph Bienfang, *The Subtle Sense,* and Lorus and Margery Milne, *The Senses of Animals and Men,* Chapter 10.

not more than ten common ones—to designate the act of either giving off odors (it SMELLS or SMELLS OF—intransitive) or taking in odors (he SMELLS the rose—transitive) and very few nouns, possibly thirty, to designate smells (the fragrance or the scent of the rose). So we have very few headwords and, as with sounds, only two methods of description—quality and comparison. Moreover, we have few adjectives that designate smells explicitly and exclusively; the commonest ones, *pungent* and *redolent*, are sadly overused and misused. Since our vocabulary is so limited, smells are less often described than implied or suggested, or they are talked about, and the talk is likely to be about the effect of the smell.

Verbs

Among the verbs possible are *smell, smell of, savor, stink, scent, sniff, snuff, perfume, reek,* and *waft,* variously transitive or intransitive or both, and all used as nouns as well as verbs. The most common by far are *smell* and *smell of.*

1. Mom put her hand on my head and I SMELLED the cold dirt and the sharp scent of tomato plants on her fingers. [Mildred Walker]
2. . . . the dentist had something on his breath that, without being either, SMELLED sweet as candy and spicy as cloves. [John Updike]
3. They all three squatted on the gallery and ate, slowly, without talking; then in the store again, they drank from a tin dipper tepid water SMELLING of the cedar bucket and of living beech trees. [William Faulkner]
4. Robert's aunt, with a kiss that SMELLED OF Kool cigarettes and starched linen, went off to catch the train to Stamford. [John Updike]
5. . . . the acrid sulphur smell of the match BURNED at my nostrils. [Alfred Kazin]
6. A dwarf chrysanthemum SPRINKLED the air with acrimony. [Glenway Wescott]

Nouns

The commonest nouns are the ten treated in the following paragraph from the college dictionary that discriminates the largest number of terms at this point. Three others could be added to this list: *fetor, must, tang.*

   —Syn. (noun) 3. *Smell, odor, scent, savor, aroma, fragrance, perfume, bouquet, stench,* and *stink* denote that which is perceived by the olfactory sense. *Smell* is the general term, to which *odor* is a close synonym. *Smell*, however, often suggests a strong and slightly un-pleasant sensation, and *odor*, a more delicate and pleasing one: the *smell* of a hospital ward, the *odor* of new-mown hay. *Scent* is always delicate: the *scent* of apple blossoms. *Savor* refers to an appetizing sensation that combines both smell and taste: the *savor* of roasting meat. *Aroma, fragrance, perfume*, and *bouquet* are pleasant. An *aroma* is delicate and spicy: the *aroma* of coffee. We speak of the *fragrance* or *perfume* of flowers; of the two, *fragrance* is the lighter and more delicate, *perfume* the stronger. *Bouquet*, in this sense, is primarily the aroma of a fine wine. *Stench* and *stink* are sickening and unpleas-ant; a *stench* is putrid or asphyxiating, and a *stink* is fetid: the *stench* of rotten eggs, the *stink* of decaying fish. [*Standard College Dictionary*]

An inventive writer will not limit himself to these nouns that des-ignate smells specifically. We have said that smells are airborne, and some nouns refer to the carrier: *breath, whiff, waft, wave, vapor, fume, exhalation, miasma, effluvium*. Some smells are faint; there is only a *suggestion*, a *reminder*, a *hint*, a *tinge*, an *aura*, even a *lurk*: at a dog show—"the sinus-penetrating LURK of animal urine." Sometimes smells do not come singly but in a *mixture*, a *concord*, or a *choke*. Finally, almost any adjective that can be used to describe an odor can be con-verted into a noun to name it—*sweetness, rifeness*—as in Faulkner's "a *rifeness* of honeysuckle."

7. The inside of the [Chinese laundryman's] store had a clean warm but fragile SCENT, like odorless flowers in a hot room. [Betty Smith]
8. . . . it is cooler here, and the ODOR of the latrine, the clammy bland SMELL of wet metal is less oppressive than the heavy sweat-ing FETOR of the troop holds. [Norman Mailer]
9. There was a powerful masculine STENCH of broad dock-leaves, a hot weedy ODOR. [Thomas Wolfe]
10. He sat in the churches as he sat in his father's church in Buffalo, amid the starchy MUST of Sunday clothes. [F. Scott Fitzgerald]
11. A sudden breeze brought the sharp TANG of a bonfire in at the window. [Jan Struther]
12. The gusty air smelt of dust and coalgas and exhausts of trucks, with an underlying singed REEK from stockyards. [John Dos Passos]
13. Within [the springhouse]—the BREATH of icy spring water, the cool, plain SMELL of naked rock, the ODORS of maidenhair and moss and lichen, the sunlight dazzling on the surface of the spring. [D. C. Peattie]
14. The soaked diaper released an invisible CLOUD of ammonia and washed tears into his eyes. [John Updike]
15. It seems to be more than a scent that emanates from the hops: it is almost a visible MIASMA, sweet yet agreeably acrid, soothing

yet tonic, which blurs the edges of one's thoughts with a greenish-gold glow. [Jan Struther]

16. An American shop-girl, laundering two changes of underwear every night, would have noticed a HINT of yesterday's reawakened sweat about Kaethe's person, less a SMELL than an ammoniacal REMINDER of the eternity of toil and decay. [F. Scott Fitzgerald]

17. . . . the elusive potato TAINT, a mixture of earth and moisture, with a remembered taste of deep-fried potato pancakes and the burlap sacking in which they had probably been stored.

18. . . . he smelled the SMELLS his father brought with him: wet wool, stale tobacco, liquor; and above all, more penetrating than any, spreading through the room and polluting everything, the echo of cheap musky perfume. . . . The TAINT of perfume seemed even stronger now. [Wallace Stegner]

19. He saw the stove in its box of pocked sand, surrounded by the nail kegs and up-ended boxes; he even smelled the rank SCORCH of recent spitting. [William Faulkner]

20. . . . in the entire car, the stale RANCOR of body sweat, pushing down on him, making him wish his ride would end.

21. Bayard shut the door behind him on the bright cold, and warmth, and rich, stale RANKNESS enveloped him like a drug. [William Faulkner]

22. . . . the acrid PUNGENCE of burned gasoline from the cars passing through the park.

The noun headwords of the examples above are variously modified. The next few examples illustrate more specifically the various methods of description—by attributes, comparisons, and, for this sense, effect.

Attributes

23. I drew a deep breath, in which I got the hawk odor, slightly bloody, slightly peppery. [Glenway Wescott]

24. The whole building was sharp with the clean nervous odor of antiseptic. [Thomas Wolfe]

25. And to show that he meant all this pleasure, he even went so far as to open the can and pour the three [tennis] balls out, releasing their fresh, inky-wooly, closed-in smell. [John Updike]

26. At their feet the cats tangle their claws and roll in the fish-smelling nets. [Benedict Thielen]

27. I could still smell the tense probing chalk smells from the classroom, the tickling high surgical odor of lysol from the open toilets. [Alfred Kazin]

Comparison

28. Under the red rag her hair came down on her neck in the frailest of ringlets, still black, and with an odor like copper. [Eudora Welty]
29. Wood smoke drifted and hung in the trees like a fragrant sky. [Eudora Welty]
30. The evening was hot; it was the fragrance of the lemon lilies that was cool, like the breath from a mountain well. [Eudora Welty]
31. . . . the fresh camphoric odor of mint. [D. C. Peattie]

Effect

32. The smell of old straw scratched his sinuses. [John Updike]
33. The wet slate [of the blackboard] had a sour claylike smell that set my teeth on edge. [Mildred Walker]
34. . . . there was something astringent in the shaving cream he used that cut into my breath. [Saul Bellow]
35. He did not like old Janet's smell. It made him a little quivery in the stomach; it was just like chicken feathers. [Katherine Anne Porter]

Sometimes the smell is neither named nor described but merely suggested or implied.

36. The old man . . . would be down at the stables, sitting there in the *ammoniac* gloom, alone or with Old Anse. [Robert Penn Warren]
37. The air was at once *bitter* and *sour* with his breathing. [Katherine Anne Porter]
38. An old Mexican was raking fallen eucalyptus leaves and scaled-off bark into a bonfire that trailed stinging sharp tonic-flavored *smoke* across the path. [John Dos Passos]

EXERCISES

A. Be prepared to discuss in class the handling of smells in these passages.

1. Robert Jordan pushed aside the saddle blanket that hung over the mouth of the cave and, stepping out, took a deep breath of the cold night air. The mist had cleared away and the stars were out. There was no wind, and, outside now of the warm air of the cave, heavy with smoke of both tobacco and charcoal, with the odor of cooked rice and meat, saffron, pimentos, and oil, the tarry, wine-spilled smell of the big skin

hung beside the door . . . , wine that spilled a little onto
the earth of the floor, settling the dust smell; out now from
the odors of different herbs whose names he did not know
that hung in bunches from the ceiling, with long ropes of garlic,
away now from the copper-penny, red wine and garlic, horse
sweat and man sweat dried in the clothing (acrid and gray the
man sweat, sweet and sickly the dried brushed-off lather of
horse sweat), of the men at the table, Robert Jordan breathed
deeply of the clear night air of the mountains that smelled
of the pines and of the dew on the grass in the meadow by
the stream. [Ernest Hemingway, *For Whom the Bell Tolls*]

2. The fall sharpened early. The first curing fires in the loaded
   [tobacco firing] barns had been lighted, and the blue smoke began
   to settle out like haze over the bare fields in the late, level light.
   Everywhere there was the thin and pervasive odor of burning,
   which, mingled with the other, more natural odors of the season,
   the dry, pungent, leather odors of earth and withering vegeta-
   tion, fed the sense of recession and finality. [Robert Penn
   Warren, *Night Rider*]

3. The sparrows floated down from the telephone wires to peck
   at every fresh pile of horse manure, and there was the smell
   of brine from the delicatessen store, of egg crates and of the milk
   scum left in the great metal cans outside the grocery, of the
   thick white paste oozing out from behind the fresh Hecker's
   Flour ad on the metal sign board. [Alfred Kazin, *A Walker in
   the City*]

B. Members of the class may bring odorants (or odorophores) to class
   and the class work together or in small groups trying to describe
   them.

C. For the writing assignment use either or both of the forms suggested for sounds: base clause containing the headword, colon or
   dash, and a series of noun clusters separated from each other by
   semicolons; or the simple inventory pattern of noun clusters punctuated as sentences.

TOUCH

We have treated sensations of sound and smell fully enough so that
we can be brief with those of touch. There are no new problems except
those posed by an even smaller vocabulary. The consequence is greater
reliance on suggestion and implication.

The entire human skin and some mucous membranes, such as

those of the mouth and lips, are receptors for tactile sensations. Strictly speaking, tactile, or tactual, sensations are notices of the pressure or motion of a solid or fluid against the sensitive areas. But we will include under touch those notices that alert us to temperature, wetness or dryness, and pain and the notices from what we call the muscle or kinesthetic sense.

The sense of touch is one of those Thoreau held made a more primitive inquisition than sight, which merely introduced us to the object. He wanted more than contact; he wanted immersion, and he wondered whether "any Roman emperor ever indulged in such luxury as . . . walking up and down a river in torrid weather with only a hat on to shade the head." Or he would himself walk in the river, noting the changing feel underfoot: "Now your feet expand on smooth sandy bottom, now contract timidly on pebbles, now slump in genial fatty mud, amid the pads."

Although touch, like the other senses, can be treated as narrative or description, the file discloses only two verbs specifically and primarily designating this sense—*feel* and *touch*. (*Feel* is linking and both transitive and intransitive.) Both of these are nouns as well as verbs, and there seem to be few other nouns specifically naming the sense of touch. Thus the headword in a noun cluster is likely to name the object rather than the quality; that is, we are more likely to find "He felt the soft nubbly CLOTH" than "He felt the soft nubbly FEEL of the cloth."

Verb Headwords

1. He TOUCHED the palm of his hand against the pine needles where he lay and he TOUCHED the bark of the pine-trunk that he lay behind. [Ernest Hemingway]
2. The rub-down, with wintergreen in it, going on icy and then turning hot, FELT good. Its sharp smell was as needles to his spirit. [W. V. T. Clark]
3. . . . the poppy seemed to come alive. She could FEEL the sticky, silky, petals, the stem, hairy like a gooseberry skin, the rough leaf and the tight glazed bud. [Katherine Mansfield]
4. She FELT his eyelid quivering against her cheek. [Katherine Mansfield]
5. . . . and he said, "Arre caballo! Go on, horse!" and FELT his big horse's chest surging with the steepening of the slope. [Ernest Hemingway]
6. There were loaded trucks moving up the road too, and all of them raised a dust that Andrés could not see in that dark but could only FEEL as a cloud that blew in his face and that he could bite between his teeth. [Ernest Hemingway]

Noun Headwords

Even though there are few nouns that name the sensations of touch specifically, the inventive writer can create a sizable vocabulary from verbs and adjectives that suggest or imply sensations of touch, and he can always have recourse to metaphor.

7. She liked the FEELING of the cold shining glass against her hot palms, and she liked to watch the funny white tops that came on her fingers when she pressed them hard against the pan. [Katherine Mansfield]

8. He felt the quick, liquid, spastic LURCHING of the [machine] gun against his shoulder. [Ernest Hemingway]

9. Then he was out in the open, over the road that was so hard under the hooves he felt the POUND of it come up all the way to his shoulders, his neck and his teeth. [Ernest Hemingway]

10. Holding his breath, he practiced drawing back the hammers, then releasing them, feeling their sinewy STRAIN against the ball of his thumb. [Christine Weston]

11. She was pushing grains of corn off the cob with her thumbs, two or three grains at a time, feeling the SPRING of the grain react to her wrist, feeling the grains yield and fall. [Elizabeth Madox Roberts]

12. Aunt Lidy held out her arms and pulled Elspeth close to her so that she felt the soft warm SPRINGINESS of the white wool dress. [Jessamyn West]

13. Tyler hurried up the stairs into the stuffy cigarette-smoky CHILL of the airconditioned restaurant. [John Dos Passos]

14. He had slipped the safety catch and he felt the worn COMFORT of the checked grip chafed almost smooth and touched the round, cool, COMPANIONSHIP of the trigger guard. [Ernest Hemingway]

15. There was an exciting incongruity between their halting, self-conscious talk and the warm, thrilling animal INTIMACY of their hot, moist palms in the long fine grass. [Ruth Suckow]

16. In a moment I have shed my clothes and am swimming out across the golden bars of moonlight, feeling the soft foamy COMMOTION of water drumming on my sides—the peerless warmth of that summer sea. [Lawrence Durrell]

Comparison

17. Her hand reached over—it felt like a petunia leaf, clinging and just a little sticky. [Eudora Welty]

18. Her fingers, as they played on the sleeve of the pongee coat, were light and fluttery as butterfly wings. [Willa Cather]

19. Her hand was warm, prehensile, like mercury in his palm, exploring softly, with delicate bones and petulant scented flesh. [William Faulkner]

20. "Feel her breast." She took my hand and held it against the [hawk's] tasseled plumage; and indeed there was a humming and stiffening in it, like a little voltage of electricity. . . . Only her grip as a whole was hard, like a pair of tight heated iron bracelets. [Glenway Wescott]

Narrative Details

The sense of touch is used so frequently for narrative details that a few examples will not be amiss. Most of these suggest or imply sensations of touch.

21. The ship rose steeply, pressing up under their feet so that their shoes seemed to weigh them down. [George Horner]

22. She walked swiftly to the house, her stockinged feet flinching and cringing from the rough earth. [William Faulkner]

23. She carried her clothes downstairs, walking silently with bare feet across floorboards still warm with yesterday's heat. [Jessamyn West]

24. He didn't want to . . . find himself sitting in his unbleached muslin nightgown, the cold September air touching him like little pieces of iron. [Jessamyn West]

25. He picked up the hem of her smock and played with it in his fingers, rubbing the grain of the raw silk against the whorls of his flesh. [Mary McCarthy]

26. He rinsed a batch of glasses in the soapy water, feeling the heat on his big red hands, feeling the ends of his fingers crinkling from the hot water. [Whitfield Cook]

27. . . . he walked to Dolly's chair, smilingly took her glass . . . , and continued up the slope, feeling the glass a bit sticky, pleasurably warm from her hand. [William Styron]

28. She opened the cellar door and went slowly down the steps, feeling the wood cool beneath her feet and the air growing damp and cool as she descended. [Mary Deasy]

It is so common for sensations of touch to be merely suggested or implied that some examples are necessary to show how it may be done.

29. His eyelids were *gritty* from so many sleepless nights. [John Dos Passos]

30. She put out her arms like wings and knew in her fingers the

thready pattern of red roses in the carpet on the stairs. [Eudora Welty]

31. Outside he inhaled *damp* snowflakes that he could no longer see against the darkening sky. [F. Scott Fitzgerald]

32. The air was *warm*, yet laced too with a thin distillation of *chill* that darkness would increase. [William Faulkner]

33. The hounds came and NUZZLED about him and he dropped his hand among their *icy* noses and the *warm* flicking of their tongues. [William Faulkner]

34. . . . his hands GRIPPED the *dry*, alien boards of the fence. The whitewash POWDERED, *furrily*, against the flesh of his hands. [Robert Penn Warren]

35. . . . with a sigh she stretched out her *hot* legs so that sheet and coverlet enveloped her body in a *soundless rush of air*, like a tent collapsing. [William Styron]

36. She saw him now clearly as he furled the *heavy* flannel cloth around the stick; the flannel hanging *blood-heavy* from the passes where it had swept over the bull's head and shoulders and the *wet* streaming shine of his withers. [Ernest Hemingway]

EXERCISES

A. Be prepared to discuss in class the senses appealed to in these passages, and the diction, the methods of description, and the use of suggestion and implication in presenting them.

   1. She pushed her hand into the brown flaky [flax] seeds. They slipped smoothly up her wrist, cool and dry, millions of polished, purple-brown, miniature guitar picks. She moved her hand and the flax swirled like heavy smooth water against her skin. [Wallace Stegner, *The Big Rock Candy Mountain*]

   2. She washed the dishes and pans which she found in the kitchen, dented, cracked, gummy, dusty, plunging her wrists into the hot hissing, swollen, delicious suds which foamed up to overflow the sink. The water was so hot it was painful—or almost painful—but at the same time it sent through her body a tingling pleasure, which, with the rising steam, flushed her cheeks and made her lips moist. For several minutes she dawdled with the dishes in the sink, not really washing them, just moving her hands under the water enough to nurse and keep alive the pulsing stimulation, the awareness of her own blood, which it provided. Then the water began to cool. The suds subsided, and grease began to coagulate murkily around the edges of the sink. [Robert Penn Warren, *At Heaven's Gate*]

3. Walking carefully, downhill, Anselmo in the lead, Augustin next, Robert Jordan placing his feet carefully so that he would not slip, feeling the dead pine needles under his rope-soled shoes, bumping a tree root with one foot and putting a hand forward and feeling the cold metal of the automatic rifle barrel and the folded legs of the tripod, then working sideways down the hill, his shoes sliding and grooving the forest floor, putting his left hand out again and touching the rough bark of a tree trunk, then as he braced himself, his hand feeling a smooth place, the base of the palm of his hand coming away sticky from the resinous sap where a blaze had been cut, they dropped down the steep wooded hillside to the point above the bridge where Robert Jordan and Anselmo had watched the first day. [Ernest Hemingway, *For Whom the Bell Tolls*]

B. For classroom practice there are ample materials at hand, especially for texture.
C. If a written exercise is to be assigned, the same two patterns can be used again. Here is an example of one pattern. Since touch is often suggested or implied rather than described, a brief narrative like the second example here may be more natural.

1. She loved to feel the ingredients that went into every batch of her cookies: the sand-like crystals of sugar rolling hard between her fingers; the silky, clean feel of flour flattening smooth under her touch; the liquid added making a sticky paste clinging to both hands, closing around them like a rubber glove; and finally the Crisco, velvet, creamy, like women's hand lotion, spreading evenly onto the cookie sheet.
2. Sometimes I lay, the sharp bones of my hips meeting only the hardness of the sand, the sun puckering my skin. My eyes closed, I lost sense of which side the sea was, which side the land, and seemed to be alive only within my own body, beating with the heat. Water came with the rising tide, gentle and shocking. I jumped with the pattern of the sand facets like the marks of rough bedclothes on my legs and cheek. Sometimes I went over to the rocks and dipped my hands in the lukewarm pools. Some of the rocks bristled with mussels and barnacles which agonized my feet; others, smooth and black and layered, shown slightly greasy with salt. Red-brown ones were dry and matte, swirled out into curves and hollows by the sea. They were warm and alive, like flesh. I sat back in an armchair of stone, resting the still-white undersides of my arms on the warmth. Sweat softened the hair in my armpits, and suddenly,

across the scent of the wind and the sea, I was conscious of
the smell of my own body. [Nadine Gordimer, *The Lying Days*]

TASTE

The sense of taste is in one way the simplest and in another the most
complex of the senses. It is the simplest in that it is the most crudely
discriminatory. We can discriminate by taste alone only sour and sweet,
bitter and salty. All the other nuances we attribute to taste, or associate
with it, we owe to the other senses—to smell, to touch, to sound even,
and to sight—so that a real banquet, or a description of one in words,
may involve appeals to all of the senses. Besides this, eating is likely to
be the focus or the occasion of a social gathering where the savoring of
food is incidental—incidental especially to talking. The talk is not likely
to be about the quality of the food; if it were, we would not have in
English such a poverty-stricken vocabulary for this sense as we do.

The vocabulary is as uncomplicated as the sense itself—two or three
verbs (*taste, savor, relish*), a small handful of nouns (*taste, savor, flavor,
sting, tang*), a few nouns derived from adjectives (such as *sweetness,
bitterness*), and the usual adjectives pressed into service for this as for
the other senses.

Most passages that purport to report the experience of eating report simply what was on the table or in the picnic hamper. They are
little more than grocery lists or menus. The items are named, and sometimes a bit of visual description is added. These are representative
examples. Identify the added modifiers and determine what sense they
appeal to.

1. In the morning they rose in a house pungent with breakfast
   cookery, and they sat at a smoking table loaded with brains and
   eggs, ham, hot biscuit, fried apples seething in their gummed syrups,
   honey, golden butter, fried steak, scalding coffee. Or there were
   stacked batter-cakes, rum-colored molasses, fragrant brown
   sausages, a bowl of wet cherries, plums, fat juicy bacon, jam. At
   the mid-day meal they ate heavily: a huge hot roast of beef, fat
   buttered lima-beans, tender corn smoking on the cob, thick red
   slabs of sliced tomatoes, rough savory spinach, hot yellow corn-
   bread, flaky biscuits, a deep-dish peach and apple cobbler spiced
   with cinnamon, tender cabbage, deep glass dishes piled with
   preserved fruits—cherries, pears, peaches. At night they might eat
   fried steaks, hot squares of grits fried in egg and butter, pork-
   chops, fish, young fried chicken.
       . . . a day or two before [Thanksgiving], the auxiliary
   dainties arrived in piled grocer's boxes—the magic of strange

foods and fruits was added to familiar fare: There were glossed
sticky dates, cold rich figs, cramped belly to belly in small boxes,
dusty raisins, mixed nuts—the almond, pecan, the meaty nigger-
toe, the walnut, sacks of assorted candies, piles of yellow Florida
oranges, tangerines, sharp, acrid, nostalgic odors. [Thomas Wolfe,
Look Homeward, Angel]

2. By sundown the streets were empty, the curtains had been drawn,
   the world put to rights. Even the kitchen walls had been scrubbed
   and now gleamed in the Sabbath candles. On the long white
   tablecloth were the "company" dishes, filled for some with *gefilte*
   fish on lettuce leaves, ringed by red horseradish, sour and half-
   sour pickles, tomato salad with a light vinegar dressing; for others,
   with chopped liver in a bed of lettuce leaves and white radishes;
   the long white khalleh, the Sabbath loaf; chicken soup with
   noodles *and* dumplings; chicken, meat loaf, prunes, and sweet
   potatoes that had been baked all day into an open pie; compote
   of prunes and quince, apricots and orange rind; applesauce; a great
   brown nutcake filled with almonds, the traditional lekakh; all
   surrounded by glasses of port wine, seltzer bottles with their
   nozzles staring down at us waiting to be pressed; a samovar of
   Russian tea, *svetouchnee* from a little red box, always served in
   tall glasses, with lemon slices floating on top. My father and
   mother sipped it in Russian fashion, through lumps of sugar held
   between the teeth. [Alfred Kazin, *A Walker in the City*]

3. Gram's cellar was the repository of a wide variety of relishes. There
   were pickled peaches, a clove stuck in the side of each. There were
   spiced crabapples, each with its own slender stem. There were
   almost transparent watermelon pickles, green tomato pickles—
   with a slight flavor of onion—sweet apple pickles, cut into quarters
   and rich in their own spiced juices. There were small pickled pears,
   for serving with ham, and tender string bean pickles, for serving
   with boiled beef. And, row on row, bottles and jars held catsup,
   chili sauce, and piccalilli. [Edward Way Teale, *Dune Boy*]

Even when a piece is labeled a dissertation on taste, it is likely to
assay fairly high in the other senses.

4. I liked the taste of beer, its live, white lather, its brass-bright
   depths, the sudden world through the wet-brown walls of the
   glass, the tilted rush to the lips and the slow swallowing down to
   the lapping belly, the salt on tongue, the foam at the corners.
   [Dylan Thomas, *Portrait of the Artist as a Young Dog*]

The file we have been drawing from does contain a few descriptions of the savor of food and drink that fall into the established patterns.

Verb and Noun Headwords

5. He ran his tongue over his teeth, TASTING the last of the molasses
   and coffee and bacon and eggs. [James Agee]
6. Then he turned the gun, with the lock open and in the dark he put
   the muzzle to his lips and blew through the barrel, the metal
   TASTING greasy and oily as his tongue touched the edge of the bore.
   [Ernest Hemingway]
7. . . . he lay there in the [barber's] chair with his eyes closed and
   the towels on his face and the sweetish TASTE of steam on his lips.
   [Robert Penn Warren]
8. The air was flat and dead. It had a metallic TASTE at the base of
   the tongue. [William Faulkner]
9. The mustard was bright yellow on the brown sausage as they ate
   it, sitting on the top of a hill, about two hours farther on. . . .
   Franklin sat with sausage and bread in his hand and felt the STING of
   mustard on his tongue like the sting of his own exhilaration.
   . . . [The chestnuts] were clean and sweet to eat after the meat
   paste and mustard, and right and beautiful with the wine.
   [H. E. Bates]
10. There was the smell of hot chokeberry patches, hillsides hot under
    the sun, and spice and bark and leaf mold and the fruity odor
    of the berries, and the puckery alum TANG of a ripe cluster stripped
    into the mouth, the feel of the pits against the palate. [Wallace
    Stegner]
11. The rich, spicy FLAVOR of the globules [of spruce pitch] had a
    slightly bitter TANG and I remember that the consistency of the
    pitch had to be just right or it stuck to my teeth with the grip of
    glue. [Edward Way Teale]

Attributes

12. And they would go across the Square to the cool depth of the
    drug-store, stand before the onyx splendor of the fountain, under
    the revolving wooden fans, and drink chill gaseous beverages,
    limeade so cold it made the head ache, or foaming ice-cream soda,
    which returned in sharp delicious belches down his tender nostrils.
    [Thomas Wolfe]
13. . . . he usually had enough left over for cold gaseous draughts
    at the soda fountain. [Thomas Wolfe]
14. . . . the opaque, sweetish, cold, licorice-tasting drink did not
    make him feel any different. [Ernest Hemingway]
15. It was buttermilk such as I had not tasted in thirty years—creamy,
    ice-cold with little flakes of butter in it. [Louis Bromfield]

16. . . . in the sun the bitter little wild crabs reach their one instant of winy, tangy, astringent perfection. [D. C. Peattie]

Comparison

17. His mouth was tastelessly dry, as though he had been eating dust, then salt and bitter as after a drink of seawater. [Joseph Conrad]
18. When I was a boy I first learned how much better water tastes when it has set a while in a cedar bucket. Warmish-cool, with a faint taste like the hot July wind in cedar trees smells. It has to set at least six hours, and be drunk from a gourd. [William Faulkner]
19. The daiquiri does have the taste of limeade, riding like oil on the top of a raw transparent taste. [John Updike]
20. She pulled back the sandwich and began unwrapping it herself. Soggy and cold, it was, and the bacon rather stiff like corrugated cardboard, once wet and dried out again. [Anne Morrow Lindbergh]

Effect

21. He was very tired and the milk, cool at first but clammy after the first drink or two, seemed to lie heavy and curdled in his throat. [H. E. Bates]
22. But I swallowed the pop thirstily, and the fizz exploded in the back of my nose and made my eyes water. It was cherry, slippery-red and fruity—more exciting by far than, years later, my first taste of whiskey. [Mary Nash]
23. Delicate tendrils of the warm-cool lime and absinthe tingled in his nose, climbed enticingly back of his temples. [John Dos Passos]
24. Sometimes Gram would bring out a quart Mason jar in a pail of cold spring water. The jar would be filled with homemade ginger ale or root beer, a beverage which brought to mind woodland tastes—of sassafras twig-tips and wintergreen berries. [Edward Way Teale]

Taste or Something Else

What we enjoy in eating and drinking, or what we are aware of whether or not we enjoy it, is often the texture (and the accompanying sound of chewing), the temperature, the smell, and, of course, the appearance of what we eat and drink. It is these we will miss when overpopulation reduces our intake to pills.

25. Dad had opened a can of pears for dessert. They were still a little cool from the root cellar and I let each piece lie on my tongue for a second. [Mildred Walker]

26. They would unlock their hands from the hoe handle, and push
    their hats back a little off the forehead. Their lips would be dry,
    and on their teeth would be the slight grittiness of dust raised
    from the dry ground. In turn, Willie Proudfit first, then Sylvestus,
    they would lift the bucket to the lips and let the cool water fill
    the mouth and slip, sweetly and purifyingly, into the throat. [Robert Penn Warren]

27. When she gave him the tumbler at last he drank the grapejuice
    in slow regular sips. It was partly sweet and very cool. Once he
    did not drink but let his lips stay in the glass, so that the coolness
    bathed them, and finally, when he lay down again, he let the
    wetness remain on the cracked dry skin. [H. E. Bates]

PART II
THE LARGER UNITS
OF COMPOSITION

7

A Short Narrative

The Flaubert who taught Maupassant so much about writing had himself to learn how to write. Early in his career, in writing *Madame Bovary*, he had to change his style to make it appropriate to the new kind of material his friend Bouilhet had persuaded him to try. Francis Steegmuller tells how Bouilhet helped him with the style:

> Together they read over sentences dozens, even hundreds of times; and then, when each sentence seemed right, they read over the paragraphs into which they were combined. Gradually, out of single sentences that were simple and direct, Flaubert learned how to construct paragraphs and pages that were also simple and solid, but shimmering and rich as well; inversions, shifts of emphasis, variety in sentence length resulted in a style that was more compelling and stronger than the monotony of the romantics. [*Flaubert and Madame Bovary, A Double Portrait*]

All of our written exercises up to this point have been designed to get the sentences right. You should have by now a good working knowledge of all the kinds of free modifiers that can be used to expand the basic sentence core. It is time to try to get the sentences to work together. In this and the next two chapters, there will be three assignments intended to solve this problem.

THE ASSIGNMENT: A PARAGRAPH

The first will be a brief narrative, from three to not more than six or eight sentences, a narrative carefully circumscribed and controlled in order to illustrate as many principles as possible. Though brief, this narrative must be a whole and of sufficient magnitude to justify so many sentences. The terms *whole* and *magnitude* are from Aristotle, and we will use his definition of a whole as an action that has a beginning, a middle, and an end. A beginning is that which is not in itself necessarily after anything and which has something else after it. An end is that which is naturally after something and with nothing else after it. From these two statements you can deduce the definition of a middle. The problem will be to use the abstract definition to identify actions that are wholes of sufficient magnitude to serve as subjects for this assignment. A single breaking ocean wave, for instance, is a natural action of sufficient magnitude, with a clearly marked beginning and end and a varied and interesting middle.

Another requirement for the action is that it shall be one you can observe over and over until you have really seen it. Learning to write is still learning to have something to say. No one needs to be at a loss for a subject. In our automated homes there is no lack. Take home two or three dozen eggs, take command of the electric mixer, and remember that no one can make an omelet without breaking the eggs. Besides the mixer, there are the juicer, the blender, the corn popper, the coffee maker, the can opener, the stereo, the tape recorder, the TV set. If your family are the do-it-yourself kind, the operation of some of the more lethal power tools makes a good subject—the saw, shaper, sander, drill, or lathe, or the welding or cutting torch. Or, if you work, you may operate machines or see them in operation, from an office duplicator to a machine-shop drop forge. Even without such a home, workshop, or job, a writer can at least find a tank toilet that he can flush over and over until he knows all its cool hydraulic movements and sounds.

If you reject the machine age and all its gadgetry, you can blow bubble gum or soap bubbles or throw a frisbee; or you can go to the pool to watch a diver, to the mountains to watch a ski jump or run, to the beach to watch the surfers, or, again, grandest subject of all, not man, not machine, but nature, the ocean wave. Keats has been praised for seeing the bubbles that slide down the back of a wave, but there are a score of such details.

Some subjects you might have expected to see here are not here. Although they have clearly marked beginnings and endings, some have no variety or interest in the middle—they have no magnitude: when you have dropped in the bread and depressed the lever, you can only stand around until the toast pops up. Although they have distinct beginnings and varied and interesting middles, some have no ends—a sprinkler or a vacuum cleaner or a typewriter just goes on and on. A clever writer, though, can bring the description of a continued or repeated action to a satisfying close. With some otherwise good subjects—such as automatic washers, dryers, and dishwashers—the interesting part of the action is concealed.

One of the first choices you will have to make is whether to use the first or third person. Some of the machines require an operator, and the operator may, indifferently, be you or someone else. But if the action is a ski or surf run or a dive, there is a vast difference between the experience of the performer and the observer. At this stage, the point of view of the observer is preferable.

The chief technical problem of the kind of narrative we are preparing to write involves the treatment of time. Objective time, ticked off by a clock or a metronome, moves at a uniform rate. The continuum is cut into arbitrary units, and all the units are accounted for at face value and in due order. We can picture it thus (each unit is a minute):

Time in a narrative cannot move at a uniform rate. If the action takes five minutes, you cannot divide it into five one-minute units, allot one sentence to each unit, and give about the same amount of detail to each sentence. Such even-handed justice would be intolerably monotonous. Narrative time is elastic, like subjective time, or like an accordion. A long novel may occupy itself with the events of a single day; in another work a single sentence—or an inch of white space—may dispose of the events of a day, a week, a year, a decade, a generation. Narrative demands what we call a change of pace. It treats intensively what the writer judges important, touches lightly on what is less important, and may skip entirely what, from the standpoint of his story, he regards as of minor or no importance. We might picture it thus:

This is pretty abstract. In describing the action you have chosen and observed exhaustively, you will be writing from three to perhaps as many as eight sentences. These will succeed one another in chronological sequence. (There is no need for flashbacks.) They may possibly overlap somewhat in time, and there may be some gaps, little segments of clock time that are just skipped. The number of sentences is the crucial problem. This depends on the analysis you make of the action. In some ultimate sense any action you may have chosen is continuous (the way our lives are, despite the birthdays), but any action of any magnitude can be divided, more or less naturally, into parts or stages. Allot one sentence to each of these stages. Each time you put down the finite verb of the base clause of a narrative sentence, that verb isolates or defines a unit of time. Make that unit of time one of the stages of your action. These units of time will not be equal in clock time. And these segments of the action will not be treated all with the same amount of detail. The texture will vary from sentence to sentence. By these two means you will achieve the change of pace that is so fundamental in narrative. You will be treating time the way the player treats his accordion.

STUDENT EXAMPLES

This is still rather abstract, so let us turn next to examples. The authors of the following examples (pages 90–91), set in parallel columns, made roughly the same analysis of the "same" subject. Author A prefaced his narrative with a sentence-length description of the appearance of the Silex coffee maker, but at the stages marked 1, 3, and 7 all four authors are together.

At the first stage, all four notice the bubbles forming on the bottom and/or sides and rising and bursting; A, B, and D notice also the steam condensing on the sides and trickling down; C alone (but C hasn't put on the upper bowl yet) notices the steam appearing and vanishing on the pouring lip. To get these items in, A and C use compound sentences; D, the shortest of all, uses up two of its four sentences; B uses only a prepositional phrase. Thus, all four recognize this stage, but vary in the amount of detail they observe in it and vary widely in the constructions they allot to it.

Note the stage marked 3. D, the simplest, has only one base clause: B has four base clauses and C has five (both spread them over two sentences); A has four parallel sentences (it is hard to tell whether the actions of 4, 5, and 6 all take place in the upper bowl). In B and C the second half of the compound sentence belongs to the next stage. Thus the sentences do not correspond to the stages of the action: some stages have more than one sentence, others less than one. The four differ considerably in the picture they present of what happens in the upper bowl; since this can be presented in relation to the rising water or the sinking coffee, the accounts differ greatly at this point. Finally, the focus at the end is quite different in the four examples: B and D focus on the grounds in the upper bowl; A and C on the brewed coffee in the lower one, but each on different details.

Although each of these narratives has its good points, no one of them is altogether successful in its sentence work.

The next set of narratives are more successful in solving the problem of relating the sentences of the narrative into stages of the action. The three appear in order of length, and the length here, as in the last examples, correlates with and is an index of the adequacy of the observation. E is superficial in its scanning of the action; G is so extraordinarily minute that one can admire the observer and the writer but wish for retrenchment. The texture is too dense to be taken in comfortably and so uniformly dense that the narrative seems to want change of pace.

E

I broke the shell of the egg, the white slipping away from the yolk like molasses sliding from a can. The yolk dropped into the blue bowl, pushing aside the egg white instead of blending with it. The motion of the beater made a circular dent in the white while the yolk whirled around, resisting the magnetic force of the blades. Soon the quickly moving metal circle drew it in, too, and broken puddles of yellow merged with the stiff peaks of egg white. Finally a yellow liquid with a mass of white froth on top filled the blue bowl—my beaten egg.

F

I poured the eggs into the bowl of the Mixmaster, watching them slip around the sides and finally settle together in the bottom, the still unbroken yolks washing against the stainless steel blades in their sea of dull, slippery jelly. Giving the ON switch a sharp click, I watched the blades spin into instant action, in perfect synchromesh, slashing at the yolks and blending them into the churning, jellylike mass of whites. In a moment, the blades were whirring smoothly, the eggs now an even, pale-yellow sea frothing and foaming about them. Soon the mass of yellow was swirling evenly with the blades, rising up in a funnel about them. I pulled the plug out of the wall and watched the blades spin suddenly to a stop, the mass of yellow washing gently around them and beginning to bubble up. I lifted the head away from the bowl, taking the blades with it, egg dripping off them and plopping into the mass below, breaking the larger bubbles which were now fizzling down into many smaller ones.

G

I lowered the beaters of the electric mixer into a bowl of egg whites, thick, clear, yellow-white, and observed a variety of meteorological phenomena in miniature: whirlpools, snow drifts, tides, flurries —each set off by me, at the controls, where I was in full charge of speeds 1, 2, and 3. At speed 1, the glutinous substance was pulled between the slowly rotating beaters, from the back toward the front of the bowl, the outer rim of the counterrevolving whirlpools rising and riding on top of the lower levels of egg white, as it all heightened and narrowed to squeeze between the beaters, quickly relaxing and returning to the pool, where it resumed its circular journey. No bubbles formed, so I turned to speed 2, its motor-hum higher pitched, its vibrations more noticeable, and its landscapes more interesting. Frothy, irregular bubbles began to appear in the wake of the beaters, backing up, and piling up behind the beater and along the sides of the bowl, the way ocean foam piles up where waves splash among big rocks. Bubbles began to work up from the bottom of the bowl, forming there, rising upward, and getting caught in the whirlpool, only to be thrown forward against the front of the bowl, returning in a backwash, riding above the revolving pool in a crescent-shaped wave. The clear pool in the center was becoming increasingly frothy when I switched recklessly to speed 3, the motor humming still higher, and the beater defying

A

(0)

Like an overgrown hour glass the Silex coffee maker stands with the dark, fragrant grains in the upper section already beginning to shimmer from the heat.

(1)

Beadlike bubbles gather on the bottom, then spring to the surface and vanish; steam fogs the glass and trickles down again to the water.

(3)

The pressure increases, forcing a clear column of water to crawl up the connecting spout and flood out among the grains, making islands, covering the islands.

(4)

Steam swirls from the dark water and foamy bubbles appear.

(5)

A brownish-white ring circles the edge.

(6)

The bubbles become larger until the whole pot rocks with their explosions.

(7)

As it cools, the thick brown water seeps and then gurgles back down the spout and fills the lower section with dark, rich coffee.

B

(1)

After the rusty, brown coils of the GE heater have become cherry-red, and pin-point bubbles have begun to collect on the sides of the glass, surge upward, hesitate at the surface, and then pop, making tiny ripples in the water,

(2)

(3)

the pressure in the lower glass of the Silex coffee maker forces the water up the tube and it begins to seep into the chocolate-colored coffee grounds in the upper glass.

(4)

Soon the water is surging up the tube, plopping and gurgling, and

(7)

when it cools, a foam collects on the surface, dotted with dark coffee grounds and iridescent bubbles that do not break.

(8)

The coffee begins trickling back down the tube in an amber-colored stream, which later becomes dark brown when the coffee cascades down.

(9)

The grounds, blanketed with the remaining foam, which is now a lacy skeleton of burst air bubbles, huddle around the strainer above.

C   D

(0)

(1)	(1)
A circular mat of little bubbles appears around the bottom of the Silex coffee maker, and	As the water becomes hot, small bubbles form on the bottom and side of the Silex, some of them rising to the surface, lingering for a moment, then bursting.

(2)

beads of perspiration fog the glass above the heating water, growing larger and sliding down the sloping glass sides like tear drops while a film of steam appears and vanishes on the pouring lip and the bubbles that had been a mat grow larger, tumbling and tossing over one another.

(2)

Drops of condensed steam, forming on the sides above the waterline, slowly trickle down.

(3)

The water swirls up through the glass tube; the seething brown mass boils and ripples; and a lighter brown scum forms along the side of the glass.

(3)

The boiling water rising in the glass tube, swirls about the coffee in the top.

(4)

Now there are but a few tablespoonfuls of water in the bottom; the gas flame is turned off, and

(5)

(6)

(7)

as the coffee cools, a yellow liquid film slides down the sides of the tube, fanning out in the water below until it too is a rich, bitter-chocolate brown.

(7)

Removed from the heat, the vacuum draws the coffee to the lower part of the Silex, leaving a mound of wet grounds, fringed with a delicate filigree of light-brown froth speckled with air bubbles.

(8)

The coffee begins to fill the tube looking like brown mercury in a thermometer, and

(9)

as it drops back down, a stream of rainbow-hued bubbles follow it to disappear beneath the surface of the liquid and boil out again while a homey, appetizing smell fills the kitchen.

complete control by jumping around a little in my hand. The froth
in the pool became whiter with fine bubbles which radiated from the
beaters toward the edge of the bowl, there pushing up a rim of larger,
frothier bubbles, as the level of whites in the bowl rose gradually,
becoming thick with minute bubbles, finer than grains of sugar, and as
white. Little circular drifts proceeded from the beaters toward the
edge of the bowl, moving more slowly as they neared the edge, an
occasional snowy peak forming and remaining until it was caught by
some undercurrent, drawn into the beater, and leveled by its force.
The miniature snowscape had reached a state where drift-cycles were
repeated and changes in contour were subtle and less interesting, so
I decided to sacrifice my fluffy white for a baked custard.

You yourself can compare and contrast the three authors' solutions
of the problem of how many sentences and how much in each. You will
note first, perhaps, that at the start E takes two two-level sentences for
what F does, with far greater precision, in one three-level sentence. But
while you are making this comparison, study the base clauses and the
relative number of words in them and in the added free modifiers. In E
there are 74 in the base clauses to 30 in the added modifiers; in F the
proportions are reversed—62 to 116. This again is an index to the texture. When the texture is dense, the base clause is generally short; it
simply indicates in general terms the subject of the next unit of time. In
sentences with two or more levels, there is a natural division of labor
between the two kinds of grammatical elements. In G the proportions
of the two are almost exactly equal. This is due to the peculiar structure of G, which is a combination of essay and narrative. The essay has
a topic sentence and conclusion and between them three subtopics—
speeds 1, 2, and 3. This essaylike framework takes about half the words.
Thus G is less typical than F.

Another problem in narrative (and in other writing as well) is the
choice of grammatical subjects for the sentences. Unlike the Silex, once
it has been set up, the Mixmaster requires an operator, and in E, F, and
G the operator is "I." If "I" were the subject of every sentence, we could
call the narration an example of *simple linear narrative.* Such narrative
is likely to become monotonous and the author is likely to search for
ways to conceal or replace the obtrusive "I." The commonest way to
conceal it is to put something before it—a sentence modifier—and the
commonest sentence modifier is the verb cluster. E has one example—
equal to "I gave the ON switch a sharp click and watched the blades
spin"; and D has one, dangling—"removed from the heat, the vacuum
draws the coffee. . . ." Initial verb clusters are used so sparingly by
professional writers that they suggest the classroom and the amateur.
The commonest way to escape "I" as a subject is to shift occasionally

to the passive; the passive has its uses, but this is not one of them. The best way is to use some part of the beater (the blades) or the beaten (the yolk, the yellow liquid). F does this once, naturally; E and G do it several times, also naturally. Finally, when you come to writing your narrative, there are three features of style you should consciously try to practice: narrative details, comparison, metaphor. You can't write an effective piece without them. Here is a brief review of the three.

EXERCISES

This assignment should be another exercise in the use of narrative details in sentences with two or more levels. Without such narrative details, you can hit only the high points of the action; or, to vary to metaphor, you will produce only the tones without the overtones. At the same time, you must get variety in the sentence structure. One of the most effective ways to do this is to vary the number and kind of parallel coordinate elements, not only the free modifiers we have been emphasizing but predicate verbs. In I notice the compound predicates *tore, flicked, felt*.

It should also be an exercise in the use of comparison. Examples A–G are not distinctive on this score, as are some of the later examples, but there are some instances: two compound adjectives (*beadlike, jellylike*); two *like* phrases describing appearances (*like an hour glass, like brown mercury in the thermometer*) and two describing action (*sliding like tear drops, slipping like molasses*); and in G two clauses, if the second is a clause, with *the way* and *than*. None of these is obtrusive—a danger when you are urged to try comparisons, but one you must risk. Most of them are accurate or appropriate, and most of them do contribute to the image.

Finally, it should be an exercise, as most writing must be, in the use of metaphor. The reason for this is simple. Metaphor is indispensable. You are dealing not only with things and familiar actions, but with appearance, for which there are no established terms. We have, and will have, no established terms for the appearances of eggs—white alone or yolks and whites—on the way from the shell to the omelet or custard. G illustrates beautifully the use of metaphor, except for the lack of one in place of *glutinous substance*.

The examples that follow are for study in class and at home to show how students have solved the various problems. The last three differ from the others. L illustrates the generalized narrative. It does not describe one operation of the lathe, but the kind of chips it produces with various metals and depths of cut. M illustrates the description of action by noun phrases. The long sentence has a parallel series of nouns modified by verb phrases. N has a pattern determined by the writer's remembrance of how, as a child, he was told how to operate a music box. It is distinctive for the large amount of description neatly woven into the narrative.

H. BATHROOM SCALE

I placed one foot on the nonskid tread of the bathroom scale and watched the black ribbon of melted numbers stream by and slow down to a legible yet indecisive rocking. While it was still rocking I placed my other foot on and snapped the legibility into motion once again, the ribbon of numbers whisking past the aperture, losing momentum abruptly, and settling roulettelike on an unlucky number. I stepped off quickly and the spring of the scale boomeranged to the zero mark, erasing its recording.

I. "LUCKIES SMOKE MILDER"

I tore a match from the book, flicked it against the striking surface, and felt it skate easily over the worn grayish strip, scraping a narrow furrow and exposing the cardboard beneath. Using the very bottom edge of the surface, I tried again and felt the match head catch hold, with a hiss and a gentle pop, as the flame sprang up. It sidled up the match, driving a film of moisture and a thin strip of darker grey before it, leaving a shriveling black waste behind. The paper at the end of my cigarette turned to flickering orange, with grey ash showing through the flame, and a black border shading into brown. The orange glow thrust cautious fingers into the dark edging, and trails of smoke, blue outside and yellow within, curled around both sides of the cigarette and met at the top in a flat ribbon which trailed away, doubling back on itself as it went. A cartwheel of pale ash appeared at the end of my Chesterfield, and I inhaled a long puff as someone on the radio informed me that "Luckies smoke milder."

J. WAVE

It was a gray afternoon and a gray-green ocean, restless and turbulent, that I surveyed from the seawall of granite boulders, spotted with green moss on the coarse surfaces between jagged edges, on which I stood, looking at the thousand ever-changing heads of wavelets shadowed by the setting sun. A wide, undulating pathway of white foam—the milky way of the Pacific—stretched parallel to the rocky barrier thirty feet offshore, dotted with floating, yellowish brown leis of seaweed and patches of bubbled foam like tufts of uncut sheep's wool, all twisting and turning, rising and falling with the expression of the ocean. A single swell, of many wavelets joined together, rose gradually, mounting ever higher as it rushed toward the seawall and broke with thunderous applause against the massive boulders, white spray, thrown twenty feet into the air, cascading over the top of the barrier followed by finely blown spume. Then the sea receded—white foam washing over the brown, marine-encrusted rocks, the shimmering water dropping from the edges of the boulders, quickly, like silver pearls slipping from rows of severed, overhanging strings into the ocean.

K. TAPE RECORDER

His eyes scanned the controls briefly, checking each for its proper prerecording position—volume indicator slightly above the center mark, speaker switch off, tape motion forward, speed 7½ feet per minute, recording light steady. Satisfied, he switched on the tape recorder motor, provoking a rustling whir from the hidden wheels and gears within the console. As the mechanism became engaged, the thin tape darted ahead like a striking snake, coiling, then receding as the slack was taken up by the slowly winding reel, settling down to a steady, measured movement, the reels synchronizing, the indicator ticking off the footage with speedometer-like precision. He spoke carefully into the microphone, watching the skittish volume needle pulsating rhythmically like a polygraphed heartbeat, fidgeting slightly at each inflection, reacting impulsively, like a startled goldfish, to a slammed door in the background, then calming down cautiously as the recording was completed, giving forth one final, jittery skip as he turned the large center dial to the off position. The plastic reels were set in reverse motion, rapidly spinning, spokes blurring and disappearing as the speed reached propellerlike intensity, whining with high-pitched frequency, the countdown on the footage indicator hurrying past zero as the rewind spool thickened with tape and the empty spool, freed of its restraining burden, spun uninhibited until the control switch forced it to an abrupt stop.

L. LATHE

A flick of the switch and the chuck transforms itself into a blur of rotating steel; the feed is engaged, the saddle begins to move, the rigid tool cuts into the work, and the lathe begins to spin its bright-colored chips. These chips will sometimes be tightly coiled like springs, or they may come off in long, loose spirals that will not break but will go twisting down the ways, down to the floor, and across it for a considerable distance, writhing like metallic serpents. Or if the cut is deep, the chips will come off in short curves—saw-edged, the outside smooth and the inside wrinkled and rough—of a gray or yellow or purple or blue color, and making a clicking noise as they break away from the parent metal. If bronze or brass is being worked, the chips will be shiny yellow, and, as the carriage moves along, the tool will perform a peculiar alchemy of its own, changing dull castings into bright gold by its polishing action.

M. SOAP BUBBLE

Blowing a soap bubble still fascinates me, though I am past the customary age limit for doing this, for in a soap bubble there seems to be a kind of escape for the mind: the thick, syrupy water lying in the bowl of the soap-bubble pipe; the gradual swelling of the flat surface of the water into the side of a bubble; the small bubbles, a sort of foam, the size of pin points, as they slide and skim from the crest of the expanding bubble, slipping down into the bowl of the pipe; the illusion created by the thinning of the soap-water on the surface of the bubble, making the bubble look as if it were spinning recklessly, whirling and bouncing on the edge of the bowl, an illusion very much like heat waves emanating from the sun-baked desert; and then the final release of the bubble in a perfect sphere with beautiful colors, the colors of the rainbow, red, orange, yellow, green, blue, indigo, and violet. Peer into that bubble, cherish the illusion it may protect, escape for a moment before it turns into a tiny water drop.

N. MUSIC BOX

You may tilt back the hinged mahogany lid (*be gentle, be careful, your great-grandfather Roessler brought this music box from Switzerland almost a hundred years ago*), tilt back the lid, with its chipped motif of lyre, mandolin, and horn so artfully grouped upon a spray of edelweiss, and stare at the intricate works beneath the glass. Yes, you may wind it now: eight pulls upon the curved steel handle, shiny where the fingers grasp the knobbed end, feeling the firm engagement of the pawl and the clicking of the ratchet as you pull, the looseness as you drop the handle back into its well. The hidden spring gains tension, and at the third stroke the brass cylinder almost imperceptibly moves; a brass pin (one of myriads which stud the cylinder, prickly to the finger's touch like a stubble beard) lifts a tooth of the steel comb, moves higher, and the tooth, released, twangs stiffly back: a solitary note of music. Five strokes: the pins are picking out a pattern—*Die Schönen Heil,* seventh of twelve tunes listed on the inner lid, in florid German script upon a paper diamond browned by time. Flip the restraining lever of the bells: now the six birds—they cannot be called a flock, this row of gilded metal larks whose wings are spread in flight but who are fixed forever to stiff wires—the six birds quiver, and when the right pin strikes, jerk forward, pecking at the row of bells (their beaks now blunted by a thousand tunes); plinking notes cascade from the springing comb; the larks strike forward; the studded cylinder revolves, snaps sideward to another tune, slows till the final pin lifts past the final vibrant tooth, and it twangs stiffly back: a solitary note of music.

8

Dominant Tone

The writing assignment for this chapter will not be a hard one to describe, but it will be a hard one for you to do well. It will be easy for us to describe because it raises no new problems of form or technique; it will be hard for you to do because it requires you to take a new attitude toward your material. Up to this point, it has been sufficient if your writing has been accurate enough and vivid enough to give the reader what Edmund Wilson called the shock of recognition. We have made accuracy and vividness an end in themselves, even while hinting that we would come to the point of requiring the details to be a means to an end beyond themselves. That time has now come. We want the details to be not only accurate and vivid but expressive.

The word *tone*, in the title of this chapter, means feeling tone or emotional tone. (Sometimes the broader term *impression* is used.) Some kinds of writing—especially that of professionals writing for professionals, scientists writing for scientists—are made as objective as possible. The tone is deliberately neutral. The principle is that an experiment, a theory, must stand or fall on its own merits; it must not be propped up by persuasive words. But much writing, including most representational writing, makes a virtue of what science takes to be a vice. It makes the control and direction of the reader's feeling or emotion one of its objectives. In literature, feeling is so important that literature itself has been defined, though perhaps extravagantly, as the science of feeling.

But what does the writer do when he wants to share or communicate feeling? Or, if sharing or communicating his own feelings is not his purpose, how does he go about arousing and controlling his reader's feelings? The first impulse, as always, is to talk about them. He can say that he is sad, as sad as sad can be, that he has never been so sad before, that he is sure no one has ever been so sad, that his sadness is deep beyond depth, and so on. All such talk is in vain. The reader is not moved. The emotions are all like happiness: it is fruitless to pursue them, you must ambush or waylay them.

TECHNIQUES

The method used in writing is suggested well by this review of a motion picture:

> All of these [characters] have been set down in a series of cramped and ugly rooms that are a distillation of the barren poverty that corrodes their spirit and paralyzes their will. The reminders are everywhere—the cracked shades at the window, the greasy linoleum around the stove, the clean square of wallpaper behind a photograph ripped from the grimy walls. And Otto Preminger has directed his film with a technique that brings them constantly into the play of the action, a camera that is constantly on the move, swinging from face to face, tracking over the bare floor boards from an unmade bed to a scaly door, binding characters and backgrounds together in a tight, almost claustrophobic unity. This is something more than the peripatetic cameras of the television studios, moving solely for the sake of movement. In *Man with the Golden Arm* the camera is ever on the prowl for the verifying detail, the revealing glance, the unguarded gesture. It will rush across the room from an extreme long-shot to a close-up of a newspaper clipping, the twitch of an unsteady hand, or the distended pupil of an addict's eye at the moment the poison enters his system. As this realism of detail, built frame by frame, moment by moment, mounts steadily through two hours the cumulative effect is one of horrified fascination—the horror of human beings writhing in the grip of forces over which they have no control, the fascination of seeing them for all their agony, for all their desperation, turning instinctively toward the sun. [Arthur Knight, *Saturday Review*, December 17, 1955]

The writing for this chapter will be essentially description—set in a brief narrative framework to bring the reader to and lead him away from the picture. The subject may be such a room or series of rooms as in *Man with the Golden Arm*. The dominant feeling—the feeling evoked in the person who reads the description of it—is of a spirit-corroding, will-paralyzing poverty. What creates this feeling, in the observer and reader, is not the room in general but the particulars of the room, the items the camera scanned—the shades at the window, the linoleum around the stove, the clean square of wallpaper, the floor-boards, the bed, the door, the newspaper clipping; and, really, not these items in general, but their attributes and details—the *cracked* shades, the *greasy* linoleum, the *scaly* doors, and so on.* The writer must have the art to select such items and to describe them in such a way that his reader will feel as the person who sees the room itself or the motion picture feels. The skillful, or conscientious, writer will not *talk about* the emotional tone. By his choice of particulars within the subject and by the way he describes them, he will *suggest* the tone. Thus, for you, the particulars you select and the attributes and details you select to describe them do not exist for themselves; they are not their own excuse for being; they are a means to an end, and the end is the emotional tone.

For a first example, a very brief one, consider again this sentence from Willa Cather's story "A Wagner Matinee." In this story a woman born and reared to a life of cultured ease in Boston lives instead as a farm wife in Nebraska. In middle age she returns to Boston for a visit and is taken to a Wagner matinee. When it is over and most of the audience have left and her companion waits for her to move, she keeps her seat. The next sentence explains why; it is the key sentence of the story.

For her, just outside the concert hall, lay the black pond with the cattle-tracked bluffs; the tall, unpainted house, with weather-curled boards, naked as a tower; the crook-backed ash seedlings where the dish-cloths hung to dry; the gaunt, moulting turkeys picking up refuse about the kitchen door.

Miss Cather might have written "For her, just outside the concert hall, lay the *dreariness of her farm home*," and someone might ask why not five words instead of forty-two? Why all this beating about the bush? The answer is not difficult. There is a pragmatic answer: read the two versions and *feel* the difference; if you don't feel any difference, you are responding as plain paper when litmus paper is called for. And there is a rational answer: "dreariness" is an abstraction; like all abstract words, as we have already said, it represents an intellectual operation on the materials of the experience; it offers the conclusion, not the evidence. Willa Cather instead offers the evidence, or what evidence she thought would produce the required effect—the four particulars (pond, house, ash seedlings, turkeys), not merely naming them in such a way as to compel the reader to reconstruct in imagination the life the woman is reluctant to return to. This imaginative reconstruction generates the feeling.

* Note that in this sentence, and in this chapter, *particulars and items* are used as synonyms (they are on the same level of generality) and that *details* is differentiated from them (it is on a lower level of generality). The terms are relative, and it would be convenient to have more of them.

We have been talking mainly about description, but the same principles apply to narration. "Gaunt" and "moulting" represent the *appearance* of the turkeys, but "picking up refuse about the kitchen door" represents their behavior. In the examples you will find now appearance, now behavior employed to generate the feeling. Hemingway said once that in his writing he tried "to put down what really happened in the action; what the actual things were which produced the emotion." Whether or not he intended it to, the statement seems to apply to both description and narration. But note that by putting down for the reader what really happened, what the actual things were, he was giving his readers the materials for the imaginative re-creation that generates the feeling. Without the cause there can be no effect.

SUBJECTS

Subjects for this assignment will not be so easy to come by as for the last. You cannot share an emotion you have not experienced yourself. People are not equally susceptible to the tone or atmosphere of a situation; and situations with such a tone or atmosphere are not part of the daily lot of most of us, and they cannot be summoned to a command performance. You may be tempted to resort to memory; the difficulty is that you may remember *how* you felt but not *what* you felt and thus know the tone but not the causes that produced it. First-hand observation is still your best resource. Here are a few suggestions.

1. You may be lucky enough to have the cooperation of the weather. In ordinary weather we see familiar things with tired eyes, but extremes of heat or cold or wet or dry, the veil of fog or rain or snow, or the agitation of wind or alterations of light put them in a new perspective and we see with fresh eyes. Sometimes the sheer intensity of the typical makes the difference, as it did for Keats on the walk which led to that serene ode, "To Autumn," one of the best examples in English literature of a dominant tone.

How beautiful the season is now [September 21]—How fine the air. A temperate sharpness about it. Really, without joking, chaste weather—Dian skies—I never lik'd stubblefields so much as now—Aye better than the chilly green of Spring. Somehow a stubble-plain looks warm—in the same way that some pictures look warm—This struck me so much in my Sunday's walk that I composed upon it.

2. Sometimes the changes wrought by time on the scenes of our childhood when we return to them are strong enough to provoke an intense emotional reaction. The changes, of course, are as likely to be in ourselves as in our former setting. This contrast is the basis of the description in Chapter 6 of *The Grapes of Wrath*, when Tom Joad returns to his home, now abandoned by his family. It is the source of much

of the feeling in books which are not merely reminiscences of childhood but which are based on an actual return to its setting, such as Alfred Kazin's *A Walker in the Streets.*

3. Another eye freshener is new horizons—a walk across the tracks or perhaps only across the hall. This is the source of Carol Kennicott's despair on her private *Seeing Main Street* tour the day she arrived in Gopher Prairie from St. Paul (see example A). You can make such a confrontation of the new an intellectual as well as an emotional experience if your city has a skidrow or a ghetto or an area marked for urban renewal, or one that ought to be. Few people can look with equanimity on urban blight—or rural, since we have much of that too. Or you can make it a practical as well as an emotional experience if you are looking for a room to rent, like the youthful American painter in the Berlin of 1931 in Katherine Anne Porter's "The Leaning Tower." Every room he saw would have afforded an adequate subject of this assignment.

Except for four winters in a minor southern university, Charles has lived at home. He had never looked for a lodging before, and he felt guilty, as if he had been peeping through cracks and keyholes, spying upon human inadequacy, its kitchen smells and airless bedrooms, the staleness of its poverty and the stuffiness of its prosperity. He had been shown spare cubbyholes back of kitchens where the baby's wash was drying on a string while the desolate room waited for a tenant. He had been ushered into regions of gilded carving and worn plush, full of the smell of yesterday's cabbage. He had ventured into bare expanses of glass brick and chromesteel sparsely set out with white leather couches and mirror-topped tables, where, it always turned out, he would be expected to stay for a year at least, at frightening expense. He peered into a sodden little den fit, he felt, only for the scene of a murder; and into another where a sullen young woman was packing up, and the whole room reeked of some nasty perfume from her underwear piled upon the bed. She had given him a deliberately dirty smile, and the landlady had said something in a very brutal tone to her. But mostly, there was a stuffy tidiness, a depressing air of constant and unremitting housewifery, a kind of repellent gentility in room after room and room, varying only in the depth of the feather bed and lavishness of draperies, and out of them all in turn he fled back to the street and the comparative freedom of the air.

This is the room he finally settled for:

The room. Well, the room. He had seen it several times before in his search. It was not what he would choose if he had a choice, but it was the least tiresome example of what he recognized now as a fixed style, with its sober rich oriental carpet, the lace curtains under looped-back velvet hangings, the large round table covered with another silky oriental rug in sweet, refined colors. One corner was occupied by deep couches heaped with silk and velvet cushions, the wall above adorned with a glass-doored cabinet filled with minute curiosities mostly in silver filigree and fine porcelain, and upon the table stood a huge lamp with an ornate pink silk shade, fluted and fringed and draped with silken tassels. The bed was massive with feather quilt and shot-silk cover, the giant wardrobe of dark polished wood was carved all out of shape.

A hell of a place, really, but he would take it. The landlady looked human, and the price was no higher than he would be asked anywhere else for such a monstrosity.

4. Another possibility is to turn the stone over and study the hidden, subterranean, other side. The public face, as T. S. Eliot put it, is a face put on to meet the faces in the street. The back yard or the back alley is often more revealing than the front yard or the street, the desk drawer more revealing than the desk top, the contents of the briefcase more than the briefcase itself. One of the most vivid memories from our careers of teaching composition is a paper with the title "After the Ball Is Over," written by a freshman who played with a dance band; another is an account of an off-season and off-hour visit to a beach amusement pier on a windy, foggy morning. Seeing the other side is not necessarily, of course, an adventure in disenchantment.

So much for the subject, some suggestions about the form. The simplest form is an enumeration of the items selected, set in a narrative framework. The framework is needed, first, for two reasons: to bring the reader to the scene, and put him into the position he is to see it from. This establishes what is called the physical point of view. Once you have established it, you must be true to it. You must not set up your camera at the front gate and proceed to record the contents of the kitchen sink. The physical point of view may be a fixed one, or it may shift (as in some of the examples), or it may remain fixed and the subject itself approach or withdraw. You must allow for such shifts; study, for example, the various descriptions of the land and the lighthouse in Stephen Crane's *The Open Boat*. The framework should also motivate the close scrutiny of the scene; the reader may take idle gaping as bad manners. It should probably also provide, as insurance against misunderstanding, a clue as to the tone intended. You must do this deftly, as the student did who came upon a sign at the end of the street he was describing, which read DEAD END.

Some textbooks make a great deal of the arrangement of the particulars in an enumeration. Whenever you have a series, whenever you have even two items, you have to settle on an order for them. The casual order in which they come to mind is not likely to be an effective one. In ordering them, it is well to have in mind that the order may be spatial, temporal, cumulative (or climactic), or psychological. It is possible for a reader to criticize the order in a given enumeration, but it is hardly realistic for a book like this to list and illustrate the possibilities. When you have settled on an order, you should indicate it very deftly or not at all (see example B). It is grotesque to give more space to telling where things are than what they are.

The term *select* used above needs some explanation. A writer cannot tell all; he must select. But the writ to select is not the same for all kinds of writing. When fidelity to fact, to things as they are, is expected, the writ is severely circumscribed. In responsible informative and persuasive writing, for example, the items selected must be *representative;* that is, they must constitute a true sample, in the statistical sense. Otherwise there is a distortion; the selection becomes card stacking. Even in personal writing where your aim is only to share an experience, the selection must be representative. Otherwise you will be a teller of tall tales. But in writing not subject to verification, whose purpose is to present not truth but the illusion of truth, the writ gives you as much freedom as you can use with effect. You are free to exclude any item, or any attribute or detail of any item, that will not contribute to the tone. (You may use such items or details for the sake of contrast.) And you are free to borrow items and details from other experiences. In professional writing, the physical traits of persons and places are far more likely than not to be composites, with some distortion to adapt the fact to the illusion. But you are not, even here, free to invent. Elizabeth Bowen did not put it too strongly when she said "Nothing physical can be invented."

Although this assignment is an extremely important one, in one respect it is a kind of tour de force. The paper you write will have to be of some length, a page or two, though it could run to several if you choose to do a private Seeing Main Street tour; but in modern fiction a set piece of such length would be a temptation to ill-trained readers to try to "skip the description." Writers, as we have said, know that the description is important for suggesting the tone, among other things; and they have to trap their readers into reading it by interweaving it with the narration, like the lean and fat in bacon. They work the way Arthur Knight describes Preminger as directing his camera, bringing the description "constantly into the play of action."

EXERCISES

The examples below are intended to suggest both subjects and techniques. The discussion above affords an outline for studying them. Notice that where the middle constitutes an enumeration, the items are often phrased in verbless sentences, commonly in noun phrases. The pattern in some examples does not involve an enumeration; it is a progressive narrative. The length of each is indicated at the end.

A. SEEING MAIN STREET

Note that in the first paragraph Lewis makes the claim that Gopher Prairie is typical or representative; this means that his description must be representative too. The thirteen descriptive paragraphs included here are only about half of the total number. After the first paragraph, all the "sentences" are noun phrases. The tone is indicated by an earlier sentence: "She stood at the corner of Main Street and Washington Avenue and despaired."

She trailed down the street on one side, back on the other, glancing into the side streets. It was a private Seeing Main Street tour. She was within ten minutes beholding not only the heart of a place called Gopher Prairie, but ten thousand towns from Albany to San Diego.

Dyer's Drug Store, a corner building of regular and unreal blocks of artificial stone. Inside the store, a greasy marble soda-fountain with an electric lamp of red and green and curdled-yellow mosaic shade. Pawed-over heaps of tooth brushes and combs and packages of shaving-soap. Shelves of soap-cartons, teething-rings, garden-seeds, and patent medicines in yellow packages—nostrums for consumption, for "women's diseases"—notorious mixtures of opium and alcohol, in the very shop to which her husband sent patients for the filling of prescriptions.

Howland & Gould's Grocery. In the display window, black, over-ripe bananas and lettuce on which a cat was sleeping. Shelves lined with red crepe paper which was now faded and torn and concentrically spotted. Flat against the wall of the second story the signs of lodges—the Knights of Pythias, the Maccabees, the Woodmen, the Masons.

Axel Egge's General Store, frequented by Scandinavian farmers. In the shallow dark window-space heaps of sleazy sateens, badly woven galateas, canvas shoes designed for women with bulging ankles, steel and red glass buttons upon cards with broken edges, a cottony blanket, a graniteware frying-pan reposing on a sun-faded crepe blouse.

Billy's Lunch. Thick handleless cups on the wet oilcloth-covered counter. An odor of onions and the smoke of hot lard. In the doorway a young man audibly sucking a toothpick.

The Ford Garage and the Buick Garage, competent one-story brick and cement buildings opposite one another. Old and new cars on grease-blackened floors. Tire advertisements. The roaring of a tested motor; a racket which beat at the nerves. Surly young men in khaki union-overalls. The most energetic and vital places in town.

A feed store, its windows opaque with the dust of bran, a patent medicine advertisement painted on its roof.

Ye Art Shoppe, Prop. Mrs. Mary Ellen Wilks, Christian Science Library open daily free. A touching fumble at beauty. A one-room shanty of boards recently covered with rough stucco. A show-window delicately rich in error: vases starting out to imitate tree trunks but running off to blobs of gilt—an aluminum ash-tray labeled "Greetings from Gopher Prairie"—a Christian Science magazine—a stamped sofa-cushion portraying a large ribbon tied to a small poppy, the correct skeins of embroidery-silk lying on the pillow. Inside the shop, glimpses of bad carbon prints of bad and famous pictures, shelves of phonograph records and camera films, wooden toys, and in the midst an anxious small woman sitting in a padded rocking chair.

A barber shop and pool room. A man in shirt sleeves, presumably Del Snafflin the proprietor, shaving a man who had a large Adam's apple.

On another side street a raw red-brick Catholic church with a varnished yellow door.

The post-office—merely a partition of glass and brass shutting off the rear of a mildewed room which must once have been a shop. A tilted writing-shelf against a wall rubbed black and scattered with official notices and army recruiting posters.

The damp, yellow-brick school building in its cindery grounds.

The State Bank, stucco masking wood.

The Farmers' National Bank. An Ionic temple of marble. Pure, exquisite, solitary. A brass plate with "Ezra Stowbody, Pres't." [Sinclair Lewis, *Main Street*, 594 words]

B. RETURN HOME

But when my turn came, what I saw—oh! it was France I saw there under the gentle French sunshine—a narrow green meadow; next to it, on one side, a rolling, half-plowed brown field, two great work horses, nodding their heads as they stepped strongly forward, throwing their shoulders against the tall collars; on the other side, a long, straight, white church tower; on the road, a farm cart with two high wheels slowly approaching, the metal trimming on the harness winking in the sun; between the railorad tracks and the meadow, a slow-moving dark green little brook bordered with silvery, pollard willows—the earth, the grass, the water, the very sky of home. [Dorothy Canfield, "The Knot Hole," 137 words]

C. A NEW WORLD

A new world, too, it was, for I had not flown in many months and the objects below me wore the freshly painted vividness of things seen

for the first time. They passed, bright and irrelevant images, slowly
under the still suspended wheel of our plane. (A wooded hill like moss,
soft gray moss to crush in one's hand. The shadow of a single elm,
flat on the ground, like a pressed fern. Pointed cedars and their shadows,
two-pronged forks—for, in this world of flat surfaces, shadows are of
equal importance with their objects. Pools in the fields as though the
earth had just risen from the flood, shaking its shoulders. The sides
of houses, hit by the morning sun, bright rectangles and squares, like
the facets of cut stones.)

My eye, unaccustomed, temporarily, to such vast expanses to
graze on, nibbled first here and then there at the scenes below, not
finishing one patch in orderly fashion before starting on a new one. The
images that attracted me were unrelated and scattered, not strung
along one thread by a road, not cupped within the rim of a lake. (The
pencil-marked shadows of telegraph poles. The neatly combed fields.
Docks and piers and bridges, flat slabs laid on the edge of a mirror.
Birds, particles of sand floating gently down the air. Cities, sudden
flashes from an apartment window or a moving car—strange that
the flash should reach a distance, like a bright speck of glass in a road,
sparkling far beyond its worth.) [Anne Morrow Lindbergh, *North
to the Orient*, 258 words]

D. WINDSWEPT

Today the snow is deep there and, according to this morning's
weather report, the cold intense and bitter. Today the blueberry fields are
discernible only as white mounds tumbling steadily downward toward
the wooded point three miles eastward from the house; the tips of
the alders, leafless and stiff, shudder in the wind; the clumps of dark,
ungainly firs and spruces at each corner of the house and on the slope
behind the barn, stand black against the snow, their shadows purple
in the sunlight. Today the sea is a purplish gray; surf foams like thick
suds about the treeless islands; the distant summit of Cadillac cuts
the western sky, sharp and keen as a new knife blade; the spruces of
Schoodic are jet-black above the tossing water; and southward the open
ocean is ridged with white at the breaking of the swells, uninhabited
now, as it is so often even in summer, by a solitary sail. [Mary Ellen
Chase, *Windswept*, 158 words]

E. "SEPTEMBER'S MY MONTH"

September's my month, thought Julie, sitting on a big flat rock at
the anchorage, her brown knees drawn up to her chin, her brown hands
clasping them. I came here in September.

Goldenrod and white asters tangled among the raspberries and
alders, growing paler, not lasting so long now in the great jars in
the living room. Fireweed, brilliant in August, that great rack of it in

the open space above the cove, flaming there, purple, violet, pink—
rose bay they called it in England, Uncle John said, growing by the slow
streams there. In September its blossoms gone, its long seed-pods
smooth like long, slim fingers, pale rose, bursting into silvery wisps of
mist, blown away in the wind, catching on the raspberries, caught
in one's hair.

"Julie, your hair is full of silver."

"It's the fireweed, Rod. You ought to see it at the cove."

Scarlet bunchberries in the damp woods, already faded in the
open stretches, still fresh and glowing among the ferns, tucked in the
napkins at night to give a festive air to supper. Tiny sea-asters, pale
lavender, growing even in the sand; the last of the pale pink bind-weed;
a solitary blue iris here and there; the rich burgundy of the wild
strawberry, three tiny brilliant leaves flat against the ground. Cran-
berries ripe and red; the leaves of the blueberries crimson, purple, rust,
bronze, so that whole patches of the long land flamed like some rare
Eastern carpet.

The ripe grasses just outside her window when she woke at sun-
rise, frail, bending with dew, growing lavender in the light, gleaming
among the juniper. Ducks in startled, silent flight across the pond,
black against the leaden water. A green and purple dragon-fly, its frail,
transparent wings one pair above the other, spread above a gray
spring of bayberry.

"See, Julie, like a tiny plane, for all the world!"

The sea pale blue at dawn, the very color of thin milk, azure as
the sun rose, sapphire at nine o'clock, a Mediterranean blue at noon,
purple at night. The moon rising like a great ripe fruit, swinging
higher, the land and sea silver. Northern lights sweeping the sky.
Windy days, still days, days of soft blue haze.

September's my month, thought Julie. [Mary Ellen Chase, *Windswept*, 242 words]

F. RAILROAD YARD

She came to the outlying spur-tracks on which strings of broken-
down boxcars had been left to fall apart, and crossed the weed-grown
rails and the mixture of oily black mud and dead willow-slashings that
filled the ditches between them and felt her way up a rock-fill to the
lights and noise of the yards. There was no feeling of triumph about it,
only a bewildered sense of having landed in a place where she was not
supposed to be, and of not knowing how to get out of it without making
it worse. Tracks gleamed everywhere, locomotives blazed headlights
on her and rolled long strings of cars into her way that took endless
walking to get around, ground-valves blew clouds of steam out at her,
lights darkened and flared up again, compressor-drills and power-
hammers rattled, a freight ground past and stopped with a thud and

groan of brakes and a banging of coupling-blocks, whistles ripped at her ears, bells clanged, block-signals overhead squeaked and clashed and changed color, cattle cars dripped green manure and dirty water from between their slats, more dirty water gushed from refrigerator cars flushing their ice chambers, men yelled and waved lanterns and stopped waving to stare after her as she waded past through the cinders and loose gravel into the nearest shadow. A crew working at some rail-changing job on the far side of the main water tank turned on an acetylene cutting-torch when she happened to be looking toward it, and as she stood blinded and helpless from the agonizing radiance it threw in her eyes one of the men came over and asked what she was looking for. [H. L. Davis, *The Distant Music*, 287 words]

G. EX LIBRIS

She left the library, the wind blowing the cold through her sweater, chilling her despite the rays of sunshine filtering through the trees, ruffling her hair, blowing her skirt against her legs first on one side and then on the other. She rested her books on the stone post, leaned her elbows against them, pausing before going down the last few steps of the walk, and surveyed the scene before her.

Leaves scurrying across the shadowed walk. A paper bag being carried across the lawn by the wind. The flag hanging in folds parallel to the pole, unfurling first in one direction and then in another, the shadows rippling in vertical lines across the horizontal stripes. A girl running across the grass, her basket held away from her, the fur collar of her car coat smoothed by the wind.

A boy with books under one arm and with the other swinging, the wind blowing open the two sides of his beige jacket, revealing a red checkered lining. A dried, brown leaf making slight scratching sounds as it skittered across the smooth stone stairs. The wind blowing the leaves of a tree together, shiny on one side, the dull undersides appearing and disappearing like the fur of a cat being rubbed back and forth.

A leaf floating through the air. The shadows of people one and a half times their size. A patch of cloud drifting out of sight. The tops of other clouds a silvery reflection of the brightness of the sun. Rays of sun sparkling through the trees like diamond lights.

The cold was reaching into her fingers and she rubbed one hand over the other to warm them. She picked up her books, holding them against her for warmth, and walked down the stairs. [297 words]

H. MIDSUMMER IN ROME

She dropped her packages on a wicker chair and ordered a Coca-Cola as the waiter seated her at the round table somewhat protected from the hot midday glare by the striped awning of the sidewalk cafe. She

fanned herself with the wine card and squinted her eyes, watching
the clerks and shoppers move along the Via Veneto, deserting the
shops until late afternoon. Shop girls in limp blouses, bare-legged and
perspiring, rings of smeared mascara beneath their eyes. Dark men
in wrinkled summer suits, unbuttoning their collars and pulling at their
ties. Red-faced seminarians, choked by stiff, white collars, their
black robes dusty at the hem. Young women in flowered voile dresses,
jutting out their chins and blowing strands of hair from their eyes,
hands grasping children shuffling along behind. Fashion models with
sculptured coiffures, their smart suits marred by damp streaks. The
waiter placed a glass of ice on the table and snapped the lid from the
bottle, his hand edged with matted hair, cuffs stained and wet. He
removed a spot of melted chocolate from the checked tablecloth,
brushed the crumbs onto the pavement, and offered her a sweet from
a tray of pastry. Narrow eclairs with yellow bubbles of grease on the
chocolate frosting, soggy, brown rum-cakes with glazed cherries crushed
in the centers, napoleons covered with magenta frosting, lying in
puddles of lumpy custard speckled with slivered almonds. She waved
away the waiter, drank her Coke in several long pulls, laid 150 lire
on the cloth, and left the cafe, passing tables decorated with silk
flags hanging motionless on red sticks.

Five minutes later, she was in the Borghese Gardens sitting on
a bench near a fountain. A man in a sleeveless undershirt rested on
the grass, moving only to brush away the flies which settled on his
forehead and chin. Beside him, a black dog scratched and panted, too
lazy to notice the orange cat licking its chest several yards away. Children splashed in a muddy pond, chasing the geese that waddled along
the bank flapping their wings and hissing with opened bills. A young
couple sat on the bank, close but not touching, too hot to make love.
A naked child climbed into the fountain and crawled onto a stone lion,
placing his hand in the spray spurting from the lion's gaping mouth.
A shouting woman, shoeless, with stocking rolled about her ankles,
hurried to the child. The girl left the bench, tramping over the yellow
grass to the street, passing through a marble arch where two old
men sweated in the narrow band of shade, drinking warm wine. [441
words]

9

The Longer Narrative

The last narrative assignment (Chapter 7) constrained you to draw harsh breath in the world of gadgets and machines—a world at once close to us and yet curiously alien to most of us. This one should free you to use the actions of human beings for your subject. But this will not make things any easier for you. We live with gadgets as much as with people, but we attend to people more. Such familiarity breeds content: we think we really know them, but we are likely to know only whatever it is that we have come to think about them. We very soon tag and label them and live with the stereotype. It is hard to see people with fresh eyes.

And of course people are infinitely more complicated than machines. Whatever the relation of body and mind, or even whether there are two entities to be related, in human behavior there is both a physical and a psychological component. We can be conscious of what we are doing—concentrating on it—and still be conscious, say, of the drag of a pencil, the alto hum of a typewriter, the sunlight lying across a page. Narrative details may be not merely picturesque but also expressive. Thus, in *The Ox-Bow Incident*, when Monty Smith left the saloon "hitching his belt," the onlookers who had humiliated him interpreted the action as a gesture "to get his conceit back." The verb cluster "hitching his belt to get his conceit back" includes both the external physical action and an *interpretation* of the psychological component. The author did not leave it to the reader to infer the motive of the action. He might have, and some discerning readers might have seen its significance; others would have seen it only as picturesque.

TECHNIQUES

With two components at his command, the writer has several possibilities:

110

1. He can present the actions of a person, as you did those of a gadget (unless you personified it), for their own interest, without any concern for the psychological component, as if it did not exist. The bowler is on the same plane as the ball he rolls and the pins it topples. A narrative of this sort can be interesting as spectacle, but it lacks depth.
2. He can do the opposite; he can emphasize the other component and treat his characters as if they were disembodied souls or sensibilities, moving about perhaps, but in worlds not realized for the reader. There are many ways of making the inner man rather than the outer man the subject of narration, but such considerations belong in advanced courses in the writing of fiction.
3. He may, instead, consider the two components as of equal or nearly equal importance. The question then is how to represent the psychological component.

One way is for him to put himself, from time to time, within the mind or consciousness of the subject and either *report* what is going on there—what the character thinks and feels and notices—or *comment* on it. If he reports, the result is a kind of interior narration; if he comments, it is a kind of interior exposition. For an example of reporting the interior action, consider Hemingway's "The Snows of Kilimanjaro." For two pages the opening scene is dramatized; dialog alternates with narrative or descriptive bits like this, the first example of several:

The cot the man lay on was in the wide shade of a mimosa tree and as he looked out past the shade onto the glare of the plain there were three of the big birds squatted obscenely, while in the sky a dozen more sailed, making quick-moving shadows as they passed.

Then Hemingway shifts to interior monolog:

So now it was all over, he thought. So now he would never have a chance to finish it. So this was the way it ended in a bickering over a drink. Since the gangrene started in his right leg he had no pain and with the pain the horror had gone and all he felt now was a great tiredness and anger that this was the end of it. For this, that now was coming, he had very little curiosity. For years it had obsessed him; but it meant nothing in itself. It was strange how easy being tired enough made it.

Now he would never write the things that he had saved to write until he knew enough to write them well. Well, he would not have to fail at trying to write them either. Maybe you could never write them, and that was why you put them off and delayed the starting. Well he would never know, now.

After another page of dramatized action, the reverie resumes in a different vein. The dying man begins to recount to himself some of the experiences he had saved to write.

Now in his mind he saw a railway station at Karagatch and he was standing with his pack and that was the headlight of the Simplon-Orient cutting the dark now and he was leaving Thrace after the retreat. This was one of the things he had saved to write.

About one-third of the story consists of reminiscences of this sort, identified by being set in italics.

If the author who puts himself inside the consciousness of his characters chooses to comment instead of report, the effect will be quite different, as this selection from Mary McCarthy shows. The second paragraph here affords a brief example of interior exposition.

The room had been redone, to cite the *Alumni Bulletin,* "in the spirit of the old College," with white walls, white straight linen curtains, and black Shaker reproduction chairs. On the walls were dark paintings of the first presidents, clergymen and theologians, a primitive engraving showing William Penn and the Indians, and a pastel portrait of the Founder done by a woman friend. On a table, beside the catalogue and a brown glass ash-tray, was a framed snapshot of Maynard, fishing in a local stream. Donna indicated this, and John gave a short laugh, which came out over-loud, like a bray. To cover himself, he got up and pretended to examine the picture. Donna became immersed in the catalogue.

Each in his own mind was sorting out the arguments at his disposal and setting them aside, provisionally, in hopes that the other would take the initiative. They did not know each other well, but the constraint of their detention was beginning to draw them together, like pupils called before the Principal, and to invoke in each a silent trust that the other was the bolder and stronger of the two. . . . Though an ocean and a gulf of class had separated their childhoods, their upbringing had much in common in strictness and isolation; both held the advanced ideas that had been current in the eighteen-sixties and that remained advanced in the present era, though with a certain pathos, like an old hat that has never been worn. [Mary McCarthy, *The Groves of Academe*]

The first paragraph begins with description and ends with narration. In both it is an objective report, without comment except in the word "pretended" and in the infinitive phrase "to cover himself." Such infinitive phrases (= *in order to* cover himself) express purpose and are necessarily comment. In the second paragraph the author is definitely inside the minds of both of the two teachers who are waiting to see the president (Maynard). The first sentence is report (narrative). The second is comment (exposition). The third is comment too: it not only reaches back into the childhood of the two teachers to explain the ideas they now share, but wittily disparages these ideas. There are novels and stories that consist almost entirely of such picking over and sorting and analyzing what is going on or might be thought to have gone on in the interior lives of the characters.

Some authors reject as unnatural this invasion of privacy, but without rejecting the possibility of making something of the interior life of their subjects. They treat the external as an index to the internal. They concentrate on the outward (appearance and behavior) and handle it in such a way as to *imply* and *suggest* the inward. (Note that this is the language of our last chapter.) When T. S. Eliot first read Joyce's *Ulysses* he felt that the method of giving the psychology did not work. "It doesn't tell as much as some casual glance from outside often tells" (Virginia Woolf, *A Writer's Diary*, September 26, 1922). In "The Killers" Hemingway uses the "glance from outside" with absolute purity. There is not one word that gives even a momentary glimpse into the mind of any one of the six principal characters, yet the reader knows that three of them are seething inwardly and three are stone cold. Although he presents only the external, Hemingway succeeds in conveying the impression of a corroding evil so secure that it paralyzes the will to live.

Another way to make an unplotted narrative more than a surface record is to *invest* it with meaning. Here the meaning is in the eye of the beholder, not in the event itself or in the minds of the actors. A good example is a *New Yorker* piece by E. B. White, called "A Letter from the South" and dated from near Sarasota, Florida, where John Ringling North winters his circus. The narrative part describes an older woman in conical hat and high-heeled shoes training a horse to go round and round in a ring, and then a girl of sixteen or seventeen, barefooted, coming to the ring and for ten minutes riding the horse. Besides the horse, the woman, and the girl, White attempts to describe something else, something not in the scene itself, not in the thoughts of the woman or the girl, but in his own mind as he watched them.

His mind projected the girl twenty-five years ahead, . . . Then it returned to the present, to the girl "at that enviable moment in life when she believes she can go once around the ring, make one complete circuit, and at the end be exactly the same age as at the start."

It is impossible to summarize his meditation on time and the exuberance and gravity of youth. White knows that what he felt is indescribable, but he believes that a writer, like an acrobat, must occasionally try a stunt that is too much for him and that he also has a duty to society. He is its secretary: "I have always felt charged with the safe-keeping of all unexpected items of worldly or unworldly enchantment, as though I might be held personally responsible if even a small one were to be lost."

Is it too much to hope that your experience of a few weeks of descriptive-narrative writing will make you feel responsible for preserving all your unexpected items of enchantment?

In this chapter we have now suggested three ways of approaching your subject: (1) treat it simply as a physical spectacle, (2) give it a psychological dimension by making the externals suggest the thoughts and feelings of the subjects, (3) invest the event with the meaning it has for you the spectator.

These three ways are obviously useful in what we set apart as creative writing; they are equally useful in what we call expository writing. We have only to look at a recent *Harper's Magazine* or *Atlantic Monthly* to be reassured, or even at a current newspaper. The trend in exposition is to use the techniques of the novelist to give force to the insights of the reporter. There is an immediacy in the description of a crumpled child that cannot be achieved by a recitation of the number of casualties in a disaster, a moving quality in an account of one child's experience in an academic wonderland that cannot be equaled by an enumeration of the failures of our school systems.

The trend does not reduce exposition to a less exact craft, but rather enhances the craft: it becomes a skill encouraging the writer to observe closely and report accurately; an art enriching the reader's perception and understanding.

EXERCISES

The examples below, divided into two sets, student and professional, are arranged to illustrate the three approaches analyzed above. They are intended to suggest both subjects and techniques. They exemplify all the principles of diction and sentence structure you have studied, and you should be able both to analyze them and to put them to practice.

A. A STRIKE

After marking the spare, he pushed his chair back from the scoring desk and stood up, hesitating to grind out his cigarette in the black-crusted metal ashtray before stepping up to the ball rack. He bent over, glancing at the scarred balls, spinning some of them around to see the numbers, and found his ball, the fourth one from the backstop. After wiping his hands on his levis, then blowing on them, he lifted the ball, gripping it with his right hand by the finger holes and swinging it up on his shoulder, and then stepped up to the line. A girl in the next lane was sighting her ball, ready to bowl, so he waited, looking at his feet, moving them back and forth, trying to pick just the right spot for his approach. The girl bowled, guttering it ten feet from the foul line, almost falling when she did it, and he smiled at her in sympathy as she walked back. Then he dropped into a crouch, swinging the ball down from his shoulder at the same time, and, lifting it with both hands into his line of vision, sighted, over the ball, first at the pins, then, head down, almost touching the ball, at the dark round spots arranged in an arrow in the blond wood of the alley. The ball arced forward as he started his approach, then back, then forward again and up when he released it—lofting it a little but not badly—and then rumbled down the lane, a good ball, fast, with a little backspin, hooking to the left as it went. It slammed into the 1–3 pocket, disappearing in the scattering pins, knocking them all down—a strike. He stood grinning, his hands on his hips, watching as the "X" flashed on the scoreboard, and then turned to resume his seat. [311 words]

B. PLAY BALL

He stood at the end of the yard, holding the small rubber ball loosely in his hand, turning it slowly with his thumb. The dog stood in front of him, one forepaw raised, his tail out, his mouth open, panting a little, watching him closely. The boy flicked his wrist in a feinted throw. The dog started a little and followed the ball with his eyes, but made no other motion. The boy tossed the ball into the air. Extending himself upward with a little jump, the dog caught it in midflight and returned it to his master, a little moisture on the soft rubber now. The next time the ball was higher. Arching his back, the dog leapt high into the air and caught it with a loud smack, then fell back, his large black body still curled, almost landing on his back but straightening out just in time to land on his hind paws. In a split second he was standing again, looking tall and dignified as he presented the ball, breathing heavily around it, and backed off a little to stand waiting again, ready as before to send his powerful body into action.

The boy drew his arm back and threw a long one that sailed the length of the yard and rolled down the street. Immediately the dog was after it, his ears back, his big body a black streamlined streak, his powerful legs scarcely touching the ground. Suddenly he braked and started back, the ball in his mouth, his Dalmation ears flopping as he frisked along like an overgrown puppy, his big ribs heaving a little, the saliva dripping out of his mouth around the now-wet ball as he laid it at the boy's feet and backed off again. This time the boy threw it onto the driveway, where it bounced along with little splatting noises, leaving small wet spots where it had been. The dog was waiting for it at the end of the driveway, panting a little still, his feet wide apart, his tail wagging broadly. Once more he brought it to his master's feet and backed off. But the boy looked at his wristwatch and then at the deepening gray of the sky and started toward the house. The dog picked up the ball and started after him. The boy reached down and rubbed his fingers through the dog's coat, leaving little silver droplets of saliva in the now roughened coat. They disappeared into the house together and the ball, dropped at the last possible minute, rolled over to the side of the porch, leaving a little wet trail behind it, and was soon turned from red to gold in the last rays of the setting sun. [456 words]

C. THOSE TEETH OF YOURS

"Come right in." The dental assistant motioned to the tall, sun-burned young man, who followed her into a small, square room. He hesitated a moment at the door, as if to make sure the cubicle were big enough for him, and then sat in the angular chair, balancing himself in an awkward half-reclining position, his neck too long for the unadjusted head rest. She adjusted it, smiling in a practiced manner, and spread a clean, white napkin over his chest, tying it around his neck with a metal chain which made him shiver convulsively. The doctor walked in and winked at him. Both white figures moved about the room without speaking, their shoe soles squeaking on the linoleum floor. In the chair, the young man listened to the sounds behind him: the sterilizer percolating violently, the clink of instruments dropped on a metal tray, the heavy breathing of the doctor as he studied the X-rays. Light streamed in the window and bounced off the white walls, illuminating the enameled apparatus gleaming beside the chair, silver knobs, red and green lights glowing over switches labeled ON and OFF, and a smooth bowl with water oozing over its surface. The patient's eyes watered and he closed them, trying to shut out the glaring whiteness of the room. He felt a warm movement stir beside him and opened his eyes, facing the doctor, who hovered above, his glasses reflecting images of the drill in his hand, a professional smile stretched across his face.

"Now let's see what we can do about those teeth of yours." [265 words]

D. THE RACE

The cars were lined up three bumpers abreast in ten rows, facing a one-eighth mile long straight of crushed red brick that was so tightly packed and tractable that when you walked across it you thought that you were walking on sandpaper. They were all master-pieces of surgical-like European craftsmanship from the glazed finish of their streamlined exteriors to their chrome molybdenum steel crank-shafts, capable of transmitting the brute thrust of powerful 5-liter engines into speeds of 150 miles an hour.

The crowd, responding to the fascination that is generated when-ever champions meet in face-to-face combat, kept up a steady, excited drone that murmured through the stands and spectator area like a low-keyed yet high-tensioned hum of electric current. As the drivers, conscious of the dramatic effect of their every gesture, first one, then another, put on their crash helmets with studied nonchalance, tugging, adjusting, primping like so many debutantes before the ball, the hum increased in intensity and then was lost in the reverberating boom of the sixty-second gun. One engine fired, coughed, and settled down to an undulating howl as the driver gunned it up and down; another started, then two, three, another, two more, until the hot July air was pulsing with the gruff, throaty roar of thirty open exhausts.

As the starting flag lifted and started down, the driver of the yellow Italian car in the pole position released the clutch, slammed down on the gas, and bolted forward, a good length in front of the screaming, pursuing pack. He grabbed the Maserati's crooked gearshift, banged it into second and wound the engine up tight, snatched third and ran it up to 7,000 rpm's, slid through the first corner with the ease of a boy pulling a toy around the floor on a string, and settled down into the first straight, three miles long. He stood on the throttle and locked his knee. The needle quickly shot up to 150 mph.

He had raced here before, and the road was familiar to him. It was a good road, string-straight and lined with poplars that had weathered numerous intruding crashes. The trees slid past in a smooth and solid tapestry, and the road rushed hysterically under the bellowing Maserati like the surging torrent of a river between two narrow rock walls.

A right-angle turn, one of the nasty ones, loomed ahead. He braked at the last possible tenth of a second, yards past the normal point. The engine screamed as he kicked it into third. He put the right wheel six inches from the grass and kept it there, to a hair, as the car cornered in an insanely fast four-wheel slide. He flicked it straight and roared at the hill ahead.

The yellow car left the ground at the top of the hill and sailed like a bird for fifty feet. It came down square and straight, and he grabbed fourth gear and rocketed away.

And so it went throughout the race until the final high-banked turn, a hairpin curve known as "Dutchman's Corner." He hit it at 85 miles an hour. He geared down, once, twice, and wrenched the wheel to the left, feeling the momentum pulling at him and the tires sliding jaggedly across the track, and waiting, waiting for the friction to grab as it always did and for the wheels to bite back into the track.

But this time they didn't, and suddenly the Maserati was off the track, off the ground, and he thought he saw the poplars, the crushed red brick road, the stands, the people, and the mountains far off in the distance all rush together in a kaleidoscopic nightmare. Only he

didn't recognize any of them, because they were all upside down.
[639 words]

E. EXIT

After the races, Jimmy and I took a walk through the stable area.
We stopped to watch a black thoroughbred being forced into a trailer.
Unshaven grooms and skinny stable boys pushed, pulled, and cajoled
the nervous side-stepping animal toward the trailer. Finally, with a
rope attached to both sides of the trailer, the line, tight under his tail,
trapping him, the careening animal lunged up into the trailer. The
grooms frantically, comically, rushed to lift and shut the door behind
him.

We turned away only to hear a tremendous rumble as the horse
gathered his energy and exploded inside the metal and wood box. The
trailer rattled and shook, rocking like a seesaw. Then the door crashed
open and twelve hundred pounds of mad horse flesh rolled in a
crazy backwards somersault onto the ground, the momentum of his
fall carrying him to his feet again. He stood, eyes rolling in pain, his
sides heaving violently, his black body glistening with nervous sweat.
Raw marks outlined where the halter had been. Above the left eye
dark blood oozed from an open gash, quickening into the little rivers
of sweat running the horse's face. The pitiful animal stood on three
legs, holding the fourth at an awkward angle. Just above the pastern,
a continuous burst of bright red ran off the tilted hoof, stirring up
swirls in the quiet dust. The animal's proud head hung down, flank and
neck muscles tense and quivering to keep balance as his life drained
down his foot.

One of the boys ran out from the long, shaded stable urging on
the tall man jogging awkwardly behind him because of his boots and
heavy satchel. The vet squatted down by the horse's slashed leg, quickly
applying a tourniquet, and then scooped a handful of chalk-white
alum out of the bag and pressed it against the red mass, until the
blood saturated it and started between his fingers. Puffs of white powder clouded over the kneeling man and the horse's leg. Finally, when
the bleeding had stopped, he examined the torn area and stood up, shaking his head. [356 words]

F. FLAMENCO

They walked up the steps of the Purple Onion and through the
white-painted door, surrounded by glass-cased photographs of performers, illuminated from overhead by a neon sign stating FLAMENCO,
while behind them the midnight traffic of Sunset Boulevard flashed
by. The room was dark—the darkness broken only by the dim red
glow of candle-glasses on tables—and smoke filled, a fog of cigarette

smoke swirling up around the candles and blanketing the low, heavy-beamed ceiling. No one appeared to seat them, so they set out on their own, squeezing between crowded tables, stumbling over chair legs, to an empty table near the back. A spotlight flashed on as they sat down, illuminating a small, low stage jutting out from the brick wall at the rear, and the piped-in music stopped. A voice announced the beginning of the show and conversation faded out as the performers filed onto the platform.

There were three of them: two men, both dressed in high-waisted, bell-bottomed trousers and short jackets, the Flamenco dancers' uniform, the taller of the pair in black, the other, carrying a guitar, in white; and a girl, her long hair shining black, brushed back to frame her narrow, brown face—the large black eyes accentuated by dark eyebrows, the nose straight and narrow, with flaring nostrils, the mouth wide, revealing white teeth when she smiled—wearing a white-with-purple-polka-dots, full-skirted Spanish dress.

They took seats on the bench along the wall, and the guitarist, after adjusting the microphone and tuning his instrument, began to play, opening with a few slow chords, then breaking into a Fandango, increasing the speed as he played, flaring his right hand across the strings to strum chords, holding it up, arched, to pick the solo strings, his left hand racing up and down the neck of the guitar, the fingers leaping across frets, his head bent low over the curve above the soundhole. The girl and her dancing partner began to clap, in syncopation, and after a moment he started singing in Spanish, his voice a high, cracking falsetto.

One of his verses amused the girl and she laughed and then, still smiling, leaped to her feet. She walked to the center of the stage, still clapping but without her smile now, and began to dance. The clapping stopped and her feet began tapping the floor, lightly at first, in a heel-toe motion at half the music's speed, then harder and faster, speeding to double time as she lifted her skirt above her red shoes and leaned back, her breast thrust forward, and then held her body rigid except for the feet.

The music slowed and when the girl reduced her pace the man got up and joined her, standing facing her but alongside, so that their faces were only inches apart. They stared at each other, their faces almost expressionless, the man with his arm around her waist, and when the music speeded again they parted and, still facing each other, one at a time began dancing again, each trying to outdo the other, spurred on by the audience's clapping and shouts of "Jota! asa, asa!".

The number ended and they sat again, smiling once more, laughing, joking in Spanish, some of the audience laughing with them.
[556 words]

G. WORDS WITHOUT MUSIC

It was intermission and the nightclub was a fog bank of tobacco smoke. The jazz fans—faces glistening in the close, pungent air—huddled about small, round tables, sipping cocktails out of moisture-beaded glasses. Their conversation, punctuated with laughter and the clink of glasses, hummed above the jazz record playing in the background. Waitresses, dressed in white blouses and dark slacks, weaved in and out through the tables, holding round trays of glasses over their heads. Abruptly the conversation trickled to silence as the fans turned to watch the five Black musicians file onto the bandstand.

They were dressed in black suits and ties and walked with the solemn dignity of pallbearers. They took their positions and tuned their instruments, talking among themselves and ignoring the watching audience as if the bandstand were a small island in limbo. Then the trumpeter tucked the gold-plated trumpet under his arm and shuffled to the front of the bandstand.

He turned and whispered to the musicians and patted his foot on the soft carpeting of the platform. The drummer, his small goatee looking strangely false on his young face, hunched forward over the sparkling white and silver drums and began to tap the end of the drumstick across the cymbal suspended in front of him, making it tremble and shimmer in the spotlight, edges blurring with vibration as it sounded high-pitched and sizzling through the club. The slender bassist pulled the brown varnished surface of the string bass close to his chest, one hand circling the long neck, knuckles sharp as his fingers pressed the strings, the other hand plucking the strings at the center with a rasping and pulsing throb. The pianist looked out at the audience through dark glasses and turned and followed the rapid thrumming of his brown fingers over the keys to the center in a clattering rush of treble notes, his other hand striking the bass keys with clawlike movements.

Then the trumpeter stepped forward to the microphone under the spotlight, which winked mirrorlike on his glossy hair. He placed the small, dented bulb of the silver mute into the bell of the trumpet and raised it to his lips. As he did, his face grimaced, cheeks stretching into tight lumps on his cheekbones, lips flat and pursed against the mouthpiece. He arched his fingers above the ivory-capped keys and started to blow—at first, a slurred repetition of the melody, then clusters of progressively higher notes reaching to a squeal, then falling step by step down the scale with sharp offbeat accents to a slow and guttural syncopation.

As the trumpeter repeated the low notes, the saxophonist stepped into the light beside him and raised the sax to his mouth and blew a long, sobbing echo of the trumpeter's notes, his gaunt cheeks filling and collapsing like a balloon. He blew louder, embellishing the notes, and the trumpeter moved back from the microphone, playing short rhythmic figures behind him. Then explosively, the saxophonist stamped his foot, closed his eyes, and thrusting the horn out and to his side, blew with harsh dissonance, his fingers flickering over the interlocking maze of keys, his dark forehead beaded with pale-gray dots of sweat in the bright light. Gradually the musicians played louder behind him, supporting his solo with long waves of sound, building slowly, slowly to a peak, then breaking in a sudden crash of cymbal as the saxophone finished in a soft, ebbing breath of notes. [583 words]

H. ROOM FOR TWO

The Metropolitan Transit bus rumbled to a stop and two men climbed on, distinguishable by their blue uniforms as bus drivers. The first, a young Black, playfully slapped the coin holder and, laughing, said, "Hitching a ride back to the depot, if you don't mind." He swung down the aisle, the firm muscles in his broad chest and shoulders rippling with the rhythm of his swinging arms, his skin smooth and clear over his cheeks and jaws, his eyes scanning the rows of seats. He sat down on the wide back seat, the only seat left on the bus with room enough for two people. The other driver followed. He was older, his hair slightly graying at the temples, his body becoming flabby from years of driving a bus. He sat down next to a commuter.

The Black lowered his eyes quickly, examining intently the perspiration on his wide, flat palms, wiping them on his pant legs, leaving damp smudges on his thighs. The bus jerked to a start and the Black lifted his eyes, gazing aimlessly at the advertisements above the windows. An image of the SMART AMERICAN WOMAN gazed down at him from her pinnacle above the window—blond hair, symmetrical teeth, smiling, wearing conspicuously red lipstick and a red, white, and blue collar. Another—ADOPT A CHILD—and two babies laughed at him, the white skin of one contrasting with the shiny black skin of the other. A photograph of the most courteous bus driver of the month grinned at him, looking something like his colleague, graying temples, loose white skin.

The bus stopped at the railroad tracks and passengers gazed absently at the empty expanse of railway tracks. It was all new but vaguely familiar to the young Black, something these people didn't understand, the stopping at the railroad tracks, the power of the big wheel under the hands, the pull of the gears as they shifted and shuddered in the older buses, the warm tingling on the skin from the yellow sun glaring through the thick glass windshield. Another driver swung onto the bus and sat in front of the older driver, the two men turning sideways, stretching their feet out in the aisle, talking bus talk. Drifts of the conversation floated back, "Behind schedule five minutes today . . . got caught behind a freight train." He squirmed in the empty seat, wide because it was over the motor. He wiped the perspiration off his forehead and looked around at the windows—everyone kept them shut. At the depot, the other two drivers stood up and walked together toward the front of the bus, the Black following them, his long arms swinging awkwardly. He put his hands in his pockets. The bus stopped and the men climbed off, the two drivers gesturing, talking, meandering toward the offices, the Black running past them and ahead, his strong legs stretching out in long strides, his back straight, arms clenched tightly against his side, eyes rigidly looking ahead. [503 words]

I. "I DUB THEE . . ."

When I was a child, spring meant playing baseball in the empty lot next door, hide and seek in the back yard, and dolls under the tangerine tree. But, above all, spring meant Uncle Harry. He was my mother's uncle, the family "ne'er do well," I found out later. I guess he had no home, because he lived with relatives all year. Each spring he moved into my great-aunt Helen's apartment above our garage, and each summer he left for his brother's home in San Diego. But everybody liked Uncle Harry except for my father, who only tolerated him. Once my father told my brother that Uncle Harry wasn't a "real man." My father liked to hunt and fish; Uncle Harry liked to read poetry and to garden.

Sometimes when I'd run in the yard after school, I'd see Uncle Harry kneeling by a rose bush, scooping up soil and patting it around the root, his sleeves rolled up above his elbows, flesh swinging from his forearms. He'd pretend he didn't see me until I was standing beside him; then, getting up, he'd fall on one knee, swish his straw hat, take my hand and kiss it, saying, "Ma-dum." I'd giggle, lay my other hand on his shoulder, palm flat and stiff, and sing out, "I dub thee Sir Harry, arise." He'd jump up and make a low bow from the waist, his straw hat brushing the grass. That was fun. Almost as much fun as looking in Uncle Harry's trunk that he kept in our garage. Each spring he'd "clean it out." He never threw anything away; I guess he just liked to look at his things. My brother and I would sit on the concrete floor of the garage, legs crossed, our chins cupped in our hands, and watch Uncle Harry fondle his mementos: a crumpled uniform from the first World War, a woolen uniform top-coat with half-dollar-sized moth holes near the hem; a red and yellow serape wrapped around a framed photograph of a serious young lady with her hair parted in the middle, a ringlet over each eyebrow; a looseleaf binder filled with clippings from gardening magazines; matted, fur ear-muffs; a dented bowler; and, best of all, a revolver with a wreath hammered on the butt. Then Uncle Harry would tell us about the War and about Paris, where people rode bicycles with long loaves of fresh bread tucked under their arms.

The spring when I was eleven Uncle Harry didn't come. Mother said he was in Florida in a Veteran's hospital. I didn't see him again until last year, a few months before he died. He was transferred to the Veteran's hospital in Santa Monica, and at Christmas Mother and I brought him some presents. He was sitting on a bench under a tree with three other men, a nurse wheeling a patient back and forth in front of them. At first he didn't remember me, and I hardly knew him, his hair chopped short, his face hanging in folds, and one eye half shut. After my mother told him who I was, he grinned, his eyes watering and his chin curling up. I smiled back and he pushed out his feet, side by side, from under the bench, placed a hand on the top slat, and struggled up. Then he let himself down on one knee and said in a wet voice, "Ma-dum." I laid my palm flat on his shoulder and began, "I dub thee . . ."; but then he fell on his side, his face turned down on the grass. The nurse helped him up, shouting, "You fool, do you want to break a rib?" He cried a little, and we left, my mother talking fast and a lot about where we should go for lunch. [637 words]

J. FROM *The Octopus*

The division superintendent, on the opposite side of the line, galloped past to a position at the head. For a long moment there was silence. A sense of preparedness ran from end to end of the column. All things were ready, each man in his place. The day's work was about to begin.

Suddenly, from a distance at the head of the line came the shrill trilling of a whistle. At once the foreman nearest Vanamee repeated it, at the same time turning down the line, and waving one arm. The signal was repeated, whistle answering whistle, till the sounds lost themselves in the distance. At once the line of ploughs lost its immobility, moving forward, getting slowly under way, the horses straining in the traces. A prolonged movement rippled from team to team, disengaging in its passage a multitude of sounds—the click of buckles, the creak of straining leather, the subdued clash of machinery, the cracking of whips, the deep breathing of nearly four hundred horses, the abrupt commands and cries of the drivers, and, last of all, the prolonged, soothing murmur of the thick brown earth turning steadily from the multitude of advancing shears. . . .

The ploughing, now in full swing, enveloped him in a vague, slow-moving whirl of things. Underneath him was the jarring, jolting, trembling machine; not a clod was turned, not an obstacle encountered, that he did not receive the swift impression of it through all his body, the very friction of the damp soil, sliding incessantly from the shiny surface of the shears, seemed to reproduce itself in his finger-tips and along the back of his head. He heard the horse-hoofs by the myriads crushing down easily, deeply, into the loam, the prolonged clinking of trace-chains, the working of the smooth brown flanks in the harness, the clatter of wooden hames, the champing of bits, the click of iron shoes against pebbles, the brittle stubble of the surface ground crackling and snapping as the furrows turned, the sonorous, steady breaths wrenched from the deep, labouring chests, strap-bound, shining with sweat, and all along the line the voices of the men talking to the horses. Everywhere there were visions of glossy brown backs, straining, heaving, swollen with muscle; harness streaked with specks of froth, broad, cup-shaped hoofs, heavy with brown loam, men's faces red with tan, blue overalls spotted with axle-grease; muscled hands, the knuckles whitened in their grip on the reins, and through it all the ammoniacal smell of the horses, the bitter reek of perspiration of beasts and men, the aroma of warm leather, the scent of dead stubble—and stronger and more penetrating than everything else, the heavy, enervating odour of the upturned, living earth.

At intervals, from the tops of one of the rare, low swells of the land, Vanamee overlooked a wider horizon. On the other divisions of Quien Sabe the same work was in progress. Occasionally he could see another column of ploughs in the adjoining division—sometimes so close at hand that the subdued murmur of its movements reached his ear; sometimes so distant that it resolved itself into a long, brown streak upon the grey of the ground. Farther off to the west on the Osterman ranch other columns came and went, and, once, from the crest of the highest swell on his division, Vanamee caught a distant glimpse of the Broderson ranch. There, too, moving specks indicated that the ploughing was under way. And farther away still, far off there beyond the fine line of the horizons, over the curve of the globe, the shoulder of the earth, he knew were other ranches, and beyond these others, and beyond these still others, the immensities multiplying to infinity. [Frank Norris, 628 words]

K. FROM "PIGEON FEATHERS"

"Don't smirk. You look like your father. How many did you get?"
"Six." .
She went into the barn, and [David] followed. She listened to the silence. Her hair was scraggly, perhaps from tussling with the dog. "I don't suppose the others will be back," she said wearily. "Indeed, I don't know why I let Mother talk me into it. Their cooing was such a comforting noise." She began to gather up the dead pigeons. Though

he didn't want to touch them, David went into the mow and picked
up by its tepid, horny, coral-colored feet the first bird he had killed. Its
wings unfolded disconcertingly, as if the creature had been held together
by threads that now were slit. It did not weigh much. He retrieved
the one on the other side of the barn; his mother got the three in the
middle and led the way across the road to the little southern slope of
land that went down toward the foundations of the vanished tobacco
shed. The ground was too steep to plant and mow; wild strawberries
grew in the tangled grass. She put her burden down and said, "We'll
have to bury them. The dog will go wild."

He put his two down on her three; the slick feathers let the bodies
slide liquidly on one another. He asked, "Shall I get you the shovel?"

"Get it for yourself; *you* bury them. They're your kill. And be
sure to make the hole deep enough so he won't dig them up." While he
went to the tool shed for the shovel, she went into the house. Unlike
her, she did not look up, either at the orchard to the right of her or
at the meadow on her left, but instead held her head rigidly, tilted a
little, as if listening to the ground.

He dug the hole, in a spot where there were no strawberry plants,
before he studied the pigeons. He had never seen a bird this close before. The feathers were more wonderful than dog's hair, for each
filament was shaped within the shape of the feather, and the feathers
in turn were trimmed to fit a pattern that flowed without error across
the bird's body. He lost himself in the geometrical tides as the feathers
now broadened and stiffened to make an edge for flight, now softened
and constricted to cup warmth around the mute flesh. And across
the surface of the infinitely adjusted yet somehow effortless mechanics
of the feathers played idle designs of color, no two alike, designs
executed, it seemed, in a controlled rapture, with a joy that hung level in
the air above and behind him. Yet these birds bred in the millions and
were exterminated as pests. Into the fragrant open earth he dropped
one broadly banded in slate shades of blue, and on top of it another,
mottled all over in rhythms of lilac and gray. The next was almost
wholly white, but for a salmon glaze at its throat. As he fitted the last
two, still pliant, on the top, and stood up, crusty coverings were lifted
from him, and with a feminine, slipping sensation along his nerves
that seemed to give the air hands, he was robed in this certainty: that
the God who had lavished such craft upon these worthless birds would
not destroy His whole Creation by refusing to let David live forever.
[John Updike, 570 words]

10

Paragraphing—
An Introduction
to Discursive Writing

In turning now from the sentence to the paragraph we turn also from representational to discursive writing, from picturing to talking about, from showing to explaining and persuading. Even in the last three chapters, where the aim was to get the sentences working together, there was no need to refer to paragraphing. The reason for this is that in *picturing* the sentence is the natural unit, and in *talking about* the paragraph is the natural unit. In narration—in writing that is chronologically ordered, whether in telling a story or describing a process—the sentences are all on the same level. In other words, in strictly linear narrative, where each sentence snips off a sequential unit of time, there can be, between sentences, none of the vertical movement up and down the levels of abstraction that is the essence of discursive writing. The backtracking and downshifting occur *within* the sentence; in discursive writing it occurs *both within and between* the sentences.

STRUCTURAL AND SUPPORTING SENTENCES

Paragraphs in discursive prose are of two kinds—the short paragraphs of one or two sentences that provide the structural framework of a piece of writing and the longer paragraphs that carry the burden of the discussion. Most writers do not distinguish the two kinds accurately or consistently; the frame and the framed mingle promiscuously. This complicates the problem of unraveling the structure of the "workhorse paragraphs," as they have been called, the goal of this and the next chapter.

THE CUMULATIVE NATURE OF EXTENDED SEQUENCES

The thesis of this and the next chapter is that the paragraph—or a sequence of paragraphs—is built according to the same rhetorical principles as the cumulative sentence—addition, direction of movement, levels of generality, density of texture. Without the principle of *addition*, we would have only one-sentence paragraphs; that is, we would have no paragraphing at all. When we add a sentence as an explication or illustration of our first sentence, the *direction of movement* as between the two sentences is backward, not forward. The sentence added is usually, but not always, at a lower *level of generality* than the first; at any rate, the trend of the paragraph is toward the more concrete and specific. If the paragraph has many sentences added, either parallel or subordinate to one another, then its texture may be called dense. The essential difference is this: to the base clause of a sentence we add words, phrases, and clauses; to the base sentence of a paragraph we add sentences.

For the writer there seem to be at least two ways to manage the problem of paragraphing. One way is to write continuously and paragraph afterwards. Paragraphing then means searching for the joints where the cuts can be made naturally, the way a skilled carver disjoints a fowl. By his paragraphing he interprets his intent to the reader—perhaps discovering in the process that his intent is not clear to himself. The other way is to build paragraphs sentence by sentence and to add paragraph to paragraph—the way this paragraph and this chapter are being written. Paragraphing in this case means using some notion of paragraph structure to control the process of writing. The results will depend on the adequacy of the notion and the ability of the writers to carry out their intentions.

One can study paragraphs in the same two ways. One can see how unparagraphed material could be divided and also how paragraphs are built up sentence by sentence. We will try both, beginning with the first.

THE PROBLEM OF PARAGRAPHING

But, first, what is a paragraph? The handbooks on writing make it a self-sufficient entity, an independent kingdom, like Monaco or Andorra, with its ruler and subjects and with laws governing their relationship, each kingdom developed according to one of the patterns of "paragraph development." There are two objections to this model of the paragraph. First, the so-called methods of paragraph development have no special relevance to the paragraph. They are simply methods of development— no more relevant to the paragraph than to the sentence on the shorter side or to the chapter or essay on the longer side. They are analogous to the three methods of description. They represent what it is we can say about a subject when our aim is not to describe it but to explain it, not to picture it, but to talk about .it. (We will return to these methods in Chapter 12.) Second, it is doubtful whether anybody, except as a school exercise, ever writes paragraphs the way the model suggests. No paragraph in this book was written by setting forth a topic sentence, choosing one of the methods of development, and keeping an eye on that blueprint. These chapters are an attempt to describe how paragraphs appear to be written and how paragraphs have to be read and may be written.

Meanwhile, our definition. A paragraph, as anyone can *see*, is a sentence or group of sentences whose first line is indented and whose last line is not filled out. Sometimes the indention is reversed; in hanging indention all lines are indented but the first. Sometimes the indention is omitted; in block style, common in business letters, indention is replaced by extra white space between paragraphs. Sometimes the column or page is printed solid and some typographic device, such as a ☐ , is inserted to group the sentences into paragraphs. In battering-ram styles, the paragraphs—usually single sentences or even fragments of sentences—are sometimes set off by additional typographic devices.

GRAPHIC DEVICES

This definition defines the paragraph by the graphic devices used to mark it for the eye of the reader. It is like defining a sentence as a group of words bounded by a capital letter and a period and defining a word as a group of letters bounded by white spaces. But definitions based on graphic devices are not very satisfactory. Even experts do not divide at the same points (compound words and sentences are especially problematic) and you sometimes want to know what it is you are walling in and walling out. Still they are useful. Before these sorting devices were worked out, a written text WASACONTINUOUSSERIESOFLETTERSLIKETHIS. Spaces, capital and lower-case letters, punctuation marks and indention progressively sorted out words, sentences, and paragraphs, grouping what went together and sundering what did not.

ORGANIZATION

Let us start with a passage where the words and sentences are separated but not the paragraphs. In the one-volume Columbia Encyclopedia (2d ed.) there is no paragraphing. The reader of any article, regardless of its length, must sort the sentences into groups as he reads—or rereads.

eye, 1. organ of vision, almost spherical in shape, situated in the front part of the bony orbit of the skull.   2. The eyeball or bulb of the eye is covered by a coat of three layers within which are contained the refracting media.   3. The layers which compose the wall of the eyeball consist of an outer fibrous, a middle vascular, and an inner nervous layer.   4. The outermost layer comprises the sclera and the cornea.   5. The sclera is white and opaque and covers the posterior larger portion of the eyeball.   6. The cornea is transparent and covers the front, lesser portion of the eyeball.   7. The middle layer is vascular and pigmented and consists of three structures, the chorioid (choroid), ciliary body, and iris.   8. The inner nervous layer, the retina, is a delicate membrane in which are distributed the fibers of the optic nerve.   9. The chorioid, situated between the sclera and retina, nourishes the retina and the lens.   10. The iris, behind the cornea, is a circular pigmented membrane perforated by an aperture, the pupil.   11. The ciliary body consists of the ciliary ring, ciliary processes, and ciliary muscle and connects the chorioid with the circumference of the iris.   12. The retina, innermost layer of the wall of the eyeball, is the perceptive structure of the eye.   13. The refracting media consist of the vitreous humor (vitreous body), the lens, and the aqueous humor.   14. The lens is a biconvex transparent structure, situated behind the iris and attached to the ciliary body by a suspensory ligament.   15. The vitreous humor is a transparent jelly-like substance which fills the hollow of the eyeball between the lens and the retina. 16. The aqueous humor occupies the space between the lens and the cornea; this space is divided into two chambers, an anterior chamber between the cornea and the iris and a posterior chamber between the iris and the lens.   17. The aqueous humor in both chambers is continuous through the pupil of the eye.   18. A number of muscles attached to the wall of the eyeball regulate the movements of the eye.   19. The convexity of the lens is controlled by the action of the ciliary muscle. 20. Eyestrain results from overaction of the ciliary muscle and of the muscles which move the eyeball.   21. Among the disorders of the eye are ASTIGMATISM, BLINDNESS, CATARACT, CONJUNCTIVITIS, CROSS-EYE, GLAUCOMA, and STY.

As you read this, attempting to group the sentences, you find the job growing easier toward the end. If you mark the groups by putting ₵ in the margin, you will illustrate the oldest system of marking groups of sentences, by a mark in the margin. The last sentence, on diseases of the eye, stands alone. The three sentences above it, on the muscles that regulate the movements of the eye, form a definite group. There are short paragraphs at the beginning, too; at least the first, verbless, sentence, a definition, stands alone. The next question is whether the remainder, sentences 2–17, can or may be divided. The best way to decide is to make a *structural analysis*, to establish the levels exactly as we did with sentences.

2. 1 The eyeball or bulb of the eye is covered by a coat of three layers within which are contained the refracting media.

3.   2 The layers which compose the wall of the eyeball consist of
      an outer fibrous, a middle vascular, and an inner nervous layer.

4.   3 The outermost layer comprises the sclera and the cornea

5.   4 The sclera is white and opaque and covers the posterior
         larger portion of the eyeball.

6.   4 The cornea is transparent and covers the front, lesser
         portion of the eyeball.

7.   3 The middle layer is vascular and pigmented and consists
      of three structures, the chorioid (choroid), ciliary body, and
      iris.

8.   3 The inner nervous layer, the retina, is a delicate mem-
      brane in which are distributed the fibers of the optic nerve.
      4 The chorioid . . .

Here something seems wrong. The chorioid is a part of the middle
layer (sentence 7) not of the inner layer (sentence 8). The iris (10) and
the ciliary body (11) are also part of the middle layer. Thus sentences
9, 10, and 11 go together under sentence 7. Sentence 12 supports this
analysis; it deals with the inner layer, the retina, in its proper place,
after the four sentences on the middle layer. Sentence 8 can be taken
out; it should follow sentence 12, as shown here:

9.   4 The chorioid, situated between the sclera and the retina,
         nourishes the retina and the lens.

10.   4 The iris, behind the cornea, is a circular pigmented
         membrane perforated by an aperture, the pupil.

11.   4 The ciliary body consists of the ciliary ring, ciliary
         processes, and ciliary muscle and connects the chorioid
         . . . the iris.

12.   3 The retina, innermost layer of the wall of the eyeball, is the
      perceptive structure of the eye.

[8.   4 It is a delicate membrane in which are distributed the
         fibers of the optic nerve.]

13.   2 The refracting media consist of the vitreous humor, the lens,
      and the aqueous humor.

14.   3 The lens is a biconvex transparent structure, situated behind
      the iris and attached to the ciliary body by a suspensory
      ligament.

15.   3 The vitreous humor is a transparent jelly-like substance
      which fills the hollow of the eyeball between the lens and
      the retina.

16.   3 The aqueous humor occupies the space between the lens
      and the cornea; this space is divided into two chambers, an
      anterior chamber between the cornea and the iris and a
      posterior chamber between the iris and the lens.

17.   4 The aqueous humor in both chambers is continuous
           through the pupil of the eye.

The structural analysis shows clearly that we can divide this long
group of sentences into at least two paragraphs. It has two fairly long
subgroups, marked level 2, and we can divide between them, putting
the description of the three layers in one paragraph and of the refracting
media in the other one. Sentence 2, which as level 1 introduces both of
the subordinate paragraphs, presents a problem. Logically, since it is a
part of neither, it should be marked as a one-sentence framework paragraph. Such sentences are often included, illogically, in the first of the
set of paragraphs they introduce. It would be possible, but still illogical,
to paragraph sentences 1 and 2 together.

Could we subdivide the two paragraphs we have not sorted out?
Sentences 4, 5 and 6 constitute a group on the outer layer, and 7, 9, 10,
and 11 (excluding 8, of course) are a group on the middle layer. If we
separate these two groups into paragraphs, we would have to make a
paragraph also of the two sentences on the retina (12 and the relo-
cated 8). In the paragraph on the refracting media, there are two sentences on the aqueous humor but only one each on the vitreous humor
and the lens. For both paragraphs the answer about subdividing is
surely no. We would pass the point of diminishing returns; for the
reader the problem would shift from sorting out sentences to sorting
out paragraphs.

If we set aside the framework or transitional paragraph as of a
different breed, we can say, by way of definition, that in discursive
writing *a paragraph is a sequence of sentences that are grouped and
set off because they are structurally related.* It is impossible to set limits
in either direction on the number of sentences in a sequence, or on very
long sequences divided into subsequences, each of which may satisfy the
definition just given. If the texture is dense there will be many sentences,
if thin there will be few. It is impossible to say much about how long
paragraphs ought to be. Paragraphs are too long when they leave too
much of the sorting to the reader. Sentences 2–17 made a paragraph that
was too long; it contained two sizable subsequences. Paragraphs are too
short when they confront the reader with the problem of sorting out
the paragraphs. Sentences 3–12 and 13–17, each divided into three paragraphs, would do just that.

The length of paragraphs is subject also to such external conditions as the attention span of readers and the width of columns of type.
One example will illustrate both conditions. A professor of English
wrote for his college newspaper a feature article on why Jeannie don't
write so good. His long paragraphs, of ten or twelve sentences, dis-
mayed the student editor, conscious of the narrowness of his columns

and cynical perhaps about the mental width of his readers. So he divided each of the long paragraphs into shorter ones of three or four sentences each. Fortunately, the long paragraphs were carefully structured, with clearly marked subsequences, and he did his job well. To solve the problem of sorting the paragraphs, he invented a device of his own, a row of stars at each of the original paragraph divisions. The same piece was mimeographed later for the use of high school English teachers. The editor of this version, given his choice and having a wider column and a more sophisticated group of readers, retained the original paragraphing. It cannot be maintained, unconditionally, that one version was better than the other.

When a sequence is broken up, one can sometimes guess at other causes: the desire for rhetorical emphasis, or to keep all the paragraphs about equal in length, or sometimes mere inattention.

This same passage on the eye provides examples for three other observations that are relevant to paragraphing. (Note this transitional paragraph.)

PUNCTUATION BY PARAGRAPH

3 The aqueous humor occupies the space between the lens and the cornea; this space is divided into two chambers, an anterior chamber between the cornea and the iris and a posterior chamber between the iris and the lens.

If all these were expanded to sentences, and sentence 17 added, the structural analysis at this point would run as follows:

3 The aqueous humor occupies the space between the lens and the cornea.
  4 This space is divided into two chambers.
    5 The anterior chamber lies between the cornea and the iris.
    5 The posterior chamber lies between the iris and the lens.
      6 The aqueous humor in both chambers is continuous through the pupil of the eye.

The many short sentences of this version raise again the problem of sorting and grouping. This problem makes the short sentences harder to read than the single longer sentence, and the short sentences complicate the problem of paragraphing. From this we can deduce—and this is an important principle in discursive writing—that sentences should be written (or rewritten) and punctuated with the problem of sorting in mind. The decision to combine two or more sentences into one compound sentence or to separate one compound sentence into two or more cannot be made effectively except in relation to the entire paragraph.

Punctuation should be the last step before the final typing and should be done paragraph by paragraph, not sentence by sentence.

ORDERING A SERIES

A second observation concerns the ordering of a series. In sentence 7, three "structures" and in sentence 13 three "media" are enumerated. These are introductory sentences, and each is followed by three parallel sentences, on the layers and then on the media. But the order is not the same in the introductory sentences and in the sets of follow-up sentences. Sentences such as 7 and 13 (and also 2, 3 and 4) are like promissory notes. The reader expects them to be paid off in the *number* and *order* of installments they specify. In revising a paper, the writer should match up such sets of items or else explain his departure from the order he establishes in the first place.

LIKE THINGS IN LIKE WAYS

The third observation, although it is exemplified only in a rather trivial way in this article, leads to one of the most useful of all rules for discursive writing—*put like things in like ways*. Consider sentence 2 again with its two plural terms. The next sentence begins "The layers which compose the walls of the eyeball consist of . . . ," and far down the page sentence 13 begins "The refracting media consist of. . . ." These two sentences have like functions (we put them both on the second level) and they are expressed in like ways—in like words and like constructions. To vary either the words or the constructions—in order, say, to vary the sentence beginnings—would only confuse the reader. It would be like trying to give variety to driving by varying the relative positions of the green, amber, and red lights. Note that 5 and 6 are like and that 4 and 7 are like but that neither 12 nor the misplaced 8 is like them. Again, 14, 15, and 16, which all appear at the same level in the structural analysis, are like. The next chapter will show how important this rule is.

Another, minor, example occurs in sentences 5 and 6 in the punctuation of "posterior larger portion" and "front, lesser portion." The situation is the same and the punctuation should be the same; a comma or a pair of commas or parentheses is called for. Sentence 3 presents three like situations. It could be written thus: an outer (fibrous), a middle (vascular), and an inner (nervous) layer.

The article on the eye is relatively simple. The principal topic, the *structure* of the eye, determined pretty largely the structure of the explanation. The explanation is spatially ordered. (Sometimes in discursive writing—for example, in historical accounts and in explanations of a process—the explanation is chronologically ordered.) But we should note, too, that what we might call logic entered into the ordering of the material. It was logical to separate the account of the three-layered wall from the account of the refracting media, and it was logical to start the treatment of the three layers with the outermost layer, and it was illogical to list vitreous humor, lens, and aqueous humor in that order and then start the explanations of the three with the lens. In most discursive writing, the order is determined primarily by logical considerations. This makes discursive writing difficult; the writer does not have an external spatial or time model to navigate by.

EXERCISES

A. Having learned more about the eye, possibly, than you ever hoped to know, you should be able to combine the logic of knowledge with the logic of structure, and produce a structural analysis of this article from the third edition of the *Columbia Encyclopedia*. First determine the level number of each sentence, then place a paragraph mark (¶) by each sentence that you would have begin a new paragraph.

eye,   1. organ of vision, a spheroid structure that rests in a bony cavity (socket or orbit) on the frontal surface of the skull.   2. It is filled with vitreous humor, a jellylike substance contained within three covering layers; the sclera, the choroid, and the retina. 3. The sclera is the outermost layer of eye tissue; part of it is visible as the "white" of the eye.   4. In the center of the visible sclera and projecting slightly, in the manner of a crystal raised above the surface of a watch, is the cornea, a transparent membrane that acts as the "window" of the eye.   5. A delicate membrane, the conjunctiva, covers the visible portion of the sclera.   6. Underneath the sclera is the second layer of tissue, the choroid, composed of blood vessels that nourish the tissues.   7. As this layer nears the center of the visible portion of the eye it merges with the ciliary body which contains the muscles used in focusing.   8. The ciliary body in turn merges with the iris, the pigmented area of the eye, the center of which is perforated and appears as the pupil.   9. The iris varies in color in different persons (blue, brown, gray), and the pupil dilates and contracts by muscular action, thus regulating the amount of light that enters the eye.   10. Back of the iris is the lens, a transparent but solid body essential in refraction.   11. The third and innermost layer of tissue, the retina, is a network of nerve fibers that fan out over the choroid from the optic nerve as it enters the rear of the eyeball from the brain.   12. Between the cornea and iris (anterior chambers) and between the iris and lens (posterior chamber) are small spaces filled with aqueous humor.   13. Accessory structures of the eye are the lachrymal gland and its ducts in the upper lid, which bathe the eye with tears, keeping the cornea moist, clean, and brilliant, and drainage ducts that carry the excess moisture to the interior of the nose.   14. In addition to errors of refraction (ASTIGMATISM; FARSIGHTEDNESS; NEARSIGHTEDNESS) the eye is subject to various types of injury, infection, and changes due to systemic disease.   15. A cornea damaged by accident or illness can often be replaced through surgery with a healthy one from a deceased human being. See BLINDNESS; CATARACT; CONJUNTIVITIS; CROSS-EYE; GLAUCOMA; STY; VISION.

B. Divide this *Columbia Encyclopedia* (3d ed.) article into paragraphs and be prepared to explain and defend your analysis.

syllogism (si′lujiz″um),   1. mode of argument in LOGIC consisting of two premises and the conclusion drawn from them.   2. It is the central tool of traditional logic and was defined by Aristotle who formulated the doctrine which has held for over 2,000 years as an argument in which certain things being laid down, something else follows from the being of these.   3. The categorical syllogism, composed of three categorical propositions or statements of fact, is the most common type and is the basic form of deductive reasoning.   4. An example of a categorical syllogism is: All animals are mortal (major premise). All men are animals (minor premise). Therefore all men are mortal (conclusion).   5. There are three, and only three, terms in a categorical syllogism: the major, the minor, and the middle.   6. The major term is the predicate of the conclusion, and the premise in which it occurs is called the major premise.   7. The minor term is the subject of the conclusion, and the premise in which it occurs is called the minor premise.   8. The middle term forms no part of the conclusion of a valid syllogism but occurs in both premises.   9. There are five rules governing the validity of categorical syllogisms: the middle term must be distributed at least once (a term is distributed when it refers to all the individuals in the class it denotes); no term may be distributed in the conclusion if it is not distributed in the premise; if both premises are negative, there can be no conclusion; if one premise is negative, the conclusion must be negative; if both premises are affirmative, the conclusion must be affirmative.   10. The types of syllogisms in addition to the categorical are the hypothetical and the disjunctive.   11. Each has its own rules of validity.   12. The hypothetical syllogism has as its major premise a conditional proposition indicating that, given a certain condition, a particular result necessarily follows.   13. An example is: If I am a man, then I am mortal. I am a man. Therefore, I am mortal.   14. The disjunctive syllogism has as its first premise a proposition giving two alternatives, at least one of which is true. An example is: I am either mortal or immortal. I am not immortal. Therefore, I am mortal.

C. Study the "punctuation" of these paragraphs. What changes could be made, with what gains or losses?

1

1. I found the act of creation to lie in the discovery of a hidden likeness.   2. The scientist or the artist takes two facts or experiences which are separate; he finds in them a likeness which had not been seen before; and he creates a unity by showing the likeness. [J. Bronowski, *Science and Human Values*]

2

Symbols are not only the most difficult of all signs to read because of the infinite number of ways they may be related to their verbal contexts (the words around them) and their matrices (their total environment), but they are the most valuable to us because it is by them and by them alone that we manage to differentiate ourselves from the other animals about us; by them and by them alone we can make appointments for the week after next; by them and by them alone we can tally the number of our flocks or discover that the square of the hypotenuse of a right triangle is equal to the sum of the squares of the opposite sides; by them and by them alone can we say "The Lord is my shepherd, and I shall not want." [Albert Upton, *Design for Thinking*]

3

1. Men fear thought as they fear nothing else on earth— more than ruin, more even than death.   2. Thought is subversive and revolutionary, destructive and terrible; thought is merciless to privilege, established institutions, and comfortable habits; thought is anarchic and lawless, indifferent to authority, careless of the well-tried wisdom of the ages.   3. Thought looks into the pit of hell and is not afraid.   4. It sees man, a feeble speck, surrounded by unfathomable depths of silence; yet it bears itself proudly, as unmoved as if it were lord of the universe.   5. Thought is great and swift and free, the light of the world, and the chief glory of man. [J. H. Randall, Jr., *The Making of the Modern Mind*]

4

1. But my analysis so far has been much too narrow, for all these changes could only have happened in the context of the great general events of the last fifteen years.   2. Our very survival.

3. Our mastery of space (not, of course, the relatively trivial problems of outer space but the management of our own acres). 4. The revolution that has brought about enormously improved teaching in the secondary and private schools.   5. And, most fundamental of all, the rediscovery of the high purpose of man as a living, loving, thinking, and acting moral entity which surely has been the decisive accomplishment of our society since 1960. 6. All these things—and many more—inevitably have had an enormous impact on our university life. [McGeorge Bundy, "The Easy Chair," *Harper's*, January 1962]

D. Write out a structural analysis of each of these paragraphs. In 3, consider carefully the punctuation.

1

1. People have speculated about the nature of language for a long time.   2. Both Plato and Aristotle discussed the matter, but, as one might expect, they did not agree.   3. Plato seems to have believed that the connection between a word and a meaning was a product of the nature of things—that each word had a true and real meaning established by this natural and inherent connection.   4. He was therefore interested in etymology as a process for discovering real meanings, the natural relationships between names and things.   5. The word "etymology" reflects this view, for it is derived from two Greek words which mean, in effect, "true speech."   6. Aristotle, on the other hand, regarded the connection between a word and a meaning as a product of convention, of tacit agreement among people.   7. Consequently, he had little interest in seeking "original meanings," for these would have no more validity than current meanings. [Sumner Ives and Stephen O. Mitchell, *Language, Style, Ideas*]

2

1. It is easy to like the young because they are young.   2. They have no faults, except the very ones they are asking you to eradicate: ignorance, shallowness, and inexperience.   3. The really hateful faults are those which we grown men and women have. 4. Some of these grow on us like diseases, others we build up and cherish as though they were virtues.   5. Ingrained conceit, calculated cruelty, deep-rooted cowardice, slobbering greed, vulgar self-satisfaction, puffy laziness of mind and body—these and the other real isms result from years, decades of careful cultivation. 6. They show on our faces, they ring harsh or hollow in our voices, they have become bone of our bone and flesh of our flesh.   7. The young do not sin in those ways.   8. Heaven knows they are in-

furiatingly lazy and unbelievably stupid and sometimes detestably cruel—but not for long, not all at once, and not (like grown-ups) as a matter of habit or policy.   9. They are trying to be energetic and wise and kind.   10. When you remember this, it is difficult not to like them. [Gilbert Highet, *The Art of Teaching*]

3

1. Perhaps the essential difference involved in this distinction [between the comprehension and the signification of a term] can be sharpened by considering alternative ways of putting it.   2. The comprehension of a term is sometimes called its *"extension"*—the class of things over which the term, so to speak, extends.   3. And the signification is sometimes called its "intension."   4. Or you could contrast the *implications* of a term with its *applications:* the comprehension consists of those things that the term applies *to:* and the signification consists of those characteristics that the term implies *about,* or attributes *to,* the things it comprehends.   5. Or you could say that in a sentence like "Bring me the green book," the term "green" helps to *indicate* which book is wanted (this is its comprehending function), and it also *predicates* a characteristic of that book (this is its signifying dimension). [Monroe Beardsley, *Thinking Straight*]

E. These two paragraphs are on the same topic—the semantic process of narrowing or specialization—and use some of the same words as examples. Study them for the definitions they offer and their relative density of texture, that is, the amount of detail in their discussion of examples. Potter is an Englishman, Pyles an American; what differences do you find in their handling of mechanics that are explained by these facts? Why does Pyles use both single and double quotation marks?

1

1. 1 The most obvious semantic category is that involving specialization or narrowing.
2.   2 When a speech-form is applied to a group of objects or ideas which resemble one another in some respect, it may naturally become restricted to just one object or idea, and if this particular restriction gains currency in a speech community, a specialized meaning prevails.
3.   3 *Meat,* as in *sweetmeat* and as in the archaic phrase 'meat and drink,' meant any kind of food.
4.   4 It now means 'edible flesh,' a sense formerly expressed by *flesh* and *flesh meat.*
5.   3 *Deer,* like Dutch *dier* and German *Tier,* used to mean

'animal' in general, as in Shakespeare's 'mice and rats and such small deer.'

6.   4 Latin *animal* and French *beast* have taken its place as the general words and *deer* now means 'wild ruminant of a particular (antlered) species.'

7.   3 *Fowl*, like Dutch and German *Vogel*, denoted 'bird' in general as in Chaucer's 'Parlement of Foules' and Biblical 'fowls of the air' and as in modern names of larger kinds of birds used with a qualifying adjective, such as *sea fowl, water fowl,* and *wild fowl.*

8.   4 Otherwise, of course, *fowl* normally means a domestic cock or hen, especially when full grown.

9.   3 *Hound* formerly meant a dog of any breed and not, as as now, a hunting dog in particular.

10.   3 *Disease* was still conceived in Chaucer's day as being dis-ease, 'absence of ease.'

11.   4 It might point to any kind of temporary discomfort and not, as now, to a morbid physical condition.

12.   3 *To starve*, like Dutch *sterven* and German *sterben*, meant 'to die,' not necessarily from lack of food.

13.   4 In modern Yorkshire dialect a body can still 'starve of cold.'

14.   3 A *wed* was a pledge of any kind.

15.   4 In conjunction with the suffic *-lock* forming nouns of action, it has come to be restricted to 'the marriage vow or obligation.'

16.   3 To the Elizabethans an *affection* was a feeling of any kind and both *lectures* and *lessons* were 'readings' of any kind.

17.   3 *Doctrine* was still teaching in general and *science* was still knowledge in general. [Simeon Potter, *Our Language*]

2

1. 1. The opposite of generalization is specialization, a process in which, by adding to the elements of meaning, the semantic content of a word is reduced.

2.   2 Deer, for instance, used to mean simply 'animal' (CE *déor*) as its German cognate *Tier* still does.

3.   3 Shakespeare writes of "Mice, and Rats, and such small Deare" (*King Lear* III.iv.144).

4.   4 By adding something particular (the family *Cervidae*) to the content, the scope of the word has been reduced, and it has come to mean a specific kind of animal.

5.   2 Similarly *hound* used to mean 'dog,' as does its German cognate *Hund*.

6.   3 To this earlier meaning we have in the course of time added the idea of hunting, and thereby restricted the scope of the word, which to us means a special sort of dog, a hunting dog.

7.   2 To the earlier content of *liquor* 'fluid' (compare *liquid*) we have added 'alcoholic.'

8.   2 But, generalization, the opposite tendency, has occurred in the case of the word rum, the name of a specific alcoholic drink, which in the usage of those who disapprove of all alcoholic beverages long ago came to mean strong drink in general, even though other liquors are much more copiously imbibed today.

9.   3 The word has even been personified in *Demon Rum*. [The sequence is interrupted here by paragraph indention.]

10.   2 *Meat* once meant simply 'food,' a meaning which it retains in *sweetmeat* and throughout the King James Bible ("meat for the belly," "meat and drink"), though it acquired the meaning 'flesh' earlier and had for a while both the general and the specialized meaning.

11.   2 *Starve* (CE *steorfan*) used to mean simply 'to die,' as its German cognate *sterben* still does.

12.   3 Chaucer writes, for instance, "But as hire man I wol ay lyve and sterve" (*Troilus and Criseyde* I.427).

13.   3 A specific way of dying had to be expressed by a following phrase, for example "of hunger, for cold."

14.   4 The OED cites "starving with the cold," presumably dialectal, as late as 1867.

15.   3 The word came somehow to be primarily associated with death by hunger, and for a while there existed a compound verb *hunger-starve*.

16.   4 Usually nowadays we put the stress altogether on the added idea of hunger and lose the older meaning altogether.

17.   3 Although the usual meaning of *to starve* now is 'to die of hunger,' we also use the phrase "starve to death," which in earlier times would have been tautological.

18.   3 An additional, toned-down meaning grows out of hyperbole, so that "I'm starving" may mean only 'I'm very hungry.'

19.   3 The word is of course used figuratively, as in "starving for love" which, as we have seen, once meant 'dying for love.'

20.   2 This word furnishes a striking example of specialization and proliferation of meaning. [Thomas Pyles, *The Origins and Development of the English Language*]

F. Look up the dates of all the persons named in this paragraph, then consider these questions. How do James (which James?) and Whitehead get into level 3? What is the significance of *so* at the beginning of the sixth sentence? Why, in view of the dates, are Berkeley and Hume put at the fourth level instead of the third?

1. 1 In every age, philosophical thinking exploits some dominant concepts and makes its greatest headway in solving problems conceived in terms of them.

2.   2 The seventeenth- and eighteenth-century philosophers construed knowledge, knower, and known in terms of sense data and their associations.

3.   3 Descartes's self-examination gave classical psychology *the mind and its contents* as a starting point.

4.   3 Locke set up sensory immediacy as the new criterion of the real, namely, the "really given"—James's and Whitehead's "stubborn, ineluctable fact."

5.   3 Hobbes provided the *genetic method* of building up complex ideas from simple ones, as one builds a wall of bricks or a puzzle picture from many pieces.

6.   4 So Berkeley and Hume build tables out of squareness and brownness (Russell took a final fling at this job by using "soft data" as his logical glue); and in another quarter, still true to the Hobbesian method, Pavlov built intellect out of conditioned reflexes and Leob built life out of tropisms. [Susanne K. Langer, *Philosophical Sketches*]

G. Any assignment in expository writing should be in terms of material —data to be interpreted and communicated—rather than in terms of a form to be filled. For example, when you have studied the paragraphs by Potter and Pyles and noted, and made notes of, the differences, you will have the topic and material for a substantial paragraph which will fall naturally into a coordinate sequence. As you try to make these differences explicit, you are likely to find yourself producing a mixed sequence.

A good start may be for the class to write on a common topic, preferably one with a plural key term. Use a key term such as *causes, results, reasons, ways, classes, kinds*—the kinds of books you read, the qualities you look for in a book, and so on. Remember to put like things in like ways.

11

The Structure of Paragraphs

Let us turn now from dividing unparagraphed material to see how paragraphs are built up sentence by sentence according to a number of distinctive patterns. We will still be looking at discursive writing—and at discursive writing that for the most part is logically rather than chronologically or spatially ordered.

As described in the last chapter, a paragraph is a sequence of structurally related sentences. The relations the sentences stand in to one another are the relations of coordination and subordination. We use these terms in a rather broad, but we hope not loose, sense. The relations are the same in the paragraph as in the sentence, but they are much harder to determine.

Sentences in a paragraph are coordinate when they have the same function, when they stand in the same relation to a superordinate sentence. Many are often marked as coordinates, and always should be, by parallel constructions—by opening, at least, with the same words in the same pattern, and *like things in like ways*. The writer who does not put like things in like ways—who relies entirely on the meaning, the semantic clues, to signal identity of function—invites confusion and misunderstanding.

A sentence in a paragraph is subordinate to the one next above—or to a set of coordinate sentences next above it—when it makes *some kind of comment* on it. "Some kind of comment" is very broad; it has to be broad to include the great range of things we can say when we talk about whatever it is we have chosen to assert. It blurs the distinction, for example, between inductive and deductive or synthetic and analytic, but it reflects reasonably well the way paragraphs unfold themselves. These kinds of comment are for discursive writing what the three methods of description are for the other modes. The next chapter will attempt to identify the most common of them; the usual lists of "methods of paragraph development" are altogether inadequate.

When a given sentence is not coordinate with any sentence above it and is not subordinate to—does not appear to make a comment of any kind on—the sentence next above it or a set of parallel sentences above it, then the paragraph has begun to drift, or the sentence is parenthetic and should put within parentheses or dropped to a footnote, or the writer has unwittingly begun a new sequence, a new paragraph. Some of these strictures will be modified later in the discussion of extra-sequential sentences.

SIMPLE COORDINATE SEQUENCE

The simplest kind of paragraph (note that this opening commits us to a climactic order in this section) is analogous to the two-level sentence that has at the second level a set of elements coordinate with one another, such as this:

1 One might speculate that the *idea* of the sentence has fallen into disrepute [among modern critics of poetry] for one or more of a number of possible reasons:
  2 because it suggests that an outward-pointing "statement" about the world is being made;
  2 because it suggests that the imaginative perceptions of the artist are confined by the conceptual and discursive mode of expression of the philosopher or of the scientist;
  2 because it suggests that, within the poem, the presentation of sensuous imagery and spontaneous feeling is subordinate to the expression of meaning. [Walter Sutton, "Beyond the Image," *Style*, February 1961]

This sentence is long, but no one has the right to say, as many would, that it is "too long"; it is easy to read. Only in its context, and as a matter of paragraph punctuation, could one say whether it would be advisable to make four sentences of it by dropping *because* and changing colon and semicolons to periods. But if this were done, one would have a four-sentence, two-level sequence that could be let stand as a paragraph. In form it would be what we will call a *simple coordinate sequence*. Here are some more examples.

A

1 In the name of justice, good sportsmanship, and general honesty, it is simply essential that information reported to this public press, in meetings of committees, or across lunch-tables be double-checked.

2 In engineering and industry this is a matter of profits or bank-ruptcy.

2 In medicine it is a matter of life or death.

2 In public affairs and in private life it is a matter of integrity or corruption.

2 In the laboratory it is taken for granted as a necessary and ele-mentary part of scientific behavior. [Wendell Johnson, *Verbal Man: The Enchantment of Words*]

B

1 The arbitrariness of the structuring of things and thoughts is familiar to anyone who has ever learned a foreign language.

2 That continuum of reality which English separates into two units through the labels *arm* and *hand* is treated as a single unit by the Russian label *ruká*.

2 That area of action which English divides into two units through the labels *carry* and *bear* is handled as a single unit by the French label *porter*.

2 That area of thought which English treats as a single unit through the label *remember* is divided in German into two units through the one-word label *behalten* ('remember' = 'keep in mind') and the three-word label *sich errinnern an* ('remember' = 'recall to mind'). [William G. Moulton, "Linguistics," in James Thorpe, ed., *The Aims and Methods of Scholarship in Modern Languages and Lit-eratures*]

C

1 The alternatives to asking answerable questions, and then making honest attempts to find answers to them, are clear—and disgraceful.

2 We can ask no questions at all, either out of stupor or as a dis-play of arrogance.

2 We can ask questions that are misleading, or vague, or mean-ingless—to be answered, respectively, by mountebanks, the con-fused, and the very naive.

2 Or, we may ask clear questions and then refuse to acknowledge them, as a gesture of fear, smugness, or irresponsibility. [Wen-dell Johnson, *Your Most Enchanted Listener*]

The first thing to notice is that the sentences added (level 2) are in each paragraph identical for the first three or four words. Like things have been put in like ways. The reader has been given the clues he needs to separate the second level from the first and to group as parallel to one another, and thus on the same level, all the sentences after the first. No further signals, such as *first, second, again, in addition,* are necessary. In C, *may* for *can* is a puzzle: where there is a difference in expression it should signal a difference in meaning, but one can't be sure whether a difference in meaning was intended or whether the difference in expression is an oversight. The expert writer is one whose expression, the reader soon comes to see, matches his meaning exactly.

Recall, incidentally, that in the earlier chapters we insisted that parallel items in our descriptions of sense impressions should not be structurally the same, that they must be varied. In this respect the two modes of writing—representational and discursive—are simply different.

The next major thing to notice is that the logical relation of the second-level sentences to one another is the same in each of the paragraphs and that the logical relation of the second-level sentences to the first-level sentence is different in each of the three paragraphs. In A, they all present *evidence* to support the assertion that information must be double-checked. In B, they all give *examples* of the arbitrariness of language in structuring things and thoughts. In C, they all *identify* the alternatives. (Notice the structure of this paragraph to this point.) These relations (evidence, exemplification, identification) are analogous to the methods of description (by attributes, details, and comparison). But whereas there are only three things one can do to picture something (or four, if we add by effect), there are far more, as we have already hinted, when it comes to talking about.

The next set of paragraphs have, like A, B, and C, a parallel sequence of supporting sentences, but the paragraphs are slow in getting under way. The writer is like a dog that turns round several times where he intends to lie down before he actually does it. Thus the parallel sequence is not at level 2, but at level 3, 4, or 5. The intermediate sentences may be thought of as *preliminaries*, a term we will use again later.

D

1 Linguistics has been described as being, at one and the same time, the most scientific of the humanities and the most humanistic of the sciences.
　2 In both theory and practice it shares elements of many other disciplines, even though it cannot be neatly classified with any one of them.
　　3 With the natural sciences it shares the method of observation, classification, and generalization, and the search for countable units and describable structures.
　　3 With the social sciences it shares an interest in group behavior as revealed through the actions of individuals.
　　3 And with the humanities it shares an interest in the uniquely human, in language as a phenomenon which distinguishes man

as "the talking animal" most sharply from all other living beings. [William G. Moulton, "Linguistics"]

E

1 The first motive [for using slang] is to interest and impress the people
with whom we are talking.
  2 Students of the psychology of language have found that, most
  of the time, in ordinary conversation, we are not trying to give
  information alone; we are trying to impress the other fellow.
    3 We are attempting to awaken his emotions: to gain his ap-
    proval, to win his sympathy, to surprise him, make him laugh,
    harrow his feelings, or excite his enthusiasm.
      4 That is why so many talkers use gestures—the less emotional
      peoples like the Dutch use few, the more emotional peoples
      like the Italians use many.
      4 That is why so many talkers try to get into some sort of
      physical contact (which means emotional contact) with the
      other man, tapping his knee, holding his lapel, patting his
      shoulder.
        5 Even to give a man a cigarette and light it for him estab-
        lishes that kind of emotional contact, however fragile
        it may seem.
      4 And that is why in informal conversation many people choose
      words which are not standard—because they will be more
      surprising and amusing. [Gilbert Highet, *The Anatomy
      of Slang*]

F

1 Substantially, then, the empire of Henry II remained in extent as
he found it at his accession to the English throne at the age of
twenty-one;
it was not created by him but inherited or annexed by marriage.
  2 Accordingly it is not as a conqueror but as a ruler that he can lay
  claim to greatness.
    3 But although Henry attempted little in the way of acquiring
    new territory, he did much to consolidate his possessions and
    to extend his European power and influence.
      4 His daughters were married to the greatest princes of their
      time, Henry the Lion, duke of Saxony and Bavaria, King
      Alphonso VIII of Castile, King William II of Sicily.
      4 He made an alliance with the ruler of Provence and planned
      a marriage with the house of Savoy that would have given
      him control of the passes into Italy.

4 He took his part in the struggle of Pope and anti-Pope, of
Pope and Emperor;
he corresponded with the emperor of Constantinople, refused
the crown of the kingdom of Jerusalem, and died on the eve
of his departure on a crusade.
5 No one could lay claim to greater influence upon the in-
ternational affairs of his time. [Charles Homer Haskins,
The Normans in European History]

Here are a few clues for studying these paragraphs. In D, note that
all three sentences at level 3 are linked to level 2 by the verb *shares* and
to level 1 by the nouns *humanities* and *sciences*. The fact that *sciences*
is plural makes it possible for the author to relate linguistics to both
natural and the social sciences. In E, the sentence put at level 5 is especially interesting. One's first thought might be to put it at level 4; but
the difference in structure suggests a difference in function, and "that
kind of emotional contact" goes back to "emotional contact" in the
sentence above. Thus lighting a cigarette is an *example* of a fragile sort
of emotional contact and the sentence is subordinate to the one above it.
In F, the difference in structure between the first level 4 ("His daughters
were married to" rather than "He married his daughters to") and the
others ("He made an alliance" and "He took his part") can be attributed
to idiom. The final level 4 is interesting because of the compounding:
two base clauses with similar openings ("He took" and "he corresponded"); and the second base clause with a compound predicate
("corresponded . . . refused . . . died").

These paragraphs support the generalization that in a coordinate
sequence all the coordinate sentences use the same method of development. In D, these at level 3 *explain* the statement of level 2. In E and F
those at level 4 offer *examples*.

SIMPLE SUBORDINATE SEQUENCES

The paragraphs we have already looked at show that paragraphs which
are primarily coordinate sequences may contain what we will call
subordinate sequences. In A, B, and C the first two sentences constitute
a minimum subordinate sequence in the sense that the second sentence
is some sort of comment on the sentence next above it—and we identified the sort of comment. In the same way, the first three sentences of
D, the first four of E, and the first four of F constitute subordinate sequences. And the addition in E of the sentence about offering a cigarette
makes it and the fourth-level sentence it is added to another minimum
subordinate sequence.

But the paragraphs do not only *contain* subordinate sequences, a subordinate sequence may *constitute* a paragraph. Such paragraphs as G we will call *simple subordinate sequences*.

G

1 From *age to age* the value currently put upon clearness in writing
   varies rather freely.
   2 *The times* when it has stood highest were also *times* when our
     chance of getting to know, pretty soon, whatever there is to be
     known were over-rated, as we see now.
     3 *A typical fruit of such a period,* vigorous, positive, bold, sure
       of the sufficiency of whatever data it had, impatient of doubts,
       reservations or awe, was *our received political economy of
       the middle nineteenth century*.
       4 In *it* a thin, fallacious lucidity seemed to make everything
         clear but did it by failing to see that there was anything
         to be cleared up where the worst difficulties lay. [C. E. Mon-
         tague, *A Writer's Notes on His Trade*]

The difference between a simple coordinate and a simple subordinate sequence is important enough to labor the point. Study B and G
again. In both, the sentences numbered 2 have the same relation to those
numbered 1; they are subordinate to them. But they diverge at the third
sentence; in B the third is coordinate with sentence 2 and thus is at the
same level—level 2; in G, it is subordinate to sentence 2 and thus is at
a *lower* level—level 3; and so on. To venture an analogy in B, sentences
2, 3, and 4 all join hands with sentence 1; in G, only sentence 2 joins
hands with 1; only 3 joins hands with 2; and only 4 with 3. For another
analogy—in B, all the sentences at level 2 are the children of one
mother; the base sentence, level 1; in G, the base clause is the mother
of 2, 2 the mother of 3, and 3 the mother of 4. If you were making family portraits, B would picture two generations, G would picture four.
The indenting and numbering make these relations graphic.

The fact that there are two kinds of sequences makes all the difference in what we can say about paragraphs. We have to have two.
contrasting, sets of rules for unity, coherence, and emphasis.

Unity. A coordinate sequence will be unified if all the added sentences use the same method of development—examples, causes, results,
and so on. A subordinate sequence will probably use a different method
of development for each added sentence, and it will be unified if each
sentence makes a relevant comment on the sentence next above it.

Coherence. A coordinate sequence will be coherent if like things
are put in like ways, if all the coordinate sentences begin alike. A
subordinate sequence will be coherent if each successive sentence is
linked to the one next above it by some verbal link, such as pronouns

or nouns repeated, as marked in G. Moreover, no subordinate sentence must look as if it were coordinate with any other sentence in the paragraph: if it does, it will mislead the reader.

Emphasis. In general, emphasis comes more from the form of the statements than from their arrangement. But in a coordinate sequence the repetition of structure is itself emphatic and a climactic order by its very nature is a movement from less to more emphatic. In a subordinate sequence the order is from the more to the less inclusive, from the biggest box to successively smaller boxes, so that the paragraph seems to be petering out. But at the same time it moves from the abstract or general to the concrete or specific, from the plural to the singular. The greater force of these counterbalances the lesser scope of the earlier sentences, with an effect something like that of a camera moving in for a close-up.

MIXED SEQUENCES

Paragraphs such as we have been studying, pure or nearly pure examples of coordinate or subordinate sequences, are not the only kinds. Most paragraphs are a combination of the two kinds of sequences. We can see how such a combination might come about, in the ordinary processes of writing and rewriting, if we simply change the punctuation of a paragraph.

H

1 Our purpose may become clearer if we at once emphasize certain things we do *not* seek to achieve by this recommendation of a course in the area of values.
 2 First, it is not our view that the course will necessarily make the undergraduate "better"; the moral of intellectual training must always be indirect, and it is not the function of the nonsectarian college to teach virtue by prescription.
 2 Second, we do not make this recommendation merely to counter the secularism of our age; we are inclined to think that studies of the sort we urge would be still more necessary if all our students were comfortably committed to some religious orthodoxy.
 2 Third, we most emphatically do not believe that any one syllabus should be devised to meet the requirement; there are a number of ways to approach the problem, and the choice is peculiarly dependent on the availability of teaching talent. [Harvard Committee, *General Education in School and College*]

Anyone might be excused for thinking this paragraph rather heavy. We can imagine someone on the committee that accepted the draft report suggesting that the sentences were a bit long. With five capital letters and five periods, the paragraph could have been given this multilevel form:

1 Our purpose may become clearer if we at once emphasize certain things we do *not* seek to achieve by this recommendation of a course in the area of values.
  2 First, it is not our view that this course will necessarily make the undergraduate "better."
    3 The moral effect of intellectual training must always be indirect.
    3 And it is not the function of a nonsectarian college to teach virtue by prescription.
  2 Second, we do not make this recommendation merely to counter the secularism of our age.
    3 We are inclined to think that studies of the sort we urge would be still more necessary if all of our students were comfortably committed to some religious orthodoxy.
  2 Third, we most emphatically do not believe that any one syllabus should be devised to meet the requirement.
    3 There are a number of ways to approach the problem.
      4 And the choice is peculiarly dependent on the availability of teaching talent.

What was simply a two-level paragraph with a three-part coordinate sequence still has the same basic structure, but each part of the three-part sequence is now itself a subordinate sequence. We can describe such a paragraph as a *mixed sequence*. This is the most frequent sort of paragraph. In this example, there seems to be no great advantage to either way of "punctuating" the paragraph. The long sentences are not really difficult to read, and the short sentences are easy to group.

MIXED COORDINATE SEQUENCES

Mixed sequences seem to grow out of the other two sorts, out of coordinate sequences and subordinate sequences. If a writer has laid out the paragraph as a coordinate sequence and he has an abundance of ideas or a genuine concern for communicating with his reader, either or both, preferably both, he may develop each subtopic rather fully, adding several sentences and using one or more added levels. (The more he adds, the denser the texture.) This is what happened in I below, where one or two sentences have been added to each member of the coordinate series. In paragraphs like this, the second-level sentences can be thought of as subtopic sentences, and each subtopic sentence and the sentence added to it can be regarded as a subsequence. In the articles on the eye we saw that long coordinate sequences can be divided, the subtopic sentences becoming the topic sentences of the resulting paragraphs. By such means a 500-word paper can grow out of a simple co-ordinate sequence.

I

1 Applied to language, the adjective *good* can have two meanings: (1) "effective, adequate for the purpose to which it is put" and (2) "acceptable, conforming to approved usage."

 (2) The first of these is truly a value judgment of the language itself.

  3 In this sense the language of Shakespeare, for example, is "good English" because it serves as a highly effective vehicle for his material.

  3 On the other hand, the language of a poorer writer, which does not meet adequately the demands put upon it, might be called "bad English."

 2 The second meaning of *good* is not really a judgment of the language itself but a social appraisal of the persons who use it.

  3 An expression like *I ain't got no time for youse* may be most effective in the situation in which it is used, and hence "good English" in the first sense.

   4 But most people, including those who naturally speak this way, will call it "bad English" because grammatical features like *ain't, youse,* and the double-negative construction belong to a variety of English commonly used by people with little education and low social and economic status. [W. Nelson Francis, *The English Language*]

Not all mixed coordinate sequences are as symmetrical as I. Two more paragraphs will provide grounds for further observations on the mixed coordinate sequence.

J

1 The other mode of thought is the scientific method.

 2 It subjects the conclusions of reason to the arbitrament of hard fact to build in increasing body of tested knowledge.

 2 It refuses to ask questions that cannot be answered, and rejects such answers as cannot be provided except by Revelation.

 2 It discovers the relatedness of all things in the universe—of the motion of the moon to the influence of the earth and sun, of the nature of the organism to its environment, of human civilization to the conditions under which it is made.

 2 It introduces history into everything.

  3 Stars and scenery have their history, alike with plant species or human institutions,

   and

  nothing is intelligible without some knowledge of the past.

    4 As Whitehead has said, each event is the reflection or effect of every other event, past as well as present.

2 It rejects dualism.

    3 The supernatural is in part the region of the natural that has not yet been understood, in part an invention of human fantasy, in part the unknowable.

    3 Body and soul are not separate entities, but two aspects of one organization,

        and

    Man is that portion of the universal world-stuff that has evolved until it is capable of rational and purposeful values.

    4 His place in the Universe is to continue that evaluation and to realize those values. [Julian Huxley, *Man in the Modern World*]

In the coordinate sequence Huxley observed exactly the principle of like things in like ways. What he added suggests careful calculation of what he could leave to the reader's understanding and what he would have to make explicit. With the first two items he trusted the reader, but could he trust the reader to understand rightly, for this context, "the relatedness of all things in the universe"? His answer here was not to add sentences, but to add to the sentence, making it a two-level one by adding three prepositional phrases in apposition to "of all things." He did not choose his examples at random. You can figure out yourself the reason for the three choices, and note that he repeats them in the next subsequence. For the last two items, he chose to add sentences. Thus whether to add, what to add, and the syntactic forms to use in adding are options of the writer. In order to exercise his options intelligently, he must consider the reader whose mind he is seeking to engage.

K

1. 1 A beginning poet today might well imagine that he ought to show evidences of faithful apprenticeship to more practices, principles, and examples than any but a remarkable talent could digest.

2. 2 He must, if I understand his obligations, begin by being metaphysical, though it is not clear who will supply him with a metaphysic.

3. 3 Thus he will start by aiming at the imaginative wit of Donne, the leap of the mind between surprisingly remote objects.

4. 3 Or he will endeavor to spin the thread of a poem from the developing implications of a single analogy.

5. 3 Or he will do what it seems neither God nor good sense have been able to forbid—
he will try to revive what he understands by the seventeenth-century "conceit."

6. 2 But his work is not over.
7. 3 It will be his obligation to show that the French symbolists have not passed him by without effect.
8. 2 Even now our poet has not paid all his debts.
9. 3 As a minimum of civic duty he must show that his ear has been attuned to the rhetoric of the later (by no means the earlier) Yeats.
10. 3 At the same time, by a truly alchemical feat, he must reveal that his language has been touched by the wand of Hopkins. [Theodore Morrison, " 'The Fault, Dear Brutus': Poetic Example and Poetic Practice Today," *The Pacific Spectator, Summer 1957*]

The writer of K, addressing a cultivated audience, assumed more knowledge of modern poetry and its historic origins than most college students can muster. Moreover, by not putting the members of the coordinate series in like ways, he deprived the reader of that important clue to the structure of his paragraph. Still, there are other clues. The repetition of *Or he will* binds sentences 3, 4, and 5 together. In spite of some similarity in form (*It will be his obligation*), 7 is cut off from this series by 6 and thus goes with 6. *At the same time . . . he must* makes 10 coordinate with 9. This kind of grouping shows that 2, 6 and 3 must be at level 2, and the reference to time in 2 (*begin*), in 6 (*But his work is not over*), and in 3 (*Even now*) marks these sentences as co-ordinate-grouped, rather artificially perhaps, by a time sequence.

It helps, too, in reading a paragraph like this, to catch the tone of irony. To do this, note what evidence there is, in nearly every sentence, that the writer is not urging these principles and practices on the beginning poet, that in fact he is ridiculing them.

MIXED SUBORDINATE SEQUENCES

In working out a subordinate sequence, each successive sentence being a comment on the one next above it, any doubling or multiplying of examples, causes, reasons, or the like will generate a *mixed subordinate sequence*—provided the multiple items are punctuated as sentences. Such paragraphs are much less frequent than mixed coordinate sequences, even if we count such paragraphs as D, E, and F as mixed subordinate sequences. (It is of no great moment to settle whether a mixed sequence is coordinate or subordinate; these are just convenient terms to designate recurring configurations.) In L, the last sentence is subordinate to the set at level 5. This set could, of course, be punctuated as a compound sentence. If it were, the paragraph would be a simple subordinate sequence.

L

1 No student of contemporary usage can be unmindful of the curious reprobative force which has been acquired by the term "prejudice."
  2 Etymologically it signifies nothing more than a prejudgment, or a judgment before all the facts are in;
      and
    since all of us have to proceed to a great extent on judgments of that kind, the word should not be any more exciting than "hypothesis."
  3 But in its rhetorical applications "prejudice" presumes far beyond that.
    4 It is used, as a matter of fact, to characterize unfavorably any value judgment whatever.
      5 If "blue" is said to be a better color than "red," that is prejudice.
      5 If people of outstanding cultural achievement are praised through contrast with other people, that is prejudice.
      5 If one mode of life is presented as superior to another, that is prejudice.
        6 And behind all this is the implication, if not the declaration, that it is un-American to be prejudiced. [Richard M. Weaver, *The Ethics of Rhetoric*]

THE TOPIC SENTENCE

We seem, in this analysis of the paragraph, to have forgotten the topic sentence. What about it? What is its function? Its position? Its form?

The topic sentence is sometimes called the thesis sentence of the paragraph. It is usually conceived as stating or summarizing the central thought and then being used as a plumb line to control the development of the paragraph. In some quarters, the old-fashioned ones perhaps, it is regarded almost as a talisman, as if it had the magic property of producing unity, coherence, and emphasis. In other quarters, it has become the style to disparage it, as if it were sure death to spontaneity and invention. Our method will continue to be more or less inductive. What do experienced writers do? What does one do oneself? And, on the basis of what is done, what can we say ought to be done?

Our definition of the topic sentence follows from the analogy between the cumulative sentence and the paragraph. It is analogous to the base clause and may be called the base sentence. It follows also from the definition of the paragraph as a sequence of structurally related sentences and may be called the top sentence of the paragraph. In view of the analytical diagrams we have been using, it may be said to be the sentence which the other sentences depend from; in the diagrams it is the sentence marked level 1. It is the parent which the following generation or generations issue from. It is the sentence which the other sentences comment on or develop or amplify or explicate or substantiate. It is usually stated in rather abstract or general terms or in plural terms.

In all examples so far, it has been the first sentence of the paragraph, literally the top sentence, literally the one the others depend from. But this position is not obligatory. Sometimes, but very rarely, it appears midway, as in M, and sometimes, but even more rarely, at the end, as in N.

M

    2 Quite evidently the ideal of non-resistance would, if literally and consistently followed, abandon the world to the predatory.

    2 Poverty, if universally practiced, would sink the world in squalor and darkness.

    2 Universal celibacy would extinguish human life.

1 All this is so obvious that, manifestly, these ideas, which we find in all high religion, cannot be treated as public rules of human conduct.

    2 They are, however, related to human conduct.

        3 For they affect the nature of man, in that the vision of ourselves transformed can modify our appetites and our passions. [Walter Lippmann, *The Public Philosophy*]

N

    2 Good will without clear thinking can be monstrous: men of all lands have always marched behind the bright banners of righteousness to do the killing they glorify as war,
      and always
    they have come home from battle to benedictions.

    2 Clear thinking without good will can be fully as lamentable: millions of human beings have been reduced to wasting torment by their shrewder fellows.

1 Mankind needs desperately one more great teacher—the wanted wise man—who will bring about close union of clear thinking and good will. [Wendell Johnson, *Your Most Enchanted Listener*]

One occasionally finds a paragraph with no topic sentence at all. Such a paragraph is almost without exception a coordinate sequence, either simple or mixed; since with no topic sentence there can be no level 1, the set of coordinate sentences will be at level 2. Such a paragraph is sometimes the first of an essay or article, where it makes for a rather rhetorical opening. More often it comes about from over-paragraphing. Because of the pressure, perhaps, to keep paragraphs moderate in length, a coordinate sequence is set off, and the two paragraphs make a single sequence.

O

2 It is self-interest to want to live in a society operating by the love of justice and the concept of law.

3 We have not been living in such a society.

2 It is self-interest to want all members of society to contribute as fully as possible to the enrichment of that society.

3 The structure of our society has prevented that.

2 It is self-interest to seek out friends and companions who are congenial in temperament and whose experiences and capacities extend our own.

3 Our society has restricted us in this natural quest.

2 It is self-interest to want to escape from the pressure to conform to values which we feel immoral or antiquated.

3 Our society has maintained such pressures.

2 It is self-interest to want to escape from the burden of vanity into the hard and happy realization that in the diminishment of others there is a deep diminishment of the self.

3 Our society has been organized for the diminishment of others. [Robert Penn Warren, *Who Speaks for the Negro?*]

P[1]

1 We are deeply attuned to the samenesses we hear or see in the use of language, so much so that when we unexpectedly hear a foreign language, whose rules are different from those which operate in our own language, we try to force it into our own language pattern.

2 Everyone has had this experience, an experience which testifies to the strong hold our own language has on us.

1 When we speak a foreign language, if we are not complete masters of it, we also tend to force the language into the patterns and rules with which we are familiar.

2 We find it difficult to hear distinctions which are of importance in the foreign language but are not in our own, and to ignore distinctions which are of significance only in our own.

2 We find it difficult to pronounce sounds of a foreign language with which we are not familiar.

P[2]

3 A Frenchman trying to speak English will have difficulty with our *th* in *the*, because that sound does not occur in his language.

4 He may say *ze* instead of *the* because *z* is familiar to him.

3 An American speaking French will have much difficulty with

the French word *rue* "street," because in English we have neither a uvular *r* or a front rounded vowel, as in *ue*.

3 In English, we do not use *thou* except in prayers; when we speak French, German, or Italian we find it difficult to remember that some of our *you's* should be *thou's* in the acceptable forms of the language being used. [Morton W. Bloomfield and Leonard Newmark, *A Linguistic Introduction to the History of English*]

Taken alone, out of context, P² clearly has no topic sentence. The three sentences are coordinate, each presenting an example, and there is no superordinate sentence to tell what they are examples of. That they are examples of our difficulties when we *speak* a foreign language we learn from the paragraph above.

P¹ is interesting in another way. Both the first and third sentences are marked 1, as if it had two topic sentences. Sentence 3 begins "When we speak a foreign language"; this matches up with the subordinate clause in sentence 1, "when we unexpectedly hear a foreign language." Like things have been put in like ways, but one of them has been buried deep in the sentence. We could straighten out the paragraph by making the first part of the first sentence the topic sentence, and making *When we hear* and *When we speak* subtopic sentences at level 2.

As it stands, the first paragraph, with two (not quite) equal parts and two topic sentences, could be called a *compound paragraph*. The compound paragraph is fairly common. Here is another example.

Q

1 It is hard for us to get the feel of the present dynamism of our society, because we have come to take change for granted in our world.

2 We can guess only with difficulty how different the lives and attitudes were of the generations before us.

3 We can feel the difference between ourselves and Asiatics or Europeans more easily than the differences between ourselves and our ancestors.

1 It is hard for us to feel the dynamism of our language, since we do not know the origin of the terms we use or the sentence forms we use them in.

2 Unless we have studied our language with an eye especially to the first use of words or constructions, we cannot tell which is new and which is old; they all come to us with equal authority from our community.

3 We ourselves without knowing may be the first and only users of a term or an expression; our present need for communication

brings us to the borderline of what has been said before us, and beyond it. [Donald J. Lloyd and Harry R. Warfel, *American English in the Cultural Setting*]

The purpose in presenting paragraphs with postponed topic sentences or with none at all has not been to recommend them as models. Here again the analogy with the sentence is useful. In the cumulative sentence the base clause is commonly placed first and the added elements come tumbling after. So in the paragraph; the topic sentence is commonly, and sensibly, placed first. In this chapter, written for ease of comprehension, all of the paragraphs begin with a sentence that defines the topic or points to it.

This practice has advantages for both the writer and the reader. For the writer, it is like settling in advance on the course to be taken in driving from here to there. It relieves him of the confusion of uncertain and divided purposes and keeps him on course. And it makes it possible for the reader to trace the writer's course. It is very gratifying to a reader to be able to run his eye down the pages, reading only the first sentences of the paragraphs, and get a clear sense of the form and substance of the essay or chapter. It is like following a numbered highway through a big city and finding each turn marked and after each turn and intersection finding the reassuring marker. Such marking of the course need not be mechanical; and it exhibits the kind of sympathetic imagination that shows the writer able to put himself in the reader's position.

Another topic on the topic sentence is the degree of explicitness desirable in it. Some topic sentences are like the foundations of a building. They are exactly as long and as wide as the building they are made for, and none of the added sentences project beyond the area outlined by the topic sentence. Others are more like signs merely pointing to the building. They *indicate* the topic of the paragraph rather than *state* it or *summarize* it. In this chapter, one topic sentence is merely a question ("But what is a paragraph?") and the next one is a mere fraction of a sentence ("Meanwhile, our definition"). The two sorts seem to work equally well for both the writer and the reader. If paragraphs are being written in isolation, as exercises, the topic sentence probably must be made pretty explicit. But in continuous discourse, the top-level sentences must be adapted to their function of taking the baton from the preceding paragraph and getting its own lap under way.

More important than the form he uses is for the writer to realize what his topic commits him to. The following sentences as topic sentences would awaken quite different expectations in the reader and therefore require quite different paragraphs from the author.

1. Movies are better than ever.
2. Movies are better this year than last year.

3. This year's movies have been very good.
4. This year's movies tell it like it is.

In the following set of topic sentences from an essay by Eric Hoffer ("The Practical Sense" in *The Ordeal of Change*), the underlined words are the keys to what the author undertakes to do in the paragraph.

1. Nowadays we take the practical attitude for granted.

2. The rise of the practical sense in Europe was not only slow but uneven.

3. There is some evidence that the rise of the practical sense is linked with a diffusion of individual freedom.

4. There are indications that the outburst of practical ingenuity in the Near East during the late Neolithic period was a function of individual activity.

5. A peculiar variant of the situation is to be found in the emergence of a Moslem civilization in the wake of the Arab conquest.

Even so few examples show that almost any part of the sentence (verb, predicate adjective, subject) may be the key to what the author is committing himself to. In 3, he must go on to provide evidence, not just evidence at random, but evidence as defined elsewhere in the sentence, evidence of a linkage between the rise of the practical sense and the spread of individual freedom—evidence, in short, of a causal connection. Unless he is alert to the implications of his topic sentence, the writer is likely to write the wrong paragraph, or, on an examination, the student to answer the wrong question. The same holds for the reader. If he misses the key, he will misread the paragraph.

PARAGRAPHS WITH EXTRASEQUENTIAL SENTENCES

Thus far in this chapter we have looked only at paragraphs that fit the definition of the paragraph as a sequence of structurally related sentences, and we have used the analogy with the cumulative sentence to display the structure. This analogy can be extended farther. A compound paragraph is like a compound sentence. One with the topic sentence at the end is like a periodic sentence. One with the topic sentence midway is like a sentence with initial and final free modifiers. One with no topic sentence is like a set of parallel noun phrases.

But paragraphs sometimes have *extrasequential sentences*—sentences that do not fit into the sequence but yet seem to belong to the paragraph. Here the paragraph seems less analogous to the sentence than to the essay. Up front such sentences serve the same purposes as an introduction (I); at the end they serve as a conclusion or coda (C). (The symbol C does *not* stand for "clincher." The notion of a clincher as a necessary adjunct of a paragraph is a fiction, or fixation, of textbooks and schoolrooms.) And occasionally the extrasequential sentence is simply parenthetic (P), like the two sentences just above. The writer conscious of form puts such sentences in parentheses or drops them to the foot of the pages. But not all the sentences you find in parentheses are really parenthetic. Many people who write are not conscious of form or of the conventions of form; and some adapt the conventions to their own purposes.

In a paragraph with an introduction, the topic sentence is still at the top of the sequence, but it is not the first sentence of the paragraph. The first sentence or two paves the way for the topic, usually by presenting a comparison, or by eliminating an unwanted sense of a term, as in R. Only enough of R has been given to show that it is the sentence marked 1 that is being developed.

R

(I) 1 The dictionaries still say that "language is a device for communicating ideas."
  (I) 2 The semanticists and the anthropologists agree that this is a tiny, specialized function of speech.
   1 Mainly language is an instrument for action.
    2 The meaning of a word or phrase is not its dictionary equivalent but the difference its utterance brings about in a situation.
    2 We use words to comfort and cajole ourselves, . . . [Clyde Kluckhohn, *Mirror for Man*]

Paragraph introductions are fairly rare, but conclusions, or codas, are fairly common. You suspect one when the last sentence, or the next to the last, does not comment on the sentence above it and is not parallel to any above it. You recognize it as a conclusion when you note, usually, that it is a comment on or a deduction from the paragraph as a whole. It is often signaled by such expressions as *then, thus, indeed, therefore, in short, in other words*. The coda is something like a grace note, a neat or witty way of rounding off the paragraph, as in T.

Paragraphs with a conclusion or coda, such as S and T, may have prompted the notion that some paragraphs have two topic sentences, at beginning and end, but clearly those marked C are not topic sentences.

S

  1 Thus the secondary phase of learning revolves around the problem of symbolism.

  2 There are realities
      and
there are appearances related to them.
  3 Some appearances represent the reality, as a thermometer
    represents the temperature, or, in a different way, a drama
    represents a certain kind of human conflict.
  3 Some appearances partly conceal or disguise a reality,
    like the sun "rising" in the east.
  3 And some appearances masquerade as reality, like the
    appearance of lofty intentions in a government about to
    grab someone else's territory.
(C) Learning to sort out these relationships, or in other words developing what is in the broadest sense a critical intelligence, is the
main preoccupation of students on the verge of becoming adult
citizens. [Northrop Frye, *Design for Learning*]

T

  1 In regard to its original meaning [Mind your P's and Q's] there
    has been much conjecture, with no really satisfying explanation.
  2 Some believe it was a warning of schoolteachers to those
    learning to write the alphabet or of master printers to their
    apprentices in setting type.
  2 Some think it has to do with *p*ints and *q*uarts in the alehouse
    reckoning.
  2 Some think it was an injunction of French dancing masters
    to their charges, to mind their feet (*pieds*) and pigtails or
    wigs (*queues*).
  2 And some would have solicitous wives beseeching their hus-
    bands, especially if they were seamen who often tarred their
    pigtails (*queues*), not to soil their *pea*jackets.
(C) The interpretation of linguistic obscurities, as Chaucer once drily
remarked, "is a glorious art, certeyn." [Bergen and Cornelia
Evans, *A Dictionary of Contemporary Conversation Usage*]

There is another class of extrasequential sentences. These are not
only no part of the sequence, but they are not related to it as introduction or conclusion or intruded into it as parenthetic. They *are* intruded
into it, but logically they are part of the structural framework of the
essay or chapter as a whole. They are the one- or two-sentence transitional paragraphs mentioned above that have been arbitrarily run into
the workhorse paragraphs because authors or editors have not seen or
treated them for what they are. The articles on the eye provided an
example. Here is an instructive example.
In section 2 of A. C. Bradley's chapter "Construction in Shake-

speare's Tragedies," in *Shakespearean Tragedy*, three of the first four paragraphs begin as indicated; the other, the third, is complete:

1. We come now to the conflict. And here one or two preliminary remarks are necessary. In the first place, it must be remembered. . . .
2. In the second place, we must be prepared to find. . . .
3. With these warnings, I turn to the question whether we can trace any distinct method or methods by which Shakespeare represents the rise and development of the conflict.
4. One [method] at least is obvious. . . .

It is evident that the first sentence of paragraph 1 is the thesis sentence of this section. It could be set off as a transitional (framework) paragraph. It is evident also that the next sentence, about preliminary remarks, is also a transitional sentence, embracing the two paragraphs that make the "preliminary remarks." It too could be set off as a framework paragraph. But then the writer would have two one-sentence transitional paragraphs. As a compromise, but it would be a compromise, the two could be combined. The third sentence ("In the first place . . .") matches the first sentence of paragraph 2 ("In the second place . . ."). So, although it is the third sentence of paragraph 1, it is the topic sentence; we can mark the first two T1 and T2 for Transitional. Paragraph 3 is a typical example of the short framework or transitional paragraph used to bridge over the larger divisions of a piece. The first phrase, "With these warnings" (i.e., with these preliminary remarks), looks back; the rest of the sentence sets the topic for the next set of paragraphs. The first sentence of paragraph 4 is the topic sentence, and it is stated so as to prepare the reader for a set of coordinate paragraphs arranged in climactic order, from the most obvious to the least.

The transition may, of course, come at the end of the paragraph.

U

  1 But there are two different ways in which a philosophy may seek to base itself on science.

    2 It may emphasize the most general *results* of science, and seek to give even greater generality and unity to those results.

    2 Or it may study the methods of science, and seek to apply these methods, with the necessary adaptions, to its own peculiar province.

      3 Much philosophy inspired by science has gone astray through preoccupation with the *results* momentarily supposed to have been achieved.

      3 It is not results, but *methods*, that can be transferred with profit from the sphere of the special sciences to the sphere of philosophy.

(T) What I wish to bring to your notice is the possibility and importance of applying to philosophical problems certain broad principles of methods which have been found successful in the study of scientific questions. [Bertrand Russell, *Mysticisms and Logics*]

As these examples show, any given transition may look backward or forward or both, and it may link sentence to sentence, paragraph to paragraph, or section to section, and so on. Although these examples do not show all the possibilities, a transition may take the form of a single word, a phrase, a subordinate clause, the first clause of a compound sentence, a separate sentence or two or three, or a paragraph.

A mark of the careful and considerate writer is the clarity and consistency of his transitions; a mark of the skillful writer is the brevity and deftness of his transitions.

This treatment of the paragraph has been long and detailed, but it is realistic.

The patterns described were not dreamed up but came to light only in the process of analyzing hundreds of paragraphs, a process that started with the hunch that there might be a strict analogy between the structure of long cumulative sentences and the structure of paragraphs. (There are sentences that can be converted into paragraphs, and vice versa, by a simple change in punctuation.) It is not necessary to affirm that all paragraphs fall into these patterns of simple or mixed coordinate and subordinate sequences. Some paragraphs have no discernible pattern, some long ones are more complex than this analysis can readily compass, and some would have to be described as composite —not compound with two or more coordinate parts, but simply under-paragraphing, running two or more loosely related paragraphs together. It is necessary to affirm only that these patterns are real—that they reveal the way an orderly writer works when he keeps his attention equally on his subject and the needs of his reader. Because they are real you can use them with confidence. As you write, they could give you a sense of direction. You should be able to proceed with a paragraph confident sentence by sentence you will know where you are and where you can go next. Most students do not have this sense. With a topic sentence as a point of departure, they simply, as William Hazlitt put it, "gabble at a venture," putting down as they occur whatever thoughts the topic suggests and producing a string of sentences that have about as much order and relation as the marbles in a bag. They merely touch one another; they do not grow like the branches from a trunk.

A clear sense of the structural relations of the sentences a paragraph should serve, to borrow another phrase, this from Wordsworth, both to "kindle and restrain." To kindle, because the sense of a pattern to be filled should prompt, should generate, the thoughts to fill it. To restrain, because the sense of a pattern limits you to what fulfills the pattern.

Finally, it should be recognized that every reader must discern the paragraph patterns as he reads. He must see what goes with what. He must recognize the backtracking and downshifting, the flow and ebb that gives the paragraph its movement. Unless he does, the paragraph will be a blur from which he carries away a name or a number, a striking phrase or an example, without the context that gives it its meaning. We ourselves have been brought to a stand by a complex paragraph until we took time to work out a structural analysis.

EXERCISES

The natural point for starting to master paragraph structure in writing is the simple coordinate sequence—a topic sentence followed by a series of coordinate sentences with like things put in like ways. It is a simple kind of structure, but you may have to fight an ingrained habit of putting down just what comes naturally.

Let us assume as a topic sentence Shakespeare's line "Sweet are the uses of adversity." What we have to do is illustrate the paradox of good emerging from apparent evil. The plural "uses" suggests a coordinate series. The structure thus becomes a means to stimulate invention and a guide to restrain irrelevant flights of fancy or fantasy.

With such an assignment one student wrote this paragraph:

"Sweet are the uses of adversity," for it is in misfortune that a man is truly revealed. Adversity gives rise to dreams and hopes which prosperity might never incite. Adversity educates and strengthens the mind, eliciting talents which under more fortunate circumstances might have lain dormant. Adversity following prosperity challenges a comeback, giving the future a purpose and placing a new value on the lost success. Without experiencing adversity it is difficult to appreciate prosperity. Finally, it is in adversity that the truly noble spirit shines brightest—both that of the afflicted and that of his loyal friend who stands by in spite of everything.

This student must have felt the power of the prescribed form both to kindle and restrain. She must have thought deeply about the paradox and then, *before beginning to write,* must have used the form of a simple coordinate sequence to sort out her thoughts, order them, and give them an appropriate shape. The shape is faulty at only one point: at first glance the fifth sentence seems to be at a third level, but closer inspection shows that it is not a comment on the fourth. It represents another use of adversity, but the difference in form throws the reader off. The slight variation in form is appropriate, though, for the final sentence.

This student has also used free modifiers freely in order to say much within the strict confines of the pattern.

Now consider another response to the same topic:

"Sweet are the uses of adversity." The poet, John Keats, struggled with sorrow and adversity experienced in the finite world. Keats searched for the ideal, but came to the conclusion sorrow and suffering must be accepted as part of the human experience. Beauty must die in order to have existence, for beauty fixed would be cold and inhuman. Alluding to his two poems, "To Autumn" and "Ode to a Nightingale," Keats resolved that autumn, too, has its song. Adversity is a part of living that makes one's human experiences more complete.

The failure of this paragraph matches the success of the other. Its writer evaded the discipline of form and simply gabbled at a venture, garbling some points that might have come up on a survey course. The result is, roughly, a simple *subordinate* sequence with a conclusion, but the fourth sentence is not a comment on the third. In other respects, too, it is a failure—in sentence work, diction, and punctuation. These are so closely interrelated—in this book at least—that you learn all or nothing at all.

A good coordinate sequence could, of course, be written using Keats's life as an example. But the coordinate series would probably be events in his life, such as the withering reviews of *Endymion*, that he somehow turned to advantage. It would take some searching to uncover relevant experiences, but then no one should expect to write off the top of his head. The study and reflection before writing is the nine-tenths of the iceberg that is not seen because it is under water, but that gives what we see its grand simplicity of movement.

Practice with simple coordinate sequences should continue long enough for the form to become second nature. Avoid compound sentences, but use free modifiers in order to amplify the bare statements of the base clauses.

A. For the topic sentences use sentences that include a plural term such as *uses, causes, reasons, results, ways, kinds, stages, needs*. Remember to state like things in like ways.
B. Use for topics materials you are studying in your various courses—in this one, for example, the three methods of description, or the four modes of discourse, or the three uses of internal punctuation.
C. The next paragraph pattern to try is the mixed coordinate sequence. In the successful paragraph you have devised above, a natural step would be to add an example (level 3) to each of the second-level statements. It would be a natural step, too, to elaborate on the example, adding further levels. If this budding process continues, you may find your 500-word paper—the form generating the content.

12
Methods of Support

The last two chapters mapped the channels of the paragraph—the various courses the thought takes in trickling down the levels of generalization. The purpose of this chapter is to examine the supporting thoughts that we find flowing down these channels. The aim in these chapters on the paragraph, as in the parallel treatment of the sentence, is not to control or contain, to constrict or constrain your thoughts, but (by opening up the possibilities) to help you generate thoughts. When you know the possibilities you have a range of choice. Whoever is to call the plays, you will agree, has to know what plays there are to call. And it helps the reader to know what plays have been called.

This chapter should provide for discursive writing the equivalent of the three methods of description used in representational writing. Desirable as that would be, the enormous range of what we can say when we come to *talk about* the world forbids it. The list of methods of support presented in this chapter runs to ten, but it pretends to be no more than useful practically, not to be complete theoretically.

Two circumstances complicate the problem of organization at this point. First, the so-called methods of paragraph development, we have asserted, are simply methods of development, no more relevant to paragraphs than to sentences (the units that constitute paragraphs) or to chapters and essays (the larger units that paragraphs constitute). Although this is true, we are still, in our analysis of the process of writing, at the level of the paragraph. Second, we found that the sentences of the paragraphs are of two sorts—structural and supporting. The topic sentence is structural; the head sentences of any subsequences are structural; the sentences of conclusion are structural. (Note in this paragraph the sharp differentiation of structural and supporting sentences. Three sentences [levels 1 and 2] present the authors' analysis of this problem of organization; the other sentences, giving supporting evidence, are for the reader, who cannot be expected to be a mind reader. The organization of expository units larger than the paragraph, according to our analysis, is dependent on these two sorts of sentences.)

But the repunctuation of the paragraph on the Harvard course (in the last chapter) showed that *structural* and *supporting* are relative terms. Although the terms are relative, the two sorts of sentences, having different functions as we have seen (the one to advance, the other to consolidate the discussion), are logically different. We have looked at structural sentences in the sample paragraphs; we examine now supporting sentences, treating the kinds of paragraph support we are likely to find in contemporary exposition.

The following paragraph illustrates the various facets of our problem. Although you will think it rather heavy, it is well planned. The erratic punctuation makes it especially illuminating. The overall structure is chronological, with two stages, both marked level 2 because there is no superordinate sentence; the alternative would be to call it a compound paragraph. The three sentences marked level 4 also form a chronological sequence. They do have a topic statement ("In the European countries . . . , this happened by stages."), what might, because of the punctuation, be called a "buried" one.

1. 2 Before a single standard language has arisen in any given country, the local dialects are of equal social value: in the early Middle Ages, the speech of Northeastern England, of Scotland, of Southern England were all equally acceptable,
      and
   each person spoke and wrote without hesitation in his own dialect.

2.   3 Likewise in France, Spain, Italy, and the other countries of Europe: in Italy, for instance, thirteenth- and fourteenth-century writers used their own local speech, very little modified under the influence of other Italian dialects:
   Bonvesin da Riva of Milan wrote in Milanese, Jacopone da Todi of Umbria wrote in Umbrian, the anonymous Roman author of the famous Life of Cola di Rienzo (the fourteenth-century republican rebel) used his native Roman dialect, and so forth.

3. 2 But as soon as the dialect of any particular place or region comes to acquire special prestige for nonlinguistic reasons such as political, economic, or cultural dominance, then speakers of other dialects begin to have an inferiority complex concerning their normal native speech, and want to use instead the dialect whose use carries greater prestige.

4.   3 This situation then forces the local types of speech into an
      unfavorable position vis-à-vis the standard language,
            and
      use of a local dialect comes to have the connotation of lower
      social or cultural standing.

5.   4 In the European countries in general, this happened by
      stages: there first arose regional standard languages—
      in France, those of the region around Paris (the so-called
      Ile de France, whose language is termed *Francien*), of Picardy,
      of Normandy, of Champagne, of Southern France (Proven-
      cal, itself based on the speech of several sub-regions); in
      Italy, those of Sicily, of Tuscany, of Lombardy, etc.

6.   4 Then a single region acquired political, economic, or cultural
      dominance over the others, and consequently linguistic
      dominance as well, so that the various regional standards
      were in their turn relegated to the status of inferior social
      acceptability: Francien became the basis of modern standard
      French, because Paris became the capital of France;
      Castilian became the basis of standard Spanish, because
      Madrid became the capital of Spain;
      the English of London and Middlesex became likewise the
      basis of standard English.

7.   4 Finally, with the development of literature in the standard
      language, a split occurs in the standard language itself, a
      more formal or literary variety being distinguished from
      the less formal, everyday, colloquial variety;
            and
      for some whose ideal is that of static perfection defined as a
      set of rigid forms, the literary language (or, in some in-
      stances, even a particular sub-dialect of the literary lan-
      guage, such as poetic usage) becomes the exclusive standard,
      in contrast to which even colloquial standard is unacceptable.
      [Robert A. Hall, Jr., *Linguistics and Your Language*]

In sentence 1, the second part (after the colon) presents an EX-
AMPLE to support the assertion "of equal social value." The first part of
sentence 2 (which is verbless) presents further EXAMPLES. In both sentences, the punctuation is disconcerting. Logic would dictate a period
in place of the colon in both. Periods would separate the structural
from the supporting parts of the sentences and would put the English
and the continental examples on an equal footing.

2 The local dialects are of equal social value . . .
   3 In the early Middle Ages, in England . . .
   3 Likewise in France, Spain, Italy, . . .
      4 In Italy, for instance . . .

Sentence 2 has four levels. The second level ("in Italy, for instance") is clearly labeled an "instance," that is, an EXAMPLE. The third level ("Bonevin da Riva," etc.) presents EXAMPLES of the situation in Italy. The fourth level consists of the parenthetical phrase (the fourteenth-century republican rebel); this tells who Cola di Rienzo was; the method is IDENTIFICATION.

The colon in sentence 5 is illogical in the same way as those in 1 and 2. It confuses the structural and supporting levels. A period is the remedy, and it would not introduce the problem of grouping the sentences, because *first, then,* and *Finally* clearly mark the three stages.

The part of sentence 5 after the colon has three levels. At the second level, the "regional standard languages" of France and Italy are listed. The method is IDENTIFICATION if all of them are listed or EXAMPLES if only some of them (as *etc.* suggests) are listed. In the discussion of France there are two third-level items, the parenthetical elements that IDENTIFY "the region around Paris" and "the regional standard language . . . of Southern France."

In sentence 6, the colon is not illogical. The three clauses that follow combine two kinds of support: EXAMPLES ("Francien became the basis of modern standard French") and CAUSE ("because Paris became the capital of France"). This sentence could be divided into two or four sentences, but this fragmentation would raise the problem of sorting.

The last sentence is compound; the absolute in the first part IDENTIFIES the two varieties that come from the split in the standard language, and it includes a few words of DEFINITION.

The relation of sentence 4 to sentence 3 remains. Sentence 4 describes the EFFECT of the "inferiority complex" of sentence 3.

This analysis of one closely packed paragraph yields five methods of support (identification, example, cause, definition, effect) and it lets us see, merely with differences in punctuation, how some, at least, of the grammatical constructions carrying them may be either full sentences or parts of sentences. The methods of paragraph development are simply methods of development or support. Very few paragraphs use only one method; a single sentence of a paragraph may use several.

In studying these methods, we are trying to find what it is that as writers we can offer our readers (who are not mind readers) to make our generalizations clear or credible. *We* know what our structural sentences mean; the reader doesn't know, except as we add to make them clear. What we add is what Henry James described as the material that acts as "the reader's friend." Close study of a substantial number of paragraphs, our usual inductive procedure, has revealed ten methods that recur often enough to make them worth adding to your rhetorical repertoire. The order of their listing here is roughly from those that merely identify to the more or less argumentative. This order must not be taken as absolute or fixed; analogy, for example, can be used for persuasion as well as for clarification. These methods do not account, either, for all the relations of subordinate to superordinate levels; that is, when you go down from one level to another, you cannot always use one of these labels to blaze the trail. Sometimes it takes a sentence to state the relation.

We will ourselves use one of these methods—citing an authority— to urge upon you the importance of this chapter.

The attempt to identify the form or forms of support in support- ing sentences is an extremely profitable exercise in the basic acts of reason. Their deliberate selection in the process of composition will almost certainly fertilize and refine the entire operation. Conscious em- ployment of this seven-category classification will not only generate ideas but will improve the quality, the logical relevance, of one's thinking. [Albert Upton, *Design for Thinking*]

For each method there will be a brief definition and examples showing the levels of support, first within the sentence and then within the paragraph. Except for the first method, identification, structural analyses have not been made.

IDENTIFICATION

Identification is the writer's response to the anticipated question "What does that mean?" The method is akin to definition, but the expression identified is not an unusual one or one used in a special way. It has not been made clear by the immediate context; the identification is the added level of context that does make it clear.

The identifier is sometimes itself identified, by *that is, i.e., namely.* The conjunction *or* sometimes indicates another thing and sometimes only another name for the same thing; the other name is for identifica- tion.

A. The added level, a pair of noun clusters, identifies the new Angus Wilson.

1 A new Wilson has emerged:
  2 a sympathetic, leisurely explorer of the heart and mind,
  2 an indefatigable auscultator of human sensibilities. [Charles Rolo]

B. This sentence, as the analysis shows, has five added levels, all of them for identification.

1 We were waiting for three persons to join us,
  2 all of them compatriots of ours—
    3 one a twenty-two-year-old American girl,
      4 the daughter of a friend of ours,

    3 the other two a man and his wife,
        4 friends of friends of ours,
            5 neither of whom we had ever met. [James Thurber]

    C. In the second sentence here the parenthetic nouns identify Ibsen in his symbolic disguises.

    This is especially noticeable in *The Master Builder*, where the hero is Ibsen in a symbolic disguise. The master builder (read sound dramatic craftsman) has first built churches (the early poetic plays), then houses for people to live in (the social dramas), and is finally erecting homes with steeples (the late, symbolic plays). [Mary McCarthy]

    D. Here the two added base clauses at the second level distinguish the two men.

1 A good case might be made, for instance, that Jack Straw influenced English more than Chaucer.
  2 Jack Straw was a rabble-rouser who led the mob; Chaucer was a gentleman who entertained the court. [Charlton Laird]

    E. The added sentence identifies the "physical basis" of music.

1 The appeal of music has, like that of the other arts, an explicit and obvious physical basis.
  2 The pitch of a note is determined by the rate of vibration of the air, its color is determined by the presence of overtones, its intensity is dependent upon the amplitude of vibration, its quality by its relative position in the scale. [Irwin Edman]

    F. Here there is identification in both the added compound appositive and the added compound sentence. The author is talking about logical positivism.

1 There are, however, two grave flaws, one in the flower and one in the root.
  2 Experientially, the theory does not do justice to the full nature of either poetic or religious experience;
        and
  logically, it rests upon an arbitrary (and I believe false) presupposition. [Philip Wheelwright]

    G. What the universities owe to black America is what they owe to white America:

    an atmosphere of freedom and dissent for the pursuit of higher learning. [E. D. Genovese]

DETAILS, PARTICULARS

Details are the parts of a whole; particulars are the items of a set of items or the stages of a process or procedure. It is sometimes difficult to tell this method from identification. The difference seems to be that identification does not involve analysis—the reduction of a whole or of a collection to its components. It is a one-to-one or two-to-two relation rather than one to several.

A. The second levels detail the stages when a class reads its own papers.

1 The class, directed by the teacher, should take an active part in making the decisions:
  2 first, about what the papers actually say;
  2 second, about what is commendable;
  2 third, about the serious faults, especially of obscurity, ambiguity, and incompleteness;
  2 fourth, about what might be done to make the papers better;
  2 finally, about the relative value—all things considered—of the specimens in hand. [Commission on English]

B. This expository sentence is like the two-level narrative sentences we have studied. The verb phrases give the details of Professor George Lyman Kittredge's procedure.

He would take a scene from one of Shakespeare's tragedies and go over it word by word, analyzing the precise meaning of every speech, discussing the dramatic values of every shift in the plot, bringing out new psychological undertones, and setting the whole episode in its place until his hearers, finally and unforgettably, understood what the poet had written. [Gilbert Highet, *The Art of Teaching*]

C. The particulars, the sorts of animals collected, are sorted out here into sentences. This passage (from a paragraph with several more sentences) illustrates the use of description and narration in writing whose aim is explanation. The verb phrase added to sentence 2 expresses PURPOSE. The extra sentence on the sea-urchins represents an INFERENCE.

The reef was gradually exposed as the tide went down, and on its flat top the tide pools were beautiful. We collected as widely and rapidly as possible, trying to take a cross-section of the animals we saw. There were purple pendent gorgonians like lacy fans; a number of small spine-covered puffer fish which bloat themselves when they are attacked, erecting the spines; and many starfish, including some purple and gold cushion stars. The club-spined sea-urchins were numerous in their rock niches. They seemed to move about very little, for their niches always just fit them, and have the marks of constant occupation. We took a number of the slim green and brown starfish and the large slim five-rayed starfish with plates bordering the ambulacral grooves. [John Steinbeck, *The Log from the Sea of Cortez*]

EXAMPLES, INSTANCES, ILLUSTRATIONS

All three terms are common, as well as *case, sample,* and *specimen. Illustration* is the broadest, including things other than verbal examples or instances, such as diagrams and pictures. *Example* and *instance* are interchangeable. *Example* and *illustration* have the most usable verbs (*exemplify, illustrate*) and *illustration* the most useful adjective (*illustrative*).

This is one of the most frequent and useful methods of support. As good a test as any of whether a person knows what he is reading or talking about is to ask him for an example—an original one. In writing you should anticipate the reader's demand for an adequate one. It brings you down to cases.

Examples are related to details and particulars. When you offer your readers the details or particulars, you offer them *all* the parts or items or stages; when you offer them an example, you select, as the *Standard College Dictionary* says, "a particular thing that belongs to and is typical of a group of things and that is singled out as having qualities identical with or similar to the qualities of any member of the group." The example *stands for* the group.

You may use a single example or a massed series of examples, even examples within examples (as in A and B). The example itself may be on any scale and in any form, from a single word or phrase dropped in parenthetically (as in the preceding sentence and here in this one) to a narrative of several paragraphs handled with all the artful techniques of fiction. Occasionally the example is not an actual one or one drawn from literature, but a confected or suppositious one, usually marked as such by beginning "Suppose. . . ."

There are two standards for evaluating the choice of an example: it must be truly representative (otherwise it will introduce bias) and it must be managed so as to exemplify what you intend (it must hit the target). You must not expect to establish an argument by a single example or even by a series of examples.

The example is often labeled with *like, as, such as, such . . . as, e.g., thus, for example, for instance.*

A. In the first sentence here *like* labels *talk* as an example. Sentences 2 and 3 exemplify the shift in meaning introduced in sentence 1; the sentences in parentheses are examples.

A verb like *talk* is less affected by its interreliance with the complement than is *lie,* but its meaning shifts as its relation with a complement changes. *Talk* without a complement means "to emit speech" (*He talked and talked*). With a complement *talk* may mean "to give expression to" (*He talked nonsense*). [Charlton Laird, *The Miracle of Language*]

B. The second part of this compound sentence is an example; *such . . . as* indicates that the words in quotation marks are examples of transferred meanings. The sentences in parentheses are also examples.

Many metaphors which we think are normal and self-explanatory seem quite foreign to the speakers of other languages; no speaker of French would ever use *oiseau* "bird" in such transferred meanings as "fellow, guy" (He's a queer old bird) or "a Bronx cheer, or other kind of derisive or unfavorable reception" (He gave us the bird). [Robert A. Hall, Jr., *Linguistics and Your Language*]

C. The sentence begins with elimination; the noun phrase "the psychopathology of everyday life" and "Christine" are identification; examples follow the colon. Semicolons would help sort out the examples.

But Ibsen is not very good at making big events happen; he is better at the small shocking event, the psychopathology of everyday life: Hedda and her husband's aunt's hat, Nora, when she nonchalantly pushes off the sewing on her poor widowed friend, Christine, Hjalmar, when he talks himself into letting Hedwig with her half-blind eyes do his retouching for him so that he can go off and play hunter with his father in the attic, Hjalmar cutting his father at the Werle soiree, Hjalmar eating butter obliviously while his hungry daughter watches him. [Mary McCarthy, *Sights and Spectacles*]

D. The seascape labeled here as an example is not an actual picture but a suppositious one. The example is carefully contrived, in two compound sentences, to illustrate both the negative and the positive points made in the compound head sentence.

It is not sufficient that the picture move us through the vicarious presence on the canvas of a moving object; it must stir us in a more immediate fashion through the direct appeal of sense. For example, a picture which presents us with a semblance of the sea will hold us through the power which the sea has over us; but it will not hold us so fast as a picture of the same object which in addition grips us through its greens and blues and wavy lines. The one sways only through the imagination; the other through our senses as well. [DeWitt Parker, *Principles of Aesthetics*]

E. What the following "cases" illustrate is stated in the paragraph preceding this one. There are seven examples.

But perhaps we should turn to cases. Consider the following: *The bomber blew up.* What is the meaning of *up* in this sentence? Obviously not *up* as the direction opposed to the pull of gravity. The pieces flew in all directions and eventually came down. Nor does *blew* have the meaning we normally associate with the word. *Blow up* has become a new verb, which means "explode." Similarly, *slip* and *on* have meanings in *slip on a dress*, which are different from the meanings of these words in *slip on the ice*. A gunman who *holds up a bank* is not using his biceps for the job, and the boy who *calls up a girl* does not expect her to start climbing a flight of stairs. You can *get over* a disease by lying in bed, and you can *get up* in the morning, if you occupy an upper berth, by getting down. In short, our language is now seeded with complex verbs which mean something that their parts do not mean, and we are so fond of these verbs that we are turning them out (*to turn out* is such a verb) with great industry. [Charlton Laird, *The Miracle of Language*]

DEFINITION

Definition can be handled more fully—where the emphasis is a formal logical definition and the methods of expanding a definition—but here we will consider, with one exception, only the incidental informal definitions that occupy a level in the sentence or a level or two or three in the paragraph.

Definition is akin to the methods of support already listed. Identification is sometimes the same as definition by synonym. Enumerating details or particulars and citing examples are ways of expanding a formal definition.

A. As each of the particulars (the "uses" or "functions") is listed it is defined.

Writers on logic and language usually distinguish between various "uses" or "functions" of language: the "informative" (to convey truth), the "expressive" (to vent feelings or excite them), and the "incitive" (to get people to do things). [Monroe C. Beardsley, *Thinking Straight*]

B. As each of the particulars ("the main sort of repetition") is listed, it is defined and (except the last) exemplified.

The main sorts of repetition are: alliterating, the repetition of a single initial letter (Peter Piper picked peppers); assonance and consonance, the repetition of other vowels and consonants (grave-grain; grave-grove); rhyme, the repetition of the final stressed syllable of a line plus any unstressed that may follow (cat-mat; tenderly-slenderly); and refrain, the repetition of whole phrases or whole lines, commonly at the ends of line-groups or stanzas. [Josephine Miles, *The Ways of the Poem*]

C. The definition ends with an enumeration of particulars; *voice* is defined parenthetically.

The common ingredient that I find in all of the writing I admire—excluding for now novels, plays and poems—is something that I shall reluctantly call the rhetorical stance, a stance which depends on discovering and maintaining in any writing situation a proper balance among the three elements that are at work in any communicative effort: the available arguments about the subject itself, the interests and peculiarities of the audience, and the voice, the implied character, of the speaker. [Wayne C. Booth, "The Rhetorical Stance"]

D. This is an example of the formal logical definition.

Textual criticism is a science, and, since it comprises recension and emendation, it is also an art. It is the science of discovering error in texts and the art of removing it. That is its definition, that is what the name *denotes*. [A. E. Housman, *Selected Prose*]

ELIMINATION, NEGATION

These are two terms for the same method, one in which the writer anticipates the wrong turns the reader is likely to take, the wrong interpretations he is likely to make, and attempts to forestall them. "Don't get me wrong," he seems to say. This method of support is especially common in definitions. It is a natural move for the writer to say first what he does not mean by the term. The examples have been quoted fully enough to show the positive statement that usually follows. In C, though, it comes last.

A. What do the quotation marks around *interesting* mean? Elimination by negative example accounts for what follows the dash in the same sentence.

In spite, or maybe because, of all that has been written on how to acquire friends, exude personality, and dazzle dinner parties, America today boasts pathetically few interesting people. By interesting one means, of course, quite the reverse of "interesting"—quite the reverse of travelers who give memorably minute accounts of their trips to the interior of Kenya; or people who have the ear, or hold the hand, or scratch the back of the great and celebrated. One means people—it seems sad to have to say what one means—who because of their brains, charm, liveliness, responsiveness, wit are a pleasure to be with. And a pleasure whether one wishes to talk sense or nonsense, since the test of interesting people is that the subject matter doesn't matter. [Louis Kronenberger, *Company Manners*]

B. This paragraph clinches an argument that the brain does not receive from the senses a neutral input.

Thus the message which the cat's and frog's eye sends back to the brain, and our eye too, is not an array of light and dark dots like a television tube, but is already a parcel that outlines a bounded and moving shape—a thing. A single fiber does not say to the brain, "My part of the field of vision is dark"; it says "The edge of something is crossing it." The single fiber takes note of all that is going on around a point in its field; it does not send a report from the point that by itself is meaningless; it signals a meaningful piece of a shape. [Jacob Bronowski, *The Identity of Man*]

C. Notice that two sets of three-negative statements are used. How is the second set related to the first? Note the use of identification in the last sentence.

We have seen that the mind achieves freedom, once it is able to seek out meaning in experience. But meaning is not confined to cause-and-effect relations in the physical world, nor, for that matter, to analyses of social behavior. Nor is meaning confined to economic activities. We do not grow roses merely to sell them, we do not form a collection of records just to study acoustics, we do not ask of every book we read: "How will this increase my efficiency at the office?" Meaning has another dimension: the dimension of culture. [Howard Mumford Jones, *One Great Society*]

D. This example shows the method spread over parts of four paragraphs. The first sentence follows the word *denotes* in example D under Definition; the other three are the topic sentences of the next three paragraphs. Even *non fit* in the Latin quotation is elimination.

. . . But I must also say something about what it does and does not *connote*, what attributes it does and does not imply; because here also there are false impressions abroad.

First, then, it is not a sacred mystery. It is purely a matter of. . . .

Secondly, textual criticism is not a branch of mathematics, nor indeed an exact science at all. It deals with. . . .

Textual criticism therefore is neither mystery nor mathematics: it cannot be learned either like the catechism or like the multiplication table. This science and this art require more in the learner than a simply receptive mind; and indeed the truth is that they cannot be taught at all: *criticus nascitur, non fit.* [A. E. Housman, *Selected Prose*]

E. The method may also be contracted and take up only a phrase.

. . . the function of an education is to educate, not to hope that lack of education will be compensated for by the child's natural gifts. [Harold Rosenberg]

RESTATEMENT, REPETITION

These terms are synonymous. The method requires definition. Its essence is to accommodate the reader by rewording what has been said. The shift may be in either direction along such lines as formal/informal, technical/popular, ornate/plain, literal/figurative, native/foreign, standard/nonstandard. The rewording is sometimes at the same level of generalization, sometimes at a lower one. It is akin to the method of identification and sometimes is indistinguishable from it.

A. Here the author explains the reason for restating.

Now apply this principle to the determination of the best method to help a child towards a philosophical analysis of thought. I will put it in more homely style, What is the best way to make a child clear-headed in its thoughts and its statements? [A. N. Whitehead, *The Aims of Education*]

B. This sample contrasts the effects of the automobile and television. Identification is followed by two restatements.

There may thus come about a real shift in social existence, from an all-too-active state to an all-too-passive one, from the benzedrine of being on the go to the bromide of sticking to the chair. From being mindlessly in motion, huge numbers of Americans may sit mindlessly motionless. [Louis Kronenberger, *Company Manners*]

C. Here is an example of multiple restatement. Dubedat is a character in Shaw's *The Doctor's Dilemma.* Study the quotation marks again.

Is Dubedat a great artist, as the doctors and his wife are convinced? Or is he a "great artist" in the sense that they are "eminent physicians"? That is, is he a bit of a hoax, not only in his personal dealings, but in his role of the genius? [Mary McCarthy, *Sights and Spectacles*]

D. To account for the second sentence, we could add to our list of methods INTERROGATION or QUESTION. The general question is restated at lower levels of generality. The final question is general again and serves as a transition (T).

Somewhere in this decoding, the mind takes a critical step from the individual experience to the general law which embraces it. How do we guess the law and form the concepts that underlie it? How do we decide that there are, and how do we give properties to, such invisible things as atoms? That atoms in their turn are composed of more fundamental properties? How do we convince ourselves that there is a universal quantity called energy, which is carried by single quanta, yet which spreads from place to place in a motion like a wave: And that the arrangement of atoms, and still more fundamental particles, consumes or releases energy? How do we come to picture a living process in these dead terms? [Jacob Bronowski, *The Identity of Man*]

COMPARISON-CONTRAST, ANALOGY

Comparison and contrast often go together—for example, on examinations you are asked to compare and contrast classic and romantic or metaphor and simile. The two methods, of course, are opposites: in comparing, you point out the likenesses the two subjects share; in contrasting, you point out their differences. There may be comparison without contrast and contrast without comparison just as, on a paper you have written, you may receive praise without blame or blame without praise.

In using comparison or contrast, or both, you sometimes have, so to speak, a compound subject; the two things you are analyzing (classical and romantic, say) are of equal importance. Such comparisons and contrasts may run to great length. The structure of a paragraph or a chapter or even a book may be so based. At other times, when comparison is used for support, one thing is subordinate to the other, used only as a vehicle for explaining the other. Your subject may be romanticism, but you define it by contrasting it with classicism.

A comparison, as the term is commonly used, may be either literal (young man *like* old man) or nonliteral (man *like* fox or pig or dog or chicken). Here we will be concerned only with the literal.

Analogy is a form of comparison, one used for practical purposes in discursive writing. The term is sometimes applied to literal comparisons, but we will be concerned only with the nonliteral analogy. In using a nonliteral analogy, you have only one subject; the analogy is subordinate, used only as a vehicle to explain the foxy, dogged, piggish, or chicken-hearted nature of man.

A. In this set of examples, analogy is the same as comparison in descriptive-narrative writing; the last one is very close to literal.

Unnecessary precision is pedantic and fussy, like honing a razor to cut butter. [Monroe C. Beardsley]

British taboos are curiously assorted and oftener arbitrary than logical; they correspond to the idioms rather than the grammar of a language. [Louis Kronenberger]

When George Moore began to write his style was poor; it gave you the impression that he wrote on wrapping paper with a blunt pencil. [Somerset Maugham]

Often impressive singly, many of these stories lack individuality; they tend to blur into a muted mass, like a too-lovingly laundered bleeding madras jacket. [William Peden]

His [Walter Savage Landor's] prose demands high marks from the examiner; but unfortunately it refuses to come alive. A dozen critics have noticed that it has the air of a distingiushed translation from some great classical original. [Ian Jack]

B. Analogy may be used in a more practical way—for explanation, as in this account of science in linguistic rather than engineering terms. The analogy is carried out further in the next paragraph. Note the many other methods used.

Plainly, it matters in the most practical way that we rightly understand how we ourselves are embedded in the system of science that we in part discover and in part create. Such a system describes the activity of nature, and ourselves in it; it is not a blueprint of the machinery of nature. We are an active and intimate part of our descriptions of her. Science is not so much a model of nature as a living language for describing her. It has the structure of a language: a vocabulary, a formal grammar, and a dictionary for translation. The vocabulary of science consists of its concepts, all the way from universal gravity and the neutron to the neutron and the unconscious. The rules of its grammar tell us how to arrange its concepts in sensible sentences—that atoms can capture neutrons, for example, and that heavy atoms when they split will release them. And the dictionary then translates these abstract sentences into practical observations that we can test in the everyday world: for example, in the damage that neutrons do when plutonium is split. [Jacob Bronowski, *The Identity of Man*]

C. All the examples above illustrate analogy, the nonliteral comparison. Here the contrast is literal and the two words contrasted are of equal rank. The contrast begun by addition within the first sentence is carried over to an added sentence.

But, as Fowler points out, with his incomparable clarity and subtlety, there is a useful distinction between the words: *explicit* means that something has been expressed clearly and in detail, with nothing left to implication; *express* means that and in addition means that it is worded with intention. That which is promised explicitly is unmistakable in its meaning; that which is promised expressly binds the maker of the promise inescapably. [Bergen and Cornelia Evans, *Dictionary of Contemporary American Usage*]

D. In this paragraph, there is contrast again; the method of support used in making the points of the contrast is explication. Here the subject is compound; the two subjects are not two different things, though, but two aspects of one, the contradictory aspects of art in modern society.

Art communicates, but it is more than communication. It conserves and reinforces social norms, but it destroys them. It is highly traditional and depends on the skills and techniques, the forms and patterns of the past, but it is good only when it is individual, fresh, and novel. It conveys meanings about all of human experience, but its worth is judged to a considerable extent by its internal structure. Finally, art is probably indispensable to society and yet is always a danger to the accepted, the established, and the static, so much so that it is always censored. These are paradoxes that bedevil art criticism and the sociology of art. [Ralph Ross, *Symbols and Civilization*]

EXPLICATION

Of all the methods of support, explication seems to be the commonest, and it was also the most difficult to identify and find a name for. We need both noun and verb, and in English we do not always have paired nouns and verbs that have stayed married in meaning. *Unfold* would be a suitable verb, but *unfoldment* would not do as a noun.

The base of the word *explication* is *plic* (L. *plicare*) as in *imply* and *reply*, which came to English by way of French, and such Latin polysyllables as *implicate, replicate, supplicate, duplicate, triplicate, quadruplicate*, etc., etc. The base *plic* means "to fold." To imply something is to fold that meaning in, as you fold the raisins into the cookie batter; to explicate the meaning of that passage is to unfold, for examination, what was originally folded in.

When you have advanced a generalization, you may devote the paragraph entire, or certain sentences of it, simply to unfolding its implications, going down the scale of generality level by level without ever using any of the methods we have described. It is sometimes as if the paragraph were a set of nested Chinese boxes. The outside box, the topic sentence (level 1), contains all the others; they are folded in or implicit in it. When you lift out the entire set of nested boxes, the one that is now the outermost (level 2) contains all the remaining ones. At other times, the paragraph seems structureless, and reading the sentences one after another is like taking eggs out of a nest one by one to examine them.

In a way, this method is like the category of a classification that is sometimes labeled "other" or "miscellaneous"—passenger cars, trucks, buses, other. You will be tempted to toss into this pigeonhole all the sentences that do not go readily into the others and then forget about them.

A. The two absolutes tell what is implied by "internally related."

Rhythm, sound, and meaning are thus internally related, the rhythm and sound being determined to some extent by the meaning, and the words in a line so emphasized by the rhythm and sound as to clarify and enrich meaning. [Ralph Ross, *Symbols and Civilization*]

B. In this short paragraph we have a set of nested boxes.

1 Youth is imaginative,
     and
 if the imagination be strengthened by discipline this energy of
 imagination can in great measure be preserved through life.
2 The tragedy of the world is that those who are imaginative have
   but slight experience,
      and
   those who are experienced have feeble imaginations.
   3 Fools act on imagination without knowledge; pedants act on
     knowledge without imagination.
     4 The task of a university is to weld together imagination and
       experience. [A. N. Whitehead, *The Aims of Education*]

C. Here again the boxes seem nested, except that the last one is not very clearly an explication of level 4.

1 In contrast to analytic thinking, intuitive thinking characteristically
   does not advance in careful, well-defined steps.
   2 Indeed, it tends to involve maneuvers based seemingly on an
     implicit perception of the total problem.
     3 The thinker arrives at an answer, which may be right or wrong,
       with little if any awareness of the process by which he reached it.
       4 He rarely can provide an adequate account of how he ob-
         tained his answer,
             and
         he may be unaware of just what aspects of the problem he was
         responding to.
         5 Usually intuitive thinking rests on familiarity with the
           domain of knowledge involved and with its structure,
           which makes it possible for the thinker to leap about, skip-

ping steps and employing short cuts in a manner that requires a later rechecking of conclusions by more analytic means, whether deductive or inductive. [Jerome S. Bruner, *The Process of Education*]

CAUSES OR REASONS; EFFECTS OR CONSEQUENCES

One way to look at events is to look for patterns linking event to event, not merely in time, as before and after or antecedent and consequent, but as causes and effects. We want to know what produces an event (What are the causes of freeway accidents?) and what will be produced by an event (Why should one use a seat belt?). There are degrees of precision in our ability to determine causes and effects. In the physical sciences, the procedures are refined and accurate beyond the grasp of the layman; in the other sciences and in the layman's handling of his own affairs, it is often more fitting to speak of reasons and consequences rather than of causes and effects. The difference is often the difference between opinion and fact.

In its synonymy under *reason*, the *Standard College Dictionary* compares and contrasts *reason, purpose, motive, ground*, and *argument* "as they denote the basis of human action."

Human beings have and can give reasons (often "good" rather than the "real" ones) for doing as they do, but other animals do not and nature does not. Natural events have causes rather than reasons; but human beings have reasons for believing this or that to be the cause.

The same dictionary, in the same place, gives this definition of reason:

A *reason* seeks to explain or justify an action by citing facts, circumstances, inducement, and the like, together with the workings of the mind upon them. *Reasons* may include *purpose* and *motive* as internal or subjective elements, and also *grounds* and *arguments* that are external or objective.

This dictionary also compares and contrasts *cause, determinant, antecedent, motive,* and *reason* as "events or circumstances prior to others." The key word here is *prior to* (Latin for the English *before*), but of course not all that goes before is the cause of what comes after. It gives this definition of *cause:*

A *cause*, in strict usage, produces a necessary and invariable effect; more loosely it may be used in the sense of *determinant* to mean one of the prior factors that influence the form, details, or character of an effect without being its sole cause.

Notice that a definition of *effect* is implied in this definition of cause. This dictionary compares and contrasts *effect, consequence, result, outcome,* and *upshot* as referring to "events or circumstances produced by some agency." The agency may be either human or physical. Both human and natural actions have effects or consequences or results.

It is evident that we have here many terms that cannot be really sharply discriminated. Even eminent academic writers do not keep the terms from changing lanes:

> The *reason* that antiquity did not give birth to science was not only *because* fact tended to grow more and more unreal and unimportant. There was an even more cogent *cause:* the ancient world was a place of fear. Magic forces ruled it and magic is absolutely terrifying *because* it is absolutely incalculable. [Edith Hamilton, *The Greek Way*]

The most troublesome terms are *reason* and *because;* both refer to either reasons or causes.

Statements of reason, cause, and effect sometimes provide the structural framework of paragraphs or entire chapters or essays. But reasons often and causes and effects occasionally are cited as support both within the sentence and within the paragraph. Within the sentence they may appear in coordinate clauses marked by *for* and in subordinate clauses marked by *because, since, so that.*

A. In the second sentence, note *contrast.* After the colon notice the reasons given, after the dash the particulars, and after the last comma an analogy (untouchables = rag dolls) in the role of identification.

> Many writers loathe above all sounds the closing of the door which seals them up in their privacy. [Tennessee] Williams, by contrast, welcomes it: it dispels the haze of uncertainty through which he normally converses, and releases for his pleasure the creatures who people his imaginings—desperate women, men nursing troublesome secrets, untouchables whom he touches with frankness and mercy, society's derelict rag dolls. [Kenneth Tynan, *Curtains*]

B. This paragraph is a simple coordinate sequence giving the reasons for calling television a menace. Within the reasons there are other reasons, and among the reasons are the bad effects.

> But in all it is and seemingly ever hopes to be, television is simply a menace to America's cultural and social life. It is a menace just because there it sits, a constant temptation, gratification, time killer, solace: you have it, why not use it? Your book's a wee bit boring, why

not shut it and turn on TV? It is an additional menace, of course,
for being commercially sponsored, and so not only riddled with the
imbecilities of announcers but splotched with the timidities of sponsors.
But it is perhaps most a menace in the sense that the better it is the
worse it must be; that the more skill it exhibits, the more big news
it conveys, the more big names it can boast, the more druglike must
be its hold on vast numbers of people. [Louis Kronenberger, *Company
Manners*]

C. Here *because* means "cause." Each of the three causes is explained by an example. These examples range from the general (some
people) to the specific (Semmelweis).

There are always segments of reality about which we are
ignorant, whether because we are not interested—some people feel
no urge to study history, geology, or chemistry—or because we have
had no opportunity to learn—what could the Eskimo know of life in
the tropics?—or because nobody has yet remarked, investigated, and
called attention to a particular fact—Semmelweis was assailed as a
crackpot and a subversive when he suggested that midwives could halt
the spread of puerperal fever by washing their hands between cases.
[Joseph Church, *Language and the Discovery of Reality*]

EVIDENCE AND AUTHORITY

Many of the statements by which we advance the thought of our paragraphs have an argumentative edge. They are assertions whose truth,
whose validity, whose desirability is not self-evident. The reader (let
us hope we have a critical reader) is likely to challenge them and to
ask us for the evidence for what is not self-evident. The evidence may
be facts or opinions which substantiate the assertions. The opinions
may be those of authorities assumed to be qualified.

A. The quotation dropped in parenthetically is evidence for
Keats's sensitivity.

Since Keats was exceptionally sensitive to the personalities
of his correspondents—"I wish I knew always the humor my friends
would be in at opening a letter of mine, to suit it to them as nearly as
possible"—it is natural to inquire who they were. [Ian Jack]

B. The topic sentence could begin "There is evidence. . . ." The
paragraph has only two levels plus a conclusion. The evidence is in the
form of examples.

There are even signs that the current generation of students is
rousing itself from its beauty sleep. Honor students at the University

of Wisconsin petitioned last year for more strenuous challenges. At Smith College, student sentiment seems overwhelmingly in favor of independent study starting in the freshman year. A Harvard student-council report lashed out at the idea that a "non-committed objective stance is the only one that is scholarly and scientific." We may yet see that "wholly awakened man" whom Woodrow Wilson called for. [David Boroff, *Harper's*, April 1960]

C. Here the author does label his examples as evidence, in the last sentence. The first sentence is transitional; the second states the topic.

If thinking is a wholly verbal activity, only human beings past infancy should be able to think. Yet it is perfectly clear, if only from the problem-solving behavior of chimpanzees, that animals can think. They can even think and plan ahead, as shown in an account of the chimpanzee who, whenever a new visitor came to the primate laboratory, got a mouthful of water and waited innocently until the visitor came near his cage, then he would give him a thorough spraying. Introspective accounts of creative thinking, such as those of mathematical thinking by Hadamard and Poincaré, suggest that much thinking, and sometimes the most fruitful kind, goes on unconsciously and apparently wordlessly. We all know the kind of experience described by St. Augustine: "When you do not ask me, I know; when you ask me, I do not know," indicating that though words may fail us, thought does not. There is abundant evidence that some types of human concept formation can take place without verbalization. [Joseph Church, *Language and the Discovery of Reality*]

D. Mary Shelley was an authority on Shelley, though not always an unbiased one perhaps, and her testimony and Shelley's own are cited here to remove a misconception.

It is a paradox that Shelley is often described as a "pure poet." In fact, as Mary Shelley pointed out, he combined two qualities of intellect that are not often associated in so high a development: "a brilliant imagination" and "a logical exactness of reason." As a consequence he 'deliberated at one time whether he should dedicate himself to poetry or metaphysics,' and it can only have been after anxious consideration that he decided to be a poet. Although we are told that he then began to educate himself for poetry by "engaging . . . in the study of the poets of Greece, Italy, and England," it is possible to exaggerate the extent to which he discarded "his philosophical pursuits." When he was at work on *Prometheus Unbound* he could still tell Peacock that he considered poetry "very subordinate to moral and political science," adding that he would have devoted himself to the latter study if he had been more robust. This makes it the less surprising that he is one of the most didactic of all our poets. [Ian Jack, *English Literature*, 1815–1832]

OTHER METHODS

If this set of ten methods of support leaves us out of breath with exertion, the remedy is not to cut the list, but to improve our intellectual capacity, even to the point where we can add to an admittedly limited list. Other methods that might have been included—and that you will encounter in your reading and have use for in your writing—are these: CATEGORIZATION, the opposite of particulars; LIMITATION, a narrowing of the range of the topic; various logical operations, such as INFERENCE, close to explication, the result of a deductive or inductive movement of thought, and GENERALIZATION and SUMMATION, the content often of the sentences we have marked conclusion (C); and various kinds of validation, such as CONCESSION, JUSTIFICATION, and EVALUATION.

The analogy used at the beginning of this chapter should encourage you. These methods are the plays you can call in writing. Many students write the way a bunch of kids play sandlot football. They have no repertoire of plays. When the ball is snapped, every kid is on his own and any progress the ball carrier makes is likely to come from his being ignored by everyone on both sides. Like football players, writers need chalk sessions or skull sessions. It isn't enough to gabble at a venture. You should know these methods well enough so that their use becomes habitual: you should identify, enumerate, define, explicate as naturally as you sign your name.

THE WRITER'S OBLIGATION

Sometimes it is easier to explain the obligations of the writer by considering the problems of the reader. When you read, going from sentence to sentence, you must see the relation of each sentence to the sentences that precede it. Does it advance the discussion or not; that is, does it move on to a new window, or does it look into the one you are already standing before? If it does not advance to a new position, is it subordinate to the preceding sentence? If it is not subordinate, it should be coordinate (if the paragraph is well written) with either the preceding sentence or one farther back. This is the substance of the last chapter. No one can read rapidly or well who cannot trace these twistings and turnings. It is a fair guess that many who are poor readers are poor because they lack this navigational skill. Besides recognizing these very general relations, the good reader will recognize also the more specific logical relations involved, the methods of support.

But even this is not enough. The good reader is also the critical reader. He is not a passive recipient of the writer's meaning. He reacts to it critically, testing its *validity*. One must write for a reader who will question the validity, the soundness, of whatever he reads. The gullible reader is no worthy opponent.

EXERCISES

A. All of these sentences have a common element—the familiar free noun phrase. Determine the method of support each represents.

1. Spell out all numbers if you can do it in two words—twenty-three, forty, 137.
2. I propose to offer two apologies for our species, the one defensive the other penitential. [Ernest Hooten]
3. Standard ways of speaking are like standard light bulb sockets, an efficient convenience. [Walter Loban]
4. A prejudice is a *prejudgment*, a conclusion reached *before* any real evidence is in. [W. W. Watt]
5. Intellectually he is a nothingness, like interstellar space—a vast vacuum occasionally crossed by homeless, wandering clichés. [John Gunther]
6. Just because we may have some irrational economies, treasuring scraps of orange peel, like Dr. Johnson, saving old newspapers, hats, gloves, attic rubbish of all kinds, is no reason for neglecting the virtue of economy altogether. [G. P. Krapp]
7. But conversation of this kind is really a kind of disease of language, a dysentery of words that may make one a popular orator or merely a tedious bore, in short a practitioner in mere words without control or intelligence behind them. [G. P. Krapp]
8. Such a demonstration combines two important matters, tight focus on a problem of sufficient general importance to warrant attention by the whole class and vigorous criticism by a live and varied audience. [Commission on English]
9. This is a tall order, but its size is proportionate to the one acceptable goal, that of teaching students above all to be honest in their writing. [Commission on English]
10. Then the poet makes a final ironic gesture ("Rejoic'd they were na *men* but *dogs*") before ending with the quiet matter-of-factness with which he had opened. [David Daiches]
11. I know of no test of the genuineness of art other than that suggested by Ruskin—the sense of "getting at the root" and of "holding this by the heart." [Herbert Read]
12. Some of our failures are due to causes we have already noticed —our prejudices which lead us to distort the evidence, our

keeping our minds in blinkers and thus closed against criticism
and incapable of further reflection, our habit of using words
repeated parrot-fashion, and our fear of being dragged from
the shelter of our comforting beliefs. [L. S. Stebbins]

13. The difference is not so much in the message as in the over-
    tones, the inferences we make concerning the speaker's or
    writer's intentions and frame of mind, his social and educational
    status. [Hans Guth]

14. [In the past century] we have had either ideological history,
    the search for and supposed isolation of laws manifesting them-
    selves in the flow of events, or else a drear cataloguing of
    facts, a lawyer's sifting of evidence, a bookkeeper's inventory
    of bare bones. [Sidney Alexander]

15. Inversion and variation of the uncalled for kinds are like
    stiletto heels: ugly things resorted to in the false belief that
    artificial things are more beautiful than nature. [H. W. Fowler]

B. These sentences all have a common added element, the familiar free
   verb phrase. Determine the method of support.

1. *Chipmunk* is related to the Ojibwa *atchitamon*, meaning squirrel and referring to the animal's habit of coming down a tree
   head first. [H. L. Mencken]

2. For ten lines he develops this aspect of his subject, etching
   one after another little scenes of conviviality. [David Daiches]

3. Burns has changed the key of the passage, transposed it into
   an idiom that is partly derived from folklore and partly based on
   a Scots literary tradition that owes nothing to the Bible. [David
   Daiches]

4. It is one of Burns's slighter poems, but shows him the complete master of his idiom, treating the subject with a laughing
   abandon while retaining a sure hold of his technique. [David
   Daiches]

5. In December 1941 I put the manuscript away, knowing that
   so much was going to happen to the world and to me that if I
   ever went back to the book, it would be to start all over again.
   [Walter Lippmann]

6. "Wonder for Huckleberry Finn" is the best piece in the collection, synthesizing with rare critical insight and revitalized
   interest the not inconsiderable studies of that novel which
   American scholarship and criticism have accumulated. [Philip
   Rahv]

7. A simile may be worked out at some length, involving detailed
   comparisons between several points of resemblance. [L. S. Steb-
   bins]

8. The Greek mind was free to think about the world as it pleased, to reject all traditional explanations, to disregard all the priests taught, to search unhampered by any outside authority for the truth. [Edith Hamilton]

9. A fiddler is a merry andrew, to be paid with drinks and patronizing; a violinist is a musician, admired and often richly rewarded. [Bergen Evans]

10. April is the cruelest month, breeding
    Lilacs out of the dead land, mixing
    Memory with desire, stirring
    Dull roots with spring rain.
    T. S. Eliot, "The Waste Land"

C. Each of these passages includes a variety of methods of support, both within the sentence (as in Exercises A and B) and by compounding and adding sentences. Identify the structures used for support and the method of support. There may be some sentences and sentence fractions that do not answer to any of the ten methods listed; here is an opportunity for you to round out that list. Some items may seem to answer to more than one of the ten methods; this is possible since restatement and negation, for example, may be used for definition, and details may be causes, examples, and so on.

1. The fact remains . . . that men spoke long before they wrote and that writing is still a secondary representation of speech. More precisely, we might say that writing, a secondary representation of speech, has been and is used to record only certain *kinds* of speech, not anything and everything that men say. [James Sledd]

2. The truth of *Huckleberry Finn* is of a different kind from that of *Tom Sawyer*. It is more intense truth, fiercer and more complex. *Tom Sawyer* has the truth of honesty—what it says about things and feelings is never false and always both adequate and beautiful. *Huckleberry Finn* deals directly with the virtue and depravity of man's heart. [Lionel Trilling]

3. To read *Huckleberry Finn* young is like planting a tree young—each year adds a new growth ring of meaning, and the book is as little likely as the tree to become dull. [Lionel Trilling]

4. We first notice that the statement "Helen went to Chicago last week to see her mother," is a highly condensed version of the actual event, that it omits a great deal. It does not say why Helen chose this time to visit her mother, what mode of transportation she used, what she saw or did along the way, where she stayed while in Chicago, what she and her mother talked

about, whether Helen is still in Chicago or has now returned. [Joseph Church]

5. A major distinction between primitive and advanced cultures is that the former are "closed" and the latter "open." That is, the primitive culture is static; it contains no gaps or ambiguities or mysteries; everything is accounted for; everything is ordained according to fixed principles, so that change can come about only very slowly and gradually. [Joseph Church]

6. The Freudian psychoanalysts analyze the personality topographically into a primary id, the sum of inherited impulses or cravings; the ego, which is thought of as being built upon the id through the progressive development of the sense of external reality; and the superego, the socially conditioned sum of forces which restrain the individual from the direct satisfaction of the id. [Edward Sapir]

7. I am using the word "feeling" not in the arbitrarily limited sense of "pleasure or displeasure" to which psychologists have often restricted it, but on the contrary in its widest possible sense, i.e. to designate *anything that may be felt*. In this sense it includes both sensation and emotion—the felt responses of our sense organs to the environment, of our proprioceptive mechanisms to internal changes, and of the organism as a whole to its situation as a whole, the so-called "emotive feelings." [Susanne K. Langer]

8. The best guarantee of an adequate conceptual formulation is that it suddenly does away with what may seem like a purely literary temptation—the constant temptation to use metaphors and stock phrases (such as nature's plans, nature's experiments) which embody obsolete theories. [Susanne K. Langer]

9. If the work of such literary artists as Proust, Mann, Yeats, and Eliot is difficult and complex, it is surely because it reflects a highly intellectualized consciousness, the artist's resolve not to simplify his imaginative experience and psychic obsessions, to remain true to the conviction that compels him even in the teeth of convention and tradition. [Philip Rahv]

10. In the Meredith lines—

Lovely are the curves of the white owl sweeping
   Wavy in the dusk lit by one large star—

certain contributory lures and graces are obvious—the engaging "Sing a song o' sixpence" melody, the play that is made with a few picked consonants, winged and liquidly gliding, and the winning way the second line is retarded at its close by the three stressed monosyllables, like a well-mannered horse pulled up by a well-mannered rider. [C. E. Montague]

11. But no language consists of signs that only call attention to things without saying anything about them—that is, without asserting or denying something. All languages we know have a fairly stabile vocabulary and a grammatical structure. No language is essentially exclamatory (like ah! and oh!) or emotional (like whining and yodeling), or even imperative. The normal mode of communicative speech, in every human society, is the indicative; and there is no empirical evidence, such as the correlation of increasing discursiveness with increasing culture, to support the belief that it was ever otherwise. [Susanne K. Langer]

12. There is no lack of evidence of the waning interest in poetry at this time. Within a few weeks of Byron's death we find a writer in *Blackwood's* remarking that nowadays 'few write poetry . . . and nobody at all reads it. Our poets . . . have over-dosed us.' Although Wordsworth's reputation continued to rise among people seriously interested in poetry, it took Longmans four years to exhaust the five hundred copies of the collected edition which they published in 1820. There was a reaction even against Byron, while new poetry was not in demand. Publishers did not dare to meddle with poetry: it is startling to find John Taylor, the friend and publisher of Keats, describing himself in 1830 as 'no publisher of poetry now.' [Ian Jack, *English Literature, 1815–1832*]

D. These statements are all drawn from a book on straight thinking. Choose one (or more, as your instructor directs) and imagine it to be your own, to be the topic sentence of a paragraph you must write for a paper you are working on. Your task is not to dispute or test the validity of the topic sentence but, assuming its validity, to explain it or make it persuasive to your reader. Write the paragraph with careful attention to structure and methods of support. Make it as long as you can sustain the sequence of sentences and exploit the methods of support for the reader's understanding. (Don't rely on vague and trite historical instances.)

1. Ability to read is not synonymous with ability to reflect on what is read.

2. The strength with which we hold a belief ought to have some proportion to the amount of evidence upon which it is based.

3. Enthusiasm is not necessarily the enemy of thinking; it is indispensable for achieving great and difficult tasks. The danger

arises from the feeling that the passionateness of a belief provides any guarantee of its truth.

4. The truth is rarely pure and never simple. [Oscar Wilde]
5. In some disputes the right is on one side alone.
6. A person capable of making a reasoned condemnation does not need to shout.
7. It is not emotion that annihilates the capacity to think clearly, but the urge to establish a conclusion in harmony with the emotion and regardless of the evidence.
8. I am concerned with only two broadly described varieties—those whose minds are relatively open and those whose minds are relatively closed.
9. The demand that a generalization should be applied to [i.e., tested by] particular instances often shows the need for an explicit qualification of the generalization by restricting its scope.
10. A firm belief in the righteousness of their own cause has seemed to many otherwise honest people to justify any methods of winning adherents to it.

E. A brief essay is the logical next step. You may expand on one of the quotations in D, or select from some proposed by your class or your instructor. You may not be able to outline your essay before you begin, but as you develop your thoughts on paper you will discover that you are generating the two kinds of expository sentences that build an essay: the structural ones—the introduction or preliminaries (if you have them), the topic sentence and subtopic sentences, the transitions, the conclusions; and the supporting sentences—those that give the evidence to the reader, that employ the methods of expository development that you have been studying.

Index

Absolute, the, 23, 25–28, 32–37, 48, 182
Abstraction, levels of, 8–9
Abstract term, defined, 8
Abstract words, 8
Action
  depicted by narration, 20
  described, 86–87
    by details, 33
Addition
  and multilevel sentences, 33–36
  point making and, 6–7
Adjective phrases, 47–48
  free, 23
Adjective plus adjective, 47
Adjectives, 7, 11–12, 24, 63
  descriptive, 12
  single-word, 16
Adverbs, 22, 24, 34
  describing attributes, 33
  of manner, 21
  noun, 34
  single-word, 16
"After the Ball Is Over," 102
Agee, James, 25, 48, 63, 79
Alexander, Sidney, 40, 49, 189
Analogy, 179–180
Anderson, Sherwood, 30
Appositive noun phrase, 42–51
  exercises for, 51–54
Argumentation, 19
Aristotle, 85
Atlantic Monthly, 114
Attributes, 69, 79
  adverbs describing, 33
Authority, 185–187

Bates, H. E., 79, 80, 81
Beardsley, Monroe C., 138, 175, 179
Bellow, Saul, 50–51, 61, 70
Benson, Sally, 52
Bienfang, Ralph, 66n.
Blake, William, 4
Bloomfield, Morton W., 157
Booth, Wayne C., 176
Boroff, David, 185–186
Bowen, Elizabeth, 103
Boyle, Kay, 63
Bradley, A. C., 161
Brain, mind and, 4
Bromfield, Louis, 79
Bronowski, Jacob, 136, 177, 179, 180
Bruner, Jerome S., 183
Bundy, McGeorge, 137

Cable, Mary, 47
Canfield, Dorothy, 105
Capote, Truman, 48
Carroll, Gladys H., 50
Cary, Joyce, 65
Categorization, 187
Cather, Willa, 26, 29, 30, 50, 52, 73, 99
Causes, 169, 183–185
Chase, Mary Ellen, 106–107
Church, Joseph, 5, 185, 186, 191
Clark, Walter Van Tilsburg, 13, 29, 40,
    56, 59, 61, 62, 72
Clauses, 12
  base, 16–17, 32, 36, 42–43, 46, 127, 158
  main, 7–8
  relative (RC), 23, 48

Clauses (*Continued*)
  restrictive, 11
  subordinate (SC), 17, 23, 33
Coatsworth, Elizabeth, 32
Cobb, I. J., 61
Cognition, 4
Coherence, paragraph, 148–149
Colons, 168–169
Columbia Encyclopedia, 134–135
Commas, 15–16
Commission on English, 172, 188
Comparisons, 63, 179–180
Concessions, 187
Conclusion or coda, 37
  to paragraph, 160
Concrete words, 8
Conjunctions, 170
  coordinate, 16–17
Consequences, 183–185
Consonants, 59
Contrast, 179–180
Cook, Whitfield, 74
"Cool Web, The," Graves, 5
Coordination, sentence, 142–143
"Craft of Writing, The," Erskine, 6–7
Crane, Stephen, 61, 102
Cumulative sentences, 8, 127

Daiches, David, 188, 189
Dark Labyrinth, The, Durrell, 17
Dashes, 15, 17
Data, overload of, 4
Davis, H. L., 108
Deasy, Mary, 62, 74
Definition, 175–176
  formal logical, 176
Derleth, August, 34
Description, 19
  appositive noun phrase in, 42–54
  defined, 20, 24
  dominant tone and, 98
  items and, 99, 102–103
  narration and, 46, 98, 112, 114
  three methods of, 24, 166
    by attribute, 24, 45
    by comparison, 24, 45
    by detail, 24–25, 44–45
Detail, 24–25, 99n., 172–173
  action described by, 33
  defined, 172
Direction of movement, 7–8, 127
Discursive writing, 45, 166
  explanation in, 133

introduction to, 126–141
  paragraph defined in, 131
Doctor's Dilemma, The, Shaw, 178
Dominant tone, 97–103
  and choice of subjects, 100–103
  exercises for, 103–109
  subjects for, 100–103
  techniques for, 98–100
Dos Passos, John, 68, 70, 73, 74, 80
Durrell, Lawrence, 17, 50, 60, 61, 62, 64, 65

Edman, Irwin, 171
Effects, 169, 183–185
Elegant variation, avoidance of, 29
Elimination, 176–178
Eliot, T. S., 102, 113, 190
Ellison, Ralph, 40
Emerson, 58
Emotions, 98
Emphasis
  paragraph, 149
  punctuation and, 15
English courses, 5
English language, 59
"Ensnare the Clouds," Coatsworth, 32
Erskine, John, 6–7
"Estate, The," Singer, 16
Evaluation, 187
Evans, Bergen, 161, 181, 190
Evans, Cornelia, 161, 181
Evidence, 185–187
Examples, 168–169, 173–175
  labeling of, 174
Explanation
  avoidance of, 28
  in discursive writing, 133
Explication, 181–183
Exposition, 19, 112, 114
Extended sequence, cumulative nature of, 126–127
Extrasequential sentences, 159–164

Faulkner, William, 26, 27, 33, 34–35, 38, 40, 47, 49, 50, 58, 61, 62, 67, 69, 75, 79–80
Feelings, sharing and communication of, 97–98
Fenton, Edward, 38
Finnegans Wake, Joyce, 10
Fitzgerald, F. Scott, 13, 48, 49, 51, 68, 69, 75
Flaubert, 14, 85

Fowler, H. W., 180, 189
Francis, W. Nelson, 151
Fromm, Erich, 4
Frost, Robert, 13
Frye, Northrop, 161

Generality, levels of, 8–9, 127
Generalization, 139, 166, 181, 187
General term, defined, 8
Genovese, E. D., 171
Glazier, Lyle, 58
Gordimer, Nadine, 49, 77
Grapes of Wrath, The, Steinbeck, 9, 17, 59, 100
Graphic representation, 36–37
Grau, Shirley Ann, 30, 50
Graves, Robert, 5
Great Books courses, 6
Guth, Hans, 189
Guthrie, A. B., 29

Hall, Robert A., Jr., 168, 174
Hamilton, Edith, 184, 189
Harper's Magazine, 114
Harriss, R. P., 62
Harvard Committee, 149, 167
Haskins, Charles Homer, 147
Hazlitt, William, 163
Headword, 7
  choice of, 58
  noun, 61–64, 73, 78–79
  verb, 60–61, 72, 78–79
Hemingway, Ernest, 24, 34, 37–38, 47, 57–58, 60, 62, 64, 71, 72, 73, 75, 76, 79, 111, 113
Highet, Gilbert, 138, 146, 172
Hoffer, Eric, 159
Hooten, Ernest, 188
Horner, George, 74
Housman, A. E., 176, 177
Huxley, Aldous, 36, 61
Huxley, Julian, 152

Ibsen, 171, 174
Identification, 169–171, 177–178
Illustration, 173–175
Impression, 97
Inference, 172, 187
  avoidance of, 28
Infinitive phrases, 112
Instances, 173–175
Interpolated comments, 37
Irony, 153

Items, description and, 99, 102–103
Ives, Sumner, 137

Jack, Ian, 180, 185, 187, 192
James, Henry, 13, 169
"Jockey, The," McCullers, 15
Johnson, Wendell, 144, 155
Jones, Howard Mumford, 177
Joyce, James, 10, 46, 113
Justification, 187

Kazin, Alfred, 67, 69, 71, 78, 101
Keats, John, 14, 86, 100, 165
Kittredge, George Lyman, 172
Kluckhohn, Clyde, 160
Knight, Arthur, 98, 103
Krapp, G. P., 188
Kronenberger, Louis, 177, 178, 180, 185

Laird, Charlton, 171, 174, 175
Langer, Susanne K., 141, 191, 192
Language
  defined, 5
  grammatical, 22
  mastery of, 5
  as medium of writing, 3
  as opening to reality, 6
  outwitting of, 10
  paradox of, 3–4
  of the senses, 55–81
  as a shield, 5
  use of, 3, 7, 10
Lawrence, D. H., 36, 60
"Leaning Tower, The," Porter, 101
Learning to write, 86
"Letter from the South, A," White, 113
Levels of generality, 8–9, 127
Lewis, Sinclair, 34, 104–105
Limitations, 187
Lindbergh, Anne Morrow, 53, 63, 80, 106
Lippmann, Walter, 155, 189
Lloyd, Donald J., 158
Loban, Walter, 188

McCarthy, Mary, 74, 112, 171, 174, 178
McCullers, Carson, 15
Madame Bovary, Maupassant, 85
Mailer, Norman, 68
Mansfield, Katherine, 47, 72, 73
Man with the Golden Arm, 98
Maslow, Abraham H., 5
Master Builder, The, Ibsen, 171
Maugham, Somerset, 180

Maupassant, Guy de, 14, 85
Meaning, modifiers and, 13–14
Memory, selective, 5
Mencken, H. L., 189
Metaphor, 58n.
Methods of support, 166–188
    by causes or reasons; effects or con-
        sequences, 183–185
    by comparison-contrast, analogy, 179–
        181
    by definition, 169, 175–176
    by elimination, negation, 176–178
    evidence and authority as, 185–187
    by examples, instances, and illustra-
        tions, 168–169, 173–175
    exercises for, 188–193
    by explication, 181–183
    by identification, 169–173
    other, 187
    by restatement, repetition, 178–179
Miles, Josephine, 176
Milne, Lorus, 66n.
Milne, Margery, 66n.
Mind, the, 4
Mitchell, Stephen O., 137
Mixed sequences in paragraphs, 149–150
    coordinate, 150–153, 155
    subordinate, 153–154
Modifiers
    bound, 8
    converting nouns into, 22
    free, 8, 12, 36, 43–45
        exercises in identifying, 15–18
        final, 15–16, 36
        initial, 15–16, 36
        medial, 15–16, 27n., 36
    meaning and, 13
    noun with an adverbial function, 23–24
    sentences and, 7
    single-word, 11, 22
Montague, C. E., 148
Moore, Marianne, 13
Morley, Christopher, 61
Morris, Wright, 23
Morrison, Theodore, 153
Moulton, William G., 144, 147

Narration, 19, 100
    defined, 20, 24
    description and, 46, 98, 100, 112, 114
    sense impressions in, 56–57
Narrative details, 74–75

Narratives
    action in, 86–87
        examples of, 88–89
        examples of, analyzed, 90–93
    longer, 110–114
        exercises for, 114–125
    short, 85–93
        exercises for, 93–96
    time in, 87
Narrative sentences
    multilevel, 32–39
        analyzing and writing of, 39
        discrimination of levels in, 38–39
        exercises for, 39–41
        relationship of additions to, 33–36
    two-level, 19–29
        exercises for, 29–31
Nash, Mary, 80
Nathan, Robert, 38, 63
Negation, 176–178
Nervous system, selectivity of, 4
New Yorker, 113
Norris, Frank, 124
Noun cluster, free, as sentence, 50
Noun headwords, 61–64, 73, 78–79
    literal, 61
Noun phrases, 34, 45–51, 103
    appositive, 42–54
    bound, 46
    defined, 45
    free, 23, 46, 48
Nouns
    abstract, 62
    coined, 62
    converted into modifiers, 22
    ending in -ing, derived from verbs, 61
    metaphorical, 62
    parenthetic, 171
    qualifying of, 7

O'Connor, Flannery, 47
Octopus, The, Norris, 123
Open Boat, The, Crane, 102
Ox-Bow Incident, The, Clark, 13, 23,
    27n., 59, 110

Packer, N. H., 30
Paragraph development, 127, 166, 169
Paragraphing, 126–134
    exercises for, 134–141
    problem of, 127–128
Paragraphs, 85–89
    analogy in, 180–181
    base sentence of, 127

Paragraphs (*Continued*)
  building of, 126–127
  causes or reasons in, 183–185
  complex, 163–164
  compound, 157–158
  conclusions or codas to, 160, 166
  defined, 128, 131, 142
  effects or consequences in, 183–185
  elimination in, 176–178
  evidence and authority in, 185–187
  exercises for writing, 93–96
  explication in, 181–183
  with extrasequential sentences, 159–
    164
  framework, 131
  graphic devices to mark, 128
  indentation of, 128
  introductions to, 160
  length of, 131–132
  mixed sequences in, 149–154
  with no discernible pattern, 163
  with no topic sentences, 155–157
  organization of, 128–132
  punctuation by, 12, 132–133
  punctuation of, 143, 149, 167
  restatement in, 178–179
  series of sentences in, 133
  simple coordinate sequence in, 143–147
  simple subordinate sequences in, 147–
    149
  structural analysis of, 129–133
  structure of, 142–164
    chronological, 167
    exercises for, 164–165
  student examples of, 88–89
    analysis of, 90–93
  study of, 127
  texture of, 127
  topic or thesis sentence of, 154–159
Parentheses, 15
Parker, DeWitt, 174
Particulars, 172–173
Peattie, Donald Culross, 60, 63, 68, 70, 80
Peden, William, 180
Periods, 168–169
  in place of commas, 50
Person, first or third, 86–87
Personification, avoidance of, 28
Phonemes, 59–60
Phrases, 12
  adjective, 47
  appositive noun, 42–54
  free adjective, 23

free adverbial, 23
free noun, 23, 46
  infinitive, 112
  noun, 34, 42–51
  propositional, 22, 25, 34, 47–48
  verb, 22, 25–28, 33–37, 47–48, 172
"Pigeon Feathers," Updike, 124
Point making, addition and, 6–7
Porter, Katherine Anne, 25, 27, 29, 46,
    48, 49, 52, 55, 62, 70, 101
Potter, Simeon, 138–139, 141
Predicate, the, 25
Preminger, Otto, 98, 103
Prepositional phrases, 22, 25, 34, 47–48
Prepositions, 22
Primer style, 11
Punctuation, 7, 12
  emphasis and, 15
  by paragraph, 12, 132–133
  of paragraphs, 143, 149, 167
Purpose, 172
Pyles, Thomas, 138, 141

Rahv, Philip, 189, 191
Randall, J. H., Jr., 136
Read, Herbert, 61, 188
Readers
  controlling feelings of, 97–98
  and paragraph patterns, 164
  problems of, 187–188
  writers and, 149, 152, 158–159, 167,
    169, 176
Reality, language as opening to, 6
Reasons, 183–185
Reminiscence, 112
Repetition, 178–179
Restatement, 178–179
Rhetorical analysis, 24
Rhetorical elements, 24
  grammatical elements and, 25–28
Roberts, Elizabeth Madox, 47, 73
"Rocking-Horse Winner, The,"
    Lawrence, 36
Rolo, Charles, 170
Rosenberg, Harold, 178
Ross, Ralph, 181, 182
Ruskin, John, 28
Russell, Bertrand, 163

Sapir, Edward, 191
Schorer, Mark, 23
Semicolons, 16
Senses, language of, 55–64
  exercises for, 64–66, 70–71

Sentences
   base clause in, 16–17, 32, 36, 42–43, 46, 127, 158
   cause in, 169
   comparison-contrast, analogy, in, 179–181
   compound, 9, 16, 153
   coordinate, 157
   cumulative, 8, 127, 163
   definition in, 169, 175–176
   examples in, 169, 173–175
   extrasequential, 159–164
   free elements of, 37
   grouped into paragraphs, 128–132, 144
      length of, 132
   identification in, 169–171, 177
   introductory, 133
   modifiers and, 7
   narrative. *See* Narrative sentences
   ordering a series of, 133
   punctuation of, 168
   putting like things in like ways in, 133–134, 142, 144, 152
   restatement in, 178–179
   structural and supporting, 122, 145, 166–167
   subject of, 20, 23
   subtopic, 150, 157
   topic or thesis, 154–160, 162–163, 166, 185
   transitional, 162–163, 186
   typical modern English, 7–8
   verbless, 103, 168
Sentimentality, avoidance of, 29
Severn, Joseph, 14
Shakespeare, 164
Shakespearean Tragedies, Bradley, 162
Sharp, William, 14
Shaw, G. B., 178
Shepard, Odell, 61
Sight, sense of, 56–58
Simile, 58*n*.
Simple coordinate sequence, 143–147, 155
Simple subordinate sequences, 147–149
   coherence of, 148–149
   emphasis in, 148
   unity in, 148
Singer, Isaac Bashevis, 16
Sledd, James, 190
Smell, sense of, 56–58, 66–69
   attributes and, 69
   comparison and, 70
   effect and, 70

   exercises for, 70–71
   nouns for, 67–69
   verbs for, 67
Smith, Betty, 68
"Snows of Kilimanjaro, The," Hemingway, 111
Sound, 57–64
   exercises for, 64–66
   speech as, 58
Specialization, 138–139
Speech, 7
   as sound, 58
Stafford, Jean, 47, 52
Standard College Dictionary, 173, 183
Stebbins, L. S., 189
Steegmuller, Frances, 85
Stegner, Wallace, 28, 33, 37, 47, 54, 63, 69, 75, 79
Steinbeck, John, 9, 17, 27, 48, 49, 51, 58*n*., 59–60, 61, 173
Stern, Laurence, 55
Struther, Jan, 68–69
Styron, William, 50, 74, 75
Subject
   approaches to, 114
   choice of, 100–103
   of sentence, 20, 23
Subordination, sentence, 142–143
Suckow, Ruth, 46, 73
Summation, 187
Sutton, Walter, 143
Swenson, May, 66
Syllables, 59

Taste, sense of, 56–57, 77–81
   attributes and, 79–80
   verb and noun headwords and, 78–79
Taylor, Elizabeth, 51
Teale, Edward Way, 78, 79, 80
Texture, 9–12
Thielen, Benedict, 69
Thomas, Dylan, 78
Thompson, Sylvia, 30
Thoreau, 72
Thorpe, Bernice, 62
Thoughts, supporting, 166–193
Thurber, James, 171
Time
   narrative, 87
   objective, 87
   units of, 87
"To Autumn," Keats, 100
Tone, dominant, 97–109

Topic or thesis sentences, 154–160, 162
  defined, 154
  explicitness of, 158
  postponed, 158
  and reader's expectations, 158–159
Touch, sense of, 56–58, 71–75
  exercises for, 75–77
  narrative details and, 74–75
Transitional sentences, 162–163, 186
Trilling, Lionel, 190
Tristram Shandy, Stern, 55
Twain, Mark, 58
Tynan, Kenneth, 184

Ulysses, Joyce, 113
Unity, paragraph, 148
Updike, John, 64, 67, 68, 69, 70, 80, 125
Upton, Albert, 136, 170

Validation, 187
Verb headwords, 60–61, 72, 78–79
Verb phrases, 22, 25–28, 33–37, 47–48,
    172
Verbs, 7, 20–21
  finite, 23
Visual and nonvisual senses, 56–58
Visual impressions, 56–58

Wagner Matinee, A, Cather, 99
Walker, Mildred, 67, 70, 80
Walker in the Streets, A, Kazin, 101
Warfel, Harry R., 158
Warren, Robert Penn, 27, 44, 48, 62, 63,
    64, 70–71, 75, 79, 81, 156
"Watchful Gods, The," Clark, 56
Watt, W. W., 188
Weaver, Richard M., 154

Welty, Eudora, 70, 73, 75
Wescott, Glenway, 47, 52, 63, 67, 69, 74
West, Jessamyn, 58, 60, 64, 73, 74
Weston, Christine, 63, 73
Wheelwright, Philip, 171
White, E. B., 113
Whitehead, A. N., 178, 182
Whitman, Walt, 58, 62, 63
Wilson, Edmund, 97
Wolfe, Thomas, 62, 68, 69, 78, 79
Woolf, Virginia, 113
Words, 5
  abstract, 8
  as arbitrary designations, 59
  concrete, 8
  echoic, 59
  onomatopoetic, 59
Wordsworth, Dorothy, 49
Wordsworth, William, 163
Writers
  careful and considerate, 163
  experienced, 154
  expert, 145
  obligation of, 187–188
  readers and, 149, 152, 158–159, 167,
    169, 176
Writing
  advice for, 28–29
  as an art, 3
  basic principles of, 6–18
  discursive. *See* Discursive writing
  discussion of, 19
  effective, 3
  linear movement of, 7
  representational, 20–22, 145, 166
  texture of, 9–12

76 77 78 79 80 9 8 7 6 5 4 3 2 1